T0327527

Modern Real Estate Portfolio Management

Susan Hudson-Wilson, Editor

Published by Frank J. Fabozzi Associates

ISBN: 1-883249-79-1

Table of Contents

Preface

Institutional investors' needs for portfolio diversification and risk reduction, higher returns on investment, a hedge against inflation, and the ability to construct portfolios that more closely represent the overall investment universe have made them pay greater attention to the real estate asset class. Passage of the Employee Retirement Income Security Act (ERISA) of 1974, and its implications for fiduciary responsibility, encouraged investors to better their understanding of real estate investment performance through the increased use of research and the application of quantitative analytical tools.

Cyclical volatility in real estate markets, relatively low inflation over the past 15 years, the development of public real estate markets (commercial mortgage-backed securities on the debt side and real estate investment trusts on the equity side), and a soaring stock market have added layers of complexity to investment decision making. This book chronicles the use of research and quantitative analysis to peel away some of these layers and facilitate a deeper understanding of real estate investments.

The book is divided into four parts. Part I addresses real estate investment strategy issues. *Why Real Estate?* (Chapter 1) answers the question in its title in terms of real estate's ability to produce returns, reduce risk, offset inflation, and render a portfolio more representative of the investment universe. *Strategy and Execution* (Chapter 2) discusses the structure of successful relationships between principals and their agents. *Hold versus Sell Decisions* (Chapter 3) analyzes the hold-sell question in three market environments (stable, rising, and falling) with investors characterized as return maximizers, portfolio risk reducers, or inflation hedgers. The analysis in *Timing the Real Estate Market* (Chapter 4) indicates that market timing can significantly increase returns over those achieved with a traditional buy and hold strategy in many market situations. The ability to profit from an understanding of the behavioral differences of loan portfolios underwritten at different levels of risk across property types at various times in a cycle (and an implication of further gains to be had from explicit market timing at the MSA level as well) is covered in *Commercial Mortgage Allocation Strategies* (Chapter 5). *Appraised Value versus Sale Price* (Chapter 6) challenges the conventional wisdom that appraised values lag transaction prices. *Real Estate and Stock Market Linkage* (Chapter 7) discusses the impact of shifting risk tolerance and security market volatility on the sustainability of capital market support for stock equities versus bonds and real estate. Part I closes with *Leverage in a Private Equity Real Estate Portfolio* (Chapter 8), which advocates the use of leverage by real estate portfolio managers when the spread is positive and risk management tools are carefully employed.

Part II focuses on public and private equity markets and investing. *The U.S. Office Market* (Chapter 9), *The Market for Multifamily Housing* (Chapter 10), and *Real Estate and Retailing* (Chapter 11) cover the history, current environment, and future prospects for those three property types. The feasibility and reliability of property market forecasts at the regional level, and the differences and similarities across eight regions are discussed in *Modeling Office Returns at the Regional Level* (Chapter 12). The risk characteristics of real estate investment trusts and the fact that the REIT universe does not serve as a close proxy for an index of the U.S. real estate market are set forth in *REITs' Real Estate Market Exposures* (Chapter 13). The unique investment issues associated with both forests and farmland are analyzed in *Timberland Investments* (Chapter 14) and *Agricultural Real Estate* (Chapter 15).

Part III takes up the intricacies of public and private debt market issues. In *Creating a Performance History for CMBS* (Chapter 16), the long-term behavioral differences for tranched bonds underwritten by loan pools containing various levels of mortgage risk and various property types are outlined using an econometric synthesis of history. The volatility of debt-related returns and the risk characteristics of public and private debt structures are discussed in *CMBS versus Whole Loans* (Chapter 17). Improved analytical methods that appropriately account for the factors that drive default are investigated in *Loan Pool Comparisons* (Chapter 18).

Asset allocation within the real estate investment class is the subject of Part IV. *Modern Portfolio Theory Applied to Real Estate* (Chapter 19) makes a strong case for the use of MPT in the careful and thoughtful management of real estate portfolios. Finally, the benefits of adding real estate investments in the public equity and public and private debt quadrants to those in the private equity quadrant as well as the impacts on allocation across stocks, bonds, government securities, and real estate are shown in *Cross-Quadrant Asset Allocation* (Chapter 20).

Acknowledgments

This book evolved from research performed by Property & Portfolio Research, Inc. (PPR) for its clients, for academic and trade journals, and in the course of new product development. While the indicated authors were primarily responsible for the research, analysis, and exposition of the results, I want to stress that all of the work is the product of the close collaborative efforts of the entire PPR team.

Ruijue Peng, Ph.D., Director of Economic Modeling and Forecasting, assisted by Joanna Stimpson, is responsible for the econometric foundations of much of the work presented. Her team's quantitative research is integral to PPR's unique and objective approach to analyzing, understanding, and forecasting real estate markets both in the U.S. and abroad.

Stephen Coyle, Director of Market Research, provides a bottom-up perspective on the market-level forecasts, supported by research of the markets team of Raymond Burrows, Nancy Chesley, Shannon Dawson, CFA, Olivia Fowlie, Scott Freeman, Nicole Garufi, Joshua Scoville, and Siga Snipas.

Bret Wilkerson, CFA, Director of REIT Research, and George Pappadopoulos CFA, Director of Debt Research, monitor and analyze the public equity and public and private debt markets with the help of David Burt and Suresh Maramreddy.

John Wilson, Ph.D., is responsible for monitoring and analyzing timberland and agricultural land investment.

Robert Hopkins, while Director of Portfolio Research, helped create PPR's optimization and portfolio simulation algorithms. Jeffrey Fisher, Ph.D., Director of the Center for Real Estate Studies at Indiana University, and Oral Capps, Ph.D., Professor at Texas A & M University, have served as consultants to PPR on quantitative real estate market analysis.

Finally, PPR is indebted to Christine O'Toole for her graphics and production work and William Tanski for his client service efforts.

Susan Hudson-Wilson, CFA
Editor

Part I

Real Estate Investment Strategy

Chapter 1

Why Real Estate?

Susan Hudson-Wilson, CFA

Robert E. Hopkins Jr.

The creation of commingled funds in the early 1970s granted large and small institutional investors access to the real estate asset class while the adoption of the "quadrants" definition of real estate in the 1980s and 1990s further enhanced their access. Real estate was initially viewed as a portfolio diversifier, or risk reducer. The Employee Retirement Income Security Act (ERISA) of 1974, as well as logic and good sense make diversification a serious responsibility of every institutional portfolio. Clearly the institutional investment community has moved a long way from the early seventies and so must re-visit the role of real estate periodically using new information on the behavior of the asset. As well, at this time one should rethink the definition of the asset "real estate" and assess the role of the asset as currently defined.

There are four primary reasons to consider real estate, or any category of investment, for inclusion in an investment portfolio:

- to reduce the overall risk of the portfolio by combining asset classes that respond differently to expected and unexpected events,
- to achieve a high absolute return,
- to hedge against unexpected inflation, and/or
- to constitute a part of a portfolio that is a reasonable reflection of the overall investment universe (an indexed, or market-neutral portfolio).

The determination of whether real estate can perform any of these assignments, in the short term as well as over the long haul, has not been easy. Academic and practitioner researchers have produced a number of studies addressing various aspects of the fundamental issues.[1] Despite two decades of research, however, little "bullet-proof" evidence that real estate has a significant position in an institutional portfolio has been amassed. Many investors manifest their skepticism by assigning only very small allocations to real estate in their portfolios. In the absence of simple and readily understandable proof about why they *should* invest in real estate, some institutions fall back on the "why nots." ("I got burned during the real estate crash of the late 1980s." "Real estate is too illiq-

3

uid, I may not be able to get out when I want to." "Real estate is 5% of my portfolio, but takes up 95% of my staff time.")

In light of the unclear historic evidence, the new volatility in, and concern about, the stock markets, and the emergence of a new, broader definition of real estate, it is time for a fresh look at the role of real estate in investment portfolios. Each of the four rationales cited above will be examined. But first, real estate must be defined.

---

[1] Early research tackled the difficult task of simply measuring real estate returns. See Mike E. Miles and Thomas E. McCue, "Historic Returns and Institutional Real Estate Portfolios," *AREUEA Journal*, vol. 10, no. 2 (1982) and Miles and McCue, "Diversification in the Real Estate Portfolio," *Journal of Financial Research*, vol. 7, no. 4 (1984), for examples. The quality and characteristics of the returns, particularly the apparent smoothing of the returns data, which produce seemingly low volatility and possibly lagging return cycles, were the subject of much analysis. See David Geltner, "Estimating Market Values from Appraised Values without Assuming an Efficient Market," *Journal of Real Estate Research*, vol. 8, no. 3 (1993) and Geltner, "Smoothing in Appraisal-Based Returns," *Journal of Real Estate Finance and Economics* (1991) for a "desmoothing" methodology, and Michael S. Young, David M. Geltner, Willard McIntosh, and Douglas M. Poutasse, "Defining Commercial Property Income and Appreciation Returns for Comparability to Stock Market-Based Measures," *Real Estate Finance* (Summer 1995) for a discussion of capital improvements expenditures on measured returns. Some analysts even question the applicability of appraisal-based returns. See, for example, Patric H. Hendershott and Edward J. Kane, "U.S. Office Market Values During the Past Decade: How Distorted Have Appraisals Been?" *Real Estate Economics*, vol. 23, no. 2 (1995), Michael S. Young and D. Wylie Greig, "Drums Along the Efficient Frontier," *Real Estate Review* (Winter 1993), and Michael S. Young and Richard A. Graff, "Real Estate is Not Normal: A Fresh Look at Real Estate Return Distributions," *Journal of Real Estate Finance and Economics* (May 1995).

A large body of research focuses on the within-real-estate allocation. Better allocation schemes within the private equity real estate asset class (see David Hartzell, David Shulman, and Charles Wurtzebach, "Refining the Analysis of Regional Diversification for Income-Producing Real Estate," *Journal of Real Estate Research*, vol. 2, no. 2 (1987), Glenn R. Mueller and Barry Ziering, "Real Estate Diversification Using Economic Diversification," *Journal of Real Estate Research*, vol. 7, no. 4 (1992), and Barry Ziering and Robert C. Hess, "A Further Note on Economic vs. Geographic Diversification," *Real Estate Finance* (Fall 1995) as examples) and inclusion of the quadrants [Susan Hudson-Wilson and Bernard L. Elbaum, "Diversification Benefits for Investors in Real Estate," *The Journal of Portfolio Management* (Spring 1995)], add to the ability to integrate real estate with the rest of the portfolio by offering choices as to the return and risk mix of real estate. Analysis of the other quadrants may also improve our understanding of real estate overall [see Michael Giliberto, "Measuring Real Estate Returns, The Hedged REIT Index," *Journal of Portfolio Management* (Spring 1993)].

Real estate as an inflation hedge has fallen off the radar screen of researchers as a result of 15 years of low inflation. With the increasing realization that the good CPI news cannot last forever, now may be the time to be looking for inflation-hedging ability. Miles and Mahoney reopen the question in Mike E. Miles and Joseph Mahoney, "Is Commercial Real Estate an Inflation Hedge?" *Real Estate Finance* (Winter 1997).

Even including real estate in an indexed portfolio necessitates sorting through the actual measurement of the size and allocation of the real estate market. Mike E. Miles, John Roberts, Donna Machi, and Robert E. Hopkins in "Sizing the Investment Markets: A Look at the Major Components of Public and Private Markets," *Real Estate Finance* (Spring 1994) and, later, Mike E. Miles and Nancy Tolleson in "A Revised Look at How Real Estate Compares with Other Major Components of the Domestic Investment Universe," *Real Estate Finance* (Spring 1997) compute the size of the entire investment market from a variety of sources, while *Investment Property & Real Estate Capital Markets Report* periodically publishes a time series of real estate market size.

Exhibit 1: Size and Share of the Real Estate Quadrants (in $billions) as of 1998

	Public		Private	
	Dollar	Percent	Dollar	Percent
Debt	$202	12%	$776	46%
Equity	$151	9%	$547	33%

Source: *Investment Property & Real Estate Capital Markets Report*

A NEW DEFINITION OF REAL ESTATE

Historically, real estate has been defined to include only investments in private real estate equity and private real estate debt. Pension funds and wealthy families bought and held direct investments in individual buildings and in commingled funds while insurance companies traditionally built large portfolios of individual private real estate mortgages. Both approaches required that significant investments were made and then held because there were no secondary and securitized markets for debt or equity. Today, however with the advent of securitization, the definition of real estate for institutional investors has broadened to cover four structures:

- *private commercial real estate equity,* held as individual assets or in commingled vehicles;
- *private commercial real estate debt,* held as either directly issued whole loans or commercial mortgages held in funds and/or commingled vehicles;
- *public real estate equity* structured as REITs or real estate operating companies (REOCs); and
- *public commercial real estate debt* structured as commercial mortgage-backed securities (CMBS).

These four structures comprise the quadrants of the modern real estate investment class. Exhibit 1 shows the approximate value and percentage shares of each quadrant.

It makes sense to expand the definition of real estate investment beyond the traditional private debt and equity concepts because the factors driving real estate investment performance in the private quadrants are reflected, to a greater or lesser degree, in the performance of the investments in the public quadrants. Any real estate investment, regardless of the formal quadrant in which it falls, is responsive to a common set of influences as well as to other influences specific to each quadrant.

Every real estate investment's performance is produced by a mix of equity-like and debt-like behaviors. For example, consider the polar case of a private real estate equity asset leased to a single credit tenant with a long-term triple-net lease. The payments on that lease resemble the fixed payments one associates with a bond, not with equity. The value of this asset to the investor fluctuates in step with the same factors that influence the value of a bond or a mortgage, such as interest rate movements, inflation, and the credit worthiness of the tenant. At the other extreme, an equity position in an empty, speculative multitenant property is driven almost entirely by equity forces. The value of the building is a function of supply and demand for space in that market, at that time. As the building becomes more fully leased, it changes from a "pure" equity to a debt-equity hybrid, and perhaps — if fully leased to long-term tenants — becomes very debt-like. In analogous fashion, as the net lease on the building in the first example ages, the residual value of the property at lease-end becomes a more and more important, and finally the dominant, component of the asset's value. Equity issues, such as real estate market forces, economic health, tenant demand, interest rates, and the idiosyncratic nature of the property, such as its location, history, visibility, and neighbors, increase their influence on the asset's value.[2]

Commercial mortgages also evidence debt-like and equity-like behaviors. In fact, this reality is the basis for the development of the CMBS market, which carves up the cash flows from pools of mortgages to produce high-grade bond cash flow characteristics in the senior tranches and more equity-like cash flow characteristics in the most subordinate pieces. The tranches between the most senior and most junior pieces have varying mixes of debt-like and equity-like cash flows.

The connection between the private and public sections of the quadrants is clear from the number of individual assets that have moved, in both directions, across the dividing line. The experience of the 1995–97 period showed that publicly traded REITs were the dominant competitor in the bidding for privately held real estate assets. At the same time, traditional lenders faced stiff competition for borrowers from the conduits that would lend and then securitize the mortgages. Public assets "go private" and private assets "go public" with increasing fluidity in a search for capital and relative value, encouraged by investors searching for ways to manage real estate portfolio risk.

Since the real estate investor is often explicitly or implicitly invested in all four quadrants, it makes sense to adjust the thinking on the role of real estate to account for every quadrant. Past approaches to the analysis of the role of real estate based only on the private equity quadrant reflect neither the reality of the investment structures that are available in the market nor the forces that influence those assets.

A Cap-Weighted Real Estate Index

Having argued that the true behavior of the real estate asset class is determined by the behaviors of all four quadrants, one must attempt to measure the combined performance of real estate in all the quadrants. To do so, a time series of capitalization-weighted performance for each quadrant was created and then combined to form a capitalization-weighted index of the complete real estate investment universe.

---

[2] See David G. Booth, Daniel M. Cashdan Jr., and Richard A. Graff, "Real Estate: A Hybrid of Debt and Equity," *Real Estate Review* (Spring 1989).

Exhibit 2: Returns for Components of the PPR Real Estate Index, 1982-1998

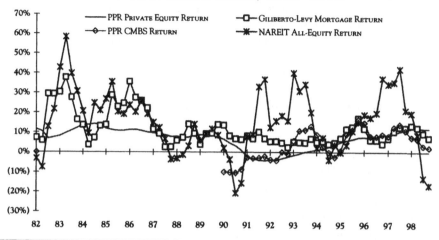

QUADRANT RETURNS

Returns for each quadrant were derived, as much as possible, from publicly available data sources. Where public data were inadequate, returns were modeled. The details of the derivation of each quadrant's performance history and the derivation of their combination into an historical performance index of the overall real estate investment universe is explained in the Appendix.

The quarterly returns for each quadrant are presented in Exhibit 2 as rolling one-year returns. The public equity quadrant is, by far, the most volatile one, with returns ranging from 60% to −21%. The private mortgage quadrant shows significant volatility during the high inflation/tight money era prior to 1986, but since then has settled down. The CMBS market, not measured before 1990 as the quadrant did not then exist, shows volatility not much different from that of the more recent mortgage era — in part because the index captures all of the tranches' behaviors and not just the behaviors of the smaller junior pieces. The least volatile quadrant is the appraisal-based private equity quadrant. Conventional wisdom suggests that the volatility of that quadrant is understated, although it is increasingly apparent that while appraisals may lag, they eventually do capture the true range of performance of individual real estate assets.[3] As well, the debt-equity hybrid nature of private equity reinforces the notion that the volatility is not understated; it is properly low because of the nature of the asset.

---

[3] For example, see Jeffrey Fisher, "Appraised Value versus Sale Price," *Real Estate/Portfolio Strategist* (March 1998). Private publication available through PPR.

QUADRANT WEIGHTS

The quadrant returns described above can be combined into a total real estate investment return index when weighted in accordance with the capitalized values of each quadrant through time. The time series of index weights were taken from the Capital Flows Database published in *Investment Property & Real Estate Capital Markets Report*. That database, which estimates the aggregate market size of each of the four quadrants and subsections of each, is available quarterly, and provided the sector totals for public and private equity and private debt and the commercial mortgage-backed security total for public debt.[4]

Prior to 1996, the private equity portion of the sample did not include the real estate owned by private financial institutions, life insurance companies, or private investors. These categories were added in 1996, with data reestimated back to 1993. However, the period prior to 1993 shows substantially lower private equity investment than the following period. The exposure to private equity was increased in the years before 1993 in line with the trend in the share of the newer categories within the total private equity quadrant.

The overall weights of each quadrant are shown in Exhibit 3. As can be seen, private debt makes up the vast majority of investable real estate in the early 1980s, comprising 82% of the institutional investor market. The current weight for private debt has fallen to 46%, much closer to today's 33% weight for private equity. As of year-end 1998 CMBS account for 12% of the index while REITs encompass 9%.

The returns in the index are capitalization-weighted in two ways. Within each quadrant, returns to each of that quadrant's components are properly weighted. For example, private equity is weighted by the value of property in the various geographies and property types comprising the private equity investment universe. The same weighting scheme is used for the mortgage series. The REIT index is compiled from the cap weights of each REIT through time as are most stock indices. Finally, the CMBS index weights are based on a simulated pattern of issuance (that replicates the distribution of real estate value in the private equity market) both over time and across markets. Next, each quadrant's returns are cap-weighted to properly account for each asset type's presence, over time, in the overall real estate investment market. The resulting real estate universe return series is shown in Exhibit 4. The average return over the 17-year period is 10.59% with a standard deviation of 7.42%.[5] It is very interesting to note that the real estate universe index never experienced negative returns; not even in the depth of the real estate depression. The mortgage returns held up during the early part of the 1980s crash and REITs started to recover by the time mortgages lost momentum. Thus, there are highly useful risk-reducing relationships across the quadrants

---

[4] The public debt market also includes government credit agencies and mortgage REITs, which were not included in this analysis.

[5] Rolling one-year returns are used in all measures.

within the overall category of real estate. The average return for the index is also considerably higher than the National Council of Real Estate Investment Fiduciaries (NCREIF) private equity-only index average of 6.77% over the same period. Risk is higher than NCREIF's 5.17%, as would be expected given the higher-risk quadrants included along with private equity in the PPR Real Estate Index. When the very high-return/high-volatility early years of the mortgage index are dropped, and the index statistics are calculated from 1987 to 1998, the index return falls to a 7.13% average return with a very low 3.62% risk. This time period was used for the rest of our analysis because the volatility of those very early years was not representative of "normal" behavior.

Exhibit 3: Real Estate Quadrant Weights, 1982–1998

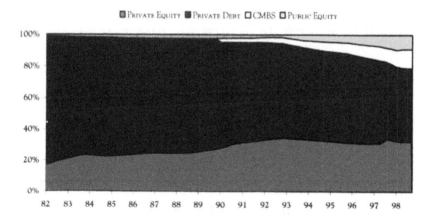

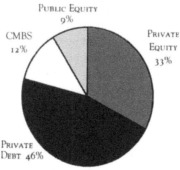

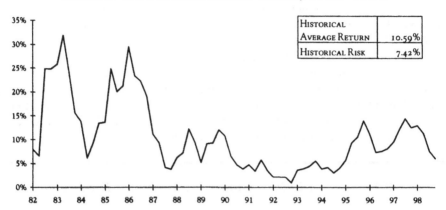

Exhibit 4: PPR Real Estate Index, 1982–1998

HISTORICAL AVERAGE RETURN	10.59%
HISTORICAL RISK	7.42%

Exhibit 5: Real Estate Return and Risk Parameters for Optimization, 1987-1998

	Return	Risk	PPR Real Estate Index	Bonds	Stocks	Cash
			Correlations			
PPR REI	7.1%	3.6%	1.000			
Bonds	8.8%	5.2%	0.284	1.000		
Stocks	17.8%	14.4%	0.547	0.317	1.000	
Cash	5.6%	1.6%	0.317	0.191	0.103	1.000

REAL ESTATE AS A
PORTFOLIO DIVERSIFIER/RISK REDUCER

Using the full quadrant real estate index (PPR REI), one can calculate the optimal allocation for real estate in a mixed asset class portfolio of stocks, bonds, and cash. The overall bond market is measured by the Lehman Corporate/Government Bond index, the stock market is measured by the S&P 500, and cash is measured by the Treasury bill rate. The parameters for the optimization (using quarterly returns from 1987 through year-end 1998) are shown in Exhibit 5.

The correlations between real estate and stocks, real estate and bonds, and real estate and cash suggest that real estate can play a significant role in a mixed asset portfolio. Whenever two assets with an imperfect relationship to each other (as shown by a correlation coefficient with a value less than 1.0) are placed together in a portfolio, there is an opportunity to earn a greater return at each level of risk or, analogously, to reduce risk for a given level of return. When the return to an asset class is high enough, the risk is low enough, and/or the correlation reflects a sufficiently different pattern of returns, the asset class earns a place in the portfolio for, at least, a portion of the return/risk spectrum. Real estate meets these tests and so does comprise a part of the well-diversified mixed asset portfolio. Real estate's role extends from the lowest risk end of the efficient frontier to just past the midpoint of the mixed asset frontier (see Exhibit 6). This makes sense as real estate is both a low-risk asset in and of itself and an excellent risk reducer in the context of a stock and bond portfolio. Clearly, if an investor wishes to simply go for broke and seek the highest possible return no matter what the risk, the investor will choose to allocate heavily toward stocks and will have no allocation to real estate (as defined here). This evidence suggests that real estate is very suitable for investors interested in capital preservation and who need to earn a useful rate of return. (Strict capital preservationists would be 100% allocated to inflation-indexed bonds and would earn very little return!) At one point along the lower half of the frontier, the model calls for an allocation of 25% to real estate. This weight drops to zero as one moves up the frontier.

Exhibit 6: Multiasset Class Efficient Frontier and Example Allocations, 1987-1999

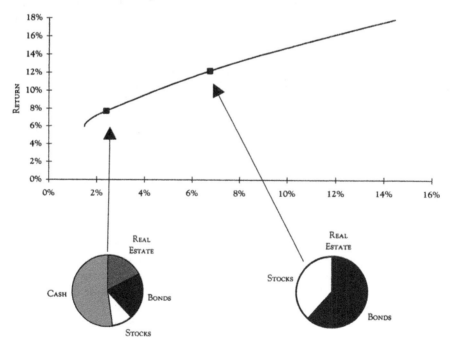

Exhibit 7: Returns and Risk-Adjusted Returns for Major Asset Classes, 1987-1998

	Return	Risk	Return per Unit of Risk	Sharpe Ratio
PPR REI	7.10%	3.60%	1.97%	0.42
Bonds	8.80%	5.20%	1.69%	0.62
Stocks	17.80%	14.40%	1.24%	0.85

REAL ESTATE AS AN ABSOLUTE RETURN ENHANCER

The second possible reason to include real estate in an investment portfolio is to bring high absolute and/or risk-adjusted returns to the portfolio. The data in Exhibit 5 show that on average, and in absolute terms, real estate did not outperform stocks and bonds over the 11-year period. When assessed in terms of total return per unit of risk, real estate outperforms both stocks and bonds. However, using the more commonly used standard Sharpe ratio and assuming a risk-free rate of 5.6% (the cash return for the period), real estate fails to outperform either stocks or bonds on a risk-adjusted basis (see Exhibit 7). The Sharpe ratio measures the excess return (above the risk-free rate) per unit of risk and does constitute a more relevant measure.

Thus, in the aggregate, it would not be justifiable to include real estate in a portfolio for the sole reason of bringing high absolute or risk-adjusted returns to the overall portfolio. There are, however, several other questions to ask about real estate's ability to deliver high absolute and risk-adjusted returns.

- Did real estate outperform stocks or bonds in some quarters? Yes. So there are periods in which the full quadrant definition of real estate is able to "bring home the bacon" relative to stocks and bonds.
- Could real estate outperform stocks or bonds again? Definitely — the drivers of stock and bond performance are different from those that propel real estate performance. Conditions could change in ways that favor the drivers for real estate but hurt those for stocks and bonds. For example (as shown below), inflation is good for real estate but not for stocks and bonds.
- Do some *components* of the PPR REI outperform stocks or bonds on average over the period? Yes — public equity real estate well outperforms bonds during the period, but none of the components of the real estate index outperform the overall stock average.
- Do each of the components of real estate outperform stocks or bonds in individual quarters? Yes — each of the four components of the PPR REI experienced periods in which the real estate components' returns were above stock or bond returns. There are a good number of quarters when

each component beats bonds during the same quarter. There are even a few quarters where all four components beat stocks as well.

The conclusion is that, in its aggregate investment universe form, real estate does not reliably produce high returns relative to the stock and bond investment classes. However, some real estate components do provide absolute return benefits and real estate's lower volatility can protect the investor from horribly low returns.

REAL ESTATE AS AN INFLATION HEDGE

Conventional wisdom has held that real estate performs as an inflation hedge. This means that if inflation is greater than expected, real estate returns will more than compensate for the surprise and will help offset the negative response of the other assets in the portfolio to the unexpected inflation. As real estate fell into disfavor through the crash of the 1980s this rationale for holding real estate assets was discredited as well. Compounding the suspicion about the rationale was a low-inflation environment and the development of a "who cares" attitude. However, even if inflation is well managed, it is not typically zero and, thus, the rationale is of importance if it is accurate. The question of whether it is or not should be answerable by empirical investigation. However, real estate returns have a complicated relationship to inflation. Inflation elicits different responses in the different property types through divergent impacts on the income and value components of return, and through variation in the effects of past and the most recent inflation. But the return-modeling process can generate a clear view of the relationship among all these components.[6] The response of private equity to inflation is presented first, below.

Past inflation is partially embedded in rents set previously as every seller of every product, including sellers of rental space, wishes to keep its price level or rising in real terms. Thus, current net operating income (NOI) is partly a function of past inflation, rising if past inflation has been greater, and falling, or rising less, if past inflation has been tame. The speed with which such inflation affects NOI, or the time lag necessary to capture inflation's impact on current NOI, depends on the structure of leases, which, in turn, varies with property type. Current office NOI reflects inflation of more than a year ago while apartment NOI reflects more recent inflation. The impact of past inflation, appropriately lagged, is positive for all four major property types.

Current inflation impacts both the level of current rents and of current expenses. Current inflation raises NOI by increasing the rental rate on new leases, but lowers NOI by raising all expenses. The model helps show which effect dominates. In the office, warehouse, and apartment markets current inflation causes NOIs to fall as the rise in current rents associated with recent leases does not fully

---

[6] The following explanation is derived from PPR's econometric model of the performance of each of the four major property types.

offset the increase in expenses, which impact the entire asset. However, in the retail sector, current inflation raises NOI, as the impact on rents and percentage rents (which apply to all, or much of the square footage in the building) more than offsets the impact on the few expenses that are not passed through. Retail then has two characteristics (percentage rents and generous passthroughs of expenses) that render it a very capable transmitter of inflation to the performance of the asset.

Inflation impacts the capital value return in two ways. First, it impacts current NOI, as described above, which feeds through to value via the capitalization rate. This "feed" is especially strong for retail assets. In addition, inflation affects the cap rate directly by influencing NOI growth expectations and so investors' demand for real estate investments. The direct capital value impact of inflation is significantly positive for apartment and office properties, but not significantly different from zero in warehouses.

Thus, the empirical assessment shows that private equity real estate is a very useful, partial inflation hedge. That said, it is also clear that the degree of inflation-hedging capacity is not uniform across the property types.

As is the case with most debt, real estate debt is not a good inflation hedge because unexpected inflation and concomitant increases in nominal interest rates negatively hit the value of outstanding securities (mortgages and CMBS). Publicly traded forms of equity real estate will capture some of the benefits of the inflation hedge, but are less successful transmitters of this value than private equity because of the links to the stock market, which is generally damaged by inflation. So, if inflation hedging is a key reason why an investor chooses an allocation to real estate, that investor must tilt the portfolio toward private equity.

REAL ESTATE AS A REFLECTION OF THE INVESTMENT UNIVERSE

Real estate belongs in a balanced investment portfolio because real estate is an important part of the investment universe. Any portfolio that does not include real estate is based on a bet that real estate will perform less well than is implied by the market-driven relative prices. Indeed, any allocation to real estate that does not reflect real estate's overall share in the investment universe implies a different bet from that of an indexed portfolio, so such an "off market" bet needs to be well justified. It is interesting, and ironic, to observe that typically the starting point to investors' thinking is a portfolio without real estate, and then to see whether any legitimate arguments support its inclusion. The starting point should be to include real estate and the other assets at their market weights and then to adjust the weights in order to best achieve the objectives of the investor. There should be a presumption that real estate has a role.

Unfortunately, determining the size of the total real estate investment universe to set the weight for real estate in an indexed portfolio has proven difficult. A summation of data on the components of the real estate investment universe is inadequate because of significant levels of double counting, conflicting data, and missing or unbelievable figures. Miles *et al.*, and, later, Miles and Tolleson tried to sort out the conflicts, but their efforts produce a result at the high end of available estimates.[7] The PPR Market Capitalization Model and the *Investment Property & Real Estate Capital Markets Report* provide comparable estimates of $1.7–1.8 trillion as the total size of the real estate market in 1998. Using those figures for the size of the market and data from the Flow of Funds report from the Federal Reserve Board for the size of the stock, bond, and cash sectors puts real estate at approximately 6% of the investment universe. Real estate had comprised as much as 10% of the overall universe in the 1980s. The rapid rise in the stock market and post-1990 declines in the real estate values combined to shrink the figure back to 6%.

A market cap-weighted and annually rebalanced portfolio of the major asset classes would have yielded an average annual return of 12.3% with a risk of 7.2% over the 1987–98 time frame. In 1998, allocation to real estate in pension fund portfolios was approximately 3.9% (3.3% in equity real estate, 0.6% in mortgages) according to a *Pension & Investments* survey. A portfolio mimicking that allocation (i.e., 3.9% of the total throughout the historical time horizon) rather than the market allocation would raise the portfolio average return by a mere 20 basis points (to 12.5% return), but would also raise portfolio risk enough to cause the risk-adjusted return to fall by one basis point. Replicating an insurance company allocation to commercial real estate (averaging 12.5% of the portfolio) would have reduced the overall portfolio return by 310 basis points to a 9.2% return. However, risk would have dropped significantly as well so that the risk-adjusted return would have risen by a very significant 22 basis points.[8] Thus, the pension funds' underweighting relative to the cap weight causes overall performance to improve very slightly while the insurance companies' overweighting relative to the cap weight causes absolute return to suffer but risk-adjusted performance to improve. Which approach makes more sense? It depends on what kind of investor you are!

RELEVANCE TO THE INVESTOR

It is clear that real estate has more than one role to play and that the investor needs to think about how to invest in real estate as well as whether to invest. But, in order to reach a conclusion about the role of real estate in a particular invest-

---

[7] See Mike E. Miles, John Roberts, Donna Machi, and Robert E. Hopkins, "Sizing the Investment Markets: A Look at the Major Components of Public and Private Markets," *Real Estate Finance* (Spring 1994); and Mike E. Miles and Nancy Tolleson, "A Revised Look at How Real Estate Compares with Other Major Components of The Domestic Investment Universe," *Real Estate Finance* (Spring 1997).

[8] The assumption in all three simulations is that the allocations across the real estate quadrants match the overall market used in the PPR REI. In fact, for example, insurance company real estate portfolios are, on average, almost 90% mortgages.

ment portfolio, one must think through the different types of investors and their needs. In this section we layer the investors' perspective over the empirical assessment of the behaviors and characteristics of real estate.

A Risk-Tolerant Investor

Real estate is a risk reducer at low- to moderate-risk and return levels and so has no role in highly risk-tolerant portfolios. Thus, an investor that is willing and able to seek the greatest return and that is not concerned with capital preservation or volatility in returns would not be inclined to allocate any part of its portfolio to real estate as defined in this chapter (there are some very high-amplitude real estate strategies that might very well be a part of a risk-tolerant investor's portfolio, but they are not addressed here). Such an investor is not concerned with real estate's size in the context of the overall investment universe and presumably is not particularly troubled by the possibility of the deleterious effects of inflation on a portfolio that would need to be heavily dominated by stock equities. While some parts of the real estate universe do periodically outperform stock equities, on average real estate is not a way to simply earn the greatest return. These investors might include individuals with true "money to burn" or extremely over-funded corporate pension funds where the corporation wishes to go for broke as a way to add to earnings. A final category of investor might be an extremely under-funded pension fund that needs to "go for the gusto" in order to bring the fund to a fully funded level (although this behavior would be inconsistent with the risk management mantra of ERISA). There are more fiduciarily responsible ways to achieve this particular objective. There are very few investors in this group because it is somewhat irresponsible to completely disregard risk.

A Risk-Sensitive Investor

The application of real estate as a partial solution to this investor's needs depends on how risk-sensitive the investor is. If the investor is mostly concerned with capital preservation and has a typical actuarial return requirement, real estate will be an important part of the portfolio. The lower the return requirement and the greater the concern about risk, the greater will be the preferred allocation to real estate, up to the 25% level indicated by the allocations presented earlier. As these investors' concern for capital preservation eases somewhat and their need for return rises, they will use less and less real estate until they have crossed the mid-point of the frontier when they will use none. The territory to the left of the mid-point (and a bit to the right) of the frontier is the area relevant to the low- to moderate-risk investor — pension funds with known liabilities and moderate actuarial rates of return, families wishing to ensure that wealth is preserved for future generations, and insurance companies and banks matching liabilities with well-understood cash flows and risk levels.

Risk-sensitive investors also generally prefer to line up with the larger investor community and so are interested in the size of the real estate market relative to the other asset classes. An allocation that is seriously over- or underweighted relative to the true investment universe represents a bet away from an important norm and begs an explanation. The explanation can be quite straightforward: "I prefer less risk and so I am deliberately overweighted in real estate relative to the value of real estate in the total investment universe." (This would suggest an allocation to real estate of between 6% and 25%.) Or, "I prefer more risk and so I am under the market weight." (This would suggest a weight of between 6% and zero.)

An Inflation-Sensitive Investor

If an investor must pay out a liability stream in real dollars, the inflation-hedging role of real estate is of interest. One of the best examples of such an investor is a defined-benefit pension fund that provides retiree medical benefits. Clearly, the cost of providing these health benefits is going to be greatly impacted by the incidence and the level of inflation. Another example would be a foundation or endowment interested in using a part of the cash flow from the investment portfolio to purchase art, provide students with scholarships, or create new physical plant (such as museums or educational facilities). These uses of the return on the portfolio are measured in real terms and would suffer from an erosion in the purchasing power of the cash flows.

Real estate is truly one of the best vehicles, and one of the only assets able to at least partially preserve its value through a period of inflation. Even when the economy seems to have inflation under control there are ways for inflation to pop up suddenly. An energy crisis, a war, or a simple miscalculation on the part of the inflation-fighting Fed could easily create a period in which the performance of the other assets in the portfolio was negatively impacted. Unfortunately the time to put a hedge in place is before inflation occurs, so investors with real liabilities really need an exposure to inflation hedges at all times.

CONCLUSIONS

This chapter has reviewed the empirical rationales for including real estate in an investment portfolio. Real estate is defined to include investments in the private equity, public equity, private debt, and public debt markets. Real estate is a risk reducer in a low- to moderate-risk portfolio, and has no role in a very highly risk-tolerant portfolio. Real estate is not reliable as a producer of the highest absolute returns and that stock equities are better suited for that task. Private equity real estate is an effective partial hedge against inflation, although different property types deliver different degrees of inflation-hedging capacity. Finally, there is a lot of real estate, so a decision to leave real estate out of a portfolio altogether is a dramatic one and requires its own rationale.

Different investors will view these reasons to use real estate differently depending on their need for return, tolerance for risk, and desire for a defense against inflation. In general, however, pension funds with fiduciary responsibilities and real liabilities; banks and insurance companies with products that can be matched against portfolios, including real estate; endowments and foundations with real uses for the proceeds of the portfolio and a need to preserve the corpus; and families with wealth intended for future generations could be well advised to consider real estate's role in how they meet their investment objectives.

APPENDIX: CALCULATION OF EACH QUADRANT'S RETURNS

Private Equity

The most commonly used return measure for private equity is the National Council of Real Estate Investment Fiduciaries (NCREIF) Property Index of unlevered real estate owned by tax-exempt institutions. While NCREIF's component returns are good measures of the performance of specific markets (provided there is a sufficient number of properties in the sample), the weights across property types and geographies in the overall index do not represent the true capitalization of real estate in the various markets around the country. Thus, the overall index is distorted to the extent that the weights are wrong. To solve this problem, we have created the PPR cap-weighted private equity index.[1] This index uses returns for all the major metropolitan markets and property types weighted by the true market capitalization in each of those markets. Good returns and good weights produce a more appropriate index.

Public Equity

Among the numerous public real estate equity indices that exist, three stand out as stronger candidates to represent the performance of this quadrant. The Morgan Stanley Real Estate Index (RMS) has a strong following, but is inappropriate for this study because of its short history. The Wilshire Real Estate Index is calculated like the Morgan Stanley index and has the advantage of including real estate operating companies. The most commonly used index, however, is the National Association of Real Estate Investment Trusts (NAREIT) index, which is a comprehensive index of all publicly traded REITs. Only the subindex of equity REITs was used.

Private Debt

There are few choices in measuring the total return to private debt. Although there are surveys of mortgage rates and numerous studies of default risk, a performance

---

[1] The PPR Cap-Weighted Return Index applies the individual MSA/property-type weights from the PPR Real Estate Market Capitalization Database to PPR's Total Derived Market Returns (DMR) at the MSA/property-type level and averages across all MSAs and property types to arrive at a single, true cap-weighted return for real estate in the 60 major metropolitan areas tracked by Property & Portfolio Research. The market capitalization data are assembled into a proprietary model of building stock inventory of each major property type in each market. A benchmark per square-foot value in each market as of the fourth quarter of 1998 was established with information obtained from a variety of local and national sources. The extent to which those prices have and will move up or down is measured by PPR's Capital Appreciation Index in each market. Multiplying the value time series by the building stock data produces our estimates of the true capitalized value of real estate, all at the local property-type level. Changes in the weights in the return index occur because of changes in these market capitalization estimates in the various markets (i.e., changes in inventory and/or changes in the value of the inventory), not because of the presence or absence of particular investors in the local markets.

index must be a consistent time series that incorporates mortgage rate, default, prepayment, and interest rate effects on value. It is possible to simulate mortgage returns based on a complete model of equity returns and a time series of historical mortgage rates by estimating each mortgage's reaction to actual historic changes in the market and interest rate environments. PPR has such a model. The most cited index, however, is the Giliberto-Levy Commercial Mortgage Performance Index. This index, which incorporates a hefty amount of modeling as well, includes the principal and interest, changes in capital value associated with interest rates and mortgage spreads, and credit loss on a portfolio of mortgage loans, and was used in this study.

Public Debt

Public debt returns are measured by the PPR CMBS model. This model applies typical CMBS structures to a variety of pools of mortgage cash flows and incorporates defaults and prepayments as well as changes in rating, spread, and overall interest rates. Other available CMBS indices, such as the new Lehman Brothers index, are either calculated at the tranche level or are too recent for this study.

Chapter 2

Strategy and Execution

Susan Hudson-Wilson, CFA

Throughout the late seventies and the eighties, as real estate evolved into an institutionally acceptable investment class (tabling, for now, the debate about whether real estate is an asset class), various structures to guide the relationships between principals and agents were developed. In the institutional world the typical principals were pension funds, endowments, and Taft Hartley funds and the agents were the advisors or money managers. In some cases they were independent companies, in others insurance companies, and in yet other cases investment banks and depository institutions. These relationships were not only national but also global. Here the focus is on principals and agents defined as sources of investment capital and service providers to the sources, although the argument may be applied to other principal/agent relationships (such as operating companies and capital sources brokers and owners, brokers and buyers, insurance companies and correspondents, conduit providers and mortgage originators, etc.).

During the great real estate depression (1989–1993) the investment vehicles and the structures and governance guiding the allocation of control over individual assets and portfolios of assets came under fire partially for excessively benefiting the agents at the expense of the principals. A new generation of vehicles is now emerging in an attempt to reallocate authority and to better align interests (and, let's face it, to entice "once burned" principals back into the game). Both parties clearly need one another; the only questions concern the rules of the game.

A brief history of the predominant structures of the past, highlighting their strengths and inadequacies, is followed by a discussion of the tools available to set the relationship between the principals and their agents. This discussion should help both sides frame the questions and reach a common understanding so that each may continue to "use" the other properly.

THE PAST

In the beginning there were insurance company separate accounts. The rules governing the relationship between principals and the insurance company advisor were very simple — the principal turned over cash, paid a fee, and got out of the way. The fee was typically set as a fixed percentage of the "value" of the assets in the portfolio, often including cash. The advisor agreed to invest the funds in "real estate." A strategy or an investment plan was not deemed necessary. There were usually rights of redemption, granted on a first-come, first-served basis; however, the redemptions were honored only if the advisor could meet the request without causing undue stress to the underlying pool of assets. It was not surprising that redemptions proved to be problematic.

These so-called open-end commingled funds were operated on the presumption, naïve in retrospect but quite modern at the time, that real estate was a somewhat generic asset and so the implicit "strategy" was to simply hold a great deal of it in lots of different places and property types. Real estate was billed as an asset whose value could only rise and which would fully hedge inflation.

The second-generation vehicle was the closed-end commingled fund, which allowed advisors to truly "lock up" the funds allocated to them for a prescribed period of time. The idea was that a portfolio could be created, operated to some maximum level of productivity, and then, at precisely the same date as the term of the fund, could be optimally liquidated. In reality the advisors weren't really thinking about liquidation, they were thinking about discretion. Also in reality, the maturity date and the market cycle came into conflict with one another. Extensions were granted and tolerated. Many of the original closed-end funds are "still running" in Energizer Bunny fashion, long past their due dates. Fees on these funds were typically a simple fixed percentage of the value of assets under management.

Another way to lock the money up was the partnership. One superficially important, but in truth overstated, difference between the two types of closed-end funds concerned governance. The limited partners, while having no decision-making authority, were at least asked periodically for their opinions on the plans of the general partners. The limiteds held the explicit right to "jaw bone" the general. Not much, but something.

The open-end concept was marginally better for the principals and worse for the agents than the closed-end funds. Better, but not good — the principals had no control over the strategy and minimal control over the decision to continue their participation in the fund: fees were paid on the value of the assets under management and the values were controlled by the agents. The advisors could plan on an annuity stream of cash flows. They held unconstrained (except by fiduciary standards of behavior) control over acquisitions, management, and dispositions; controlled the valuation process and results; and timed the ultimate sale of any asset.

At the time, the advisors rationalized this arrangement by arguing that the principals did not have the necessary skills to actively manage the pool of assets. This, compounded by the commingled nature of the pools, meant that shared decision making would have certainly been too cumbersome.

One response to this situation was the introduction of the true separate account. For large investors, these noncommingled portfolios provided a partial solution to the problem. The solution was not applicable to small investors. In some cases these separate accounts are discretionary so the improvements are diluted, but in most cases the principal has the right to be an active participant in the decision-making process — assuming that they were properly skilled and informed. An illusion of control and liquidity was in place. Again fees were set as a simple fixed percentage of the value of assets under management and the advisor controlled the valuation process.

The past can be summed up as a period in which the principal was outside of the investment process. Strategy was not articulated, fees were based on the values, the values were assessed through the agents, and liquidity was illusory and contrary to the motivations of the agents. Advisors were in the business of cumulating assets under management in order to create an annuity stream to which they were captive. The belief at the time was that real estate was a long-term investment: each asset was to be held for a long time, perhaps forever. When termination dates arrived for the closed-end vehicles, investors were told to stay a little longer — either because the assets were doing well and had not quite reached their full potential, or because they were doing poorly and so the "time is not right" to sell. Catch 22. The system was not as cynical as it now seems; advisors and principals were new at the business. They mutually agreed to an arrangement that seemed to allow both of the parties to use one another wisely.

THE FUTURE

Without belaboring the point, it is fair to say that the agreed-upon system did not weather the great real estate depression. New arrangements were needed, and indeed arrangements have been designed. We've added partnerships and private REITs with improved governance provisions. We've added fee arrangements keyed off of "knowable numbers" like NOI. But we have a way to go still. Strategy is still only weakly articulated, ventures-oriented closed-end structures abound, and fees based on NOIs still constitute an annuity concept. Nope, it's not right yet.

The next generation of new arrangements should address the following needs:

- By principals:

    to obtain from their agents a clear statement of the proposed investment strategy;

    to have a means of regularly assessing adherence to the agreed-upon strategy;

    to pay fair fees for services rendered;

    to appropriately reward those who perform ahead of expectations within the defined strategy;

    to fire underperformers without a lot of fuss and process;

    to adjust the allocation of the aggregate portfolio, including real estate, as needed;

    to adjust the allocation within the real estate portfolio as needed;

to maintain control over selected parts of the decision making; and
to have a valuation system about which they can feel confident.

• By agents:

to create and operate a business that can reliably create and grow share-
holder wealth;

to operate an agreed-upon strategy without undue constraints imposed
by the principal;

to have the principal share a clear, productive, and timely process for
joint decision making;

to earn a fair fee, appropriate to the value-added of the service rendered;
and

to work within clear and objective agent selection and performance
measurement systems.

TOOLS YOU CAN USE

What are the tools available to define a mutually beneficial relationship between
principals and agents and what are the constraints on the use of these tools?

Relationships between principals and agents are expressed in two ways
— through the processes and the economics by which they work with one
another. Here are some suggestions to make the principal/agent relationship as
beneficial as possible.

Governance. Any investment program must have a set of rules governing
decision making. Two phases of decision making are important — strategy design
and execution. Strategy design is defined to include the declaration of a portfolio's
goals and objectives, typically expressed in the manner of "CFA-speak" — required
return, risk tolerance, need for liquidity, tax considerations, and investment horizon.

The strategy setter must be as articulate as possible about the desired ends.
Real estate investors have not yet realized the need for ever greater clarity on this
issue. This may well be the most important job of the principal. Principals have
largely failed to determine and articulate why they want real estate in their portfolio.

Once the principal is clear about what is needed, it can turn to the question of execution. In setting the means the principal needs to consider such factors
as its own expertise, the availability of unbiased advice, and the trustworthiness
of the agent. The principal should, of course, feed off of the knowledge and experience of the agent to determine the agent's ability to accurately execute its needs.
Principals should be choosy.

Once the means for the execution of the strategy is determined, decisions
must be made about the execution itself. There are choices to be made about acquisitions, asset management, financing, and the timing and method of disposition. The
timeliness of decision making is also crucial. The most appropriate person, and not all

possible people, should select the means of execution. Decisions can be made individually or jointly, although too many cooks generally means too much salt in the soup.

Strategy setting and execution discretion are closely related. The clearer the statement of objectives, the less likely the agent can act inconsistently with those objectives, and the more likely the principal will be able to monitor the agent and hold it accountable for its choices. This is a high and rarely achieved standard in today's real estate investment community, but one well worth pursuing. Therefore, there is really only one reason for a principal to become involved in decision making about strategy execution — if it has a knowledge base or a skill that is truly additive and not redundant. This is likely to be rare.

Note that two subtle reasons have caused principals to be reluctant to relinquish their role in execution decision making. One is that principals do not trust their agents and the second is that principals have not understood how to best use themselves in the investment process. Sorry principals, sorry agents, but this is true.

The primary evidence of trust violated is the shortfall of sell discipline. Investment money managers are motivated to boost assets under management and to secure reliable revenue streams. Again this is not a bad thing, it is just true. Instead of ignoring this truth we should work with it.

Real estate principals have undervalued the contribution to performance that comes from setting strategy and overvalued the contribution that comes from asset-level decisions. Together the principals and the agents have a plethora of asset-level skills and a dearth of strategic training and experience. However, the principals are, in fact, accountable for strategy. Setting strategy and understanding the real estate economy should occupy 90% of every principal's day. This activity could be better accomplished by leveraging the skills of the agents, not by duplicating their skills. Governance is easy if everyone does the job for which they have the right skills and a clear understanding of the mission.

PERFORMANCE MONITORING

Accountability has two stages — execution and final outcome. Let's assume that the parties' ability to judge the final outcome is not in question so let's focus on accountability during execution. The execution period might be long or very short. In the latter case interim accountability may be a waste of time.

Accountability is pretty simple — there is a need to ensure that the agent is doing what it said it would, in the way it said it would. It is important to police the means as well as the outcome because one must distinguish luck from skill in order to make judgments about the agent's future usefulness. Again, the starting place is a clear articulation of what is going to be accomplished and how it is going to be done. Agents naturally prefer a clear playing field and will argue hard for flexibility. However, the deal is that if you want to operate without Big Brother second guessing your every decision, you must be willing to choose the "how" of execution in advance. In fact, the less certain the agent is with respect to the how, the more reluctant I would be to invest with that agent. If an agent's view on the how of execution changes in course of execution, the agent should go back to the principal and try to renegotiate the means and the monitoring tools to reflect what is achievable.

Performance monitoring must allow the principal to observe the agent's actions and the effects of these actions. The agent must report the relevant information, not all possible information — the principal does not need that level of understanding! The principal and the agent should agree in advance on one, two, three, or ten facts to be reported on a regular schedule. These facts should be selected so that they allow the principal to see what is being done and how. The principal is responsible for either having the skills necessary to review the reports or for contracting out the responsibilities. The principal is also responsible for providing feedback to the agent about possible gaps between the plan and its execution and results. This is the principal's second most important assignment.

TERM

At the outset of a relationship the time required to execute the proposed strategy must be estimated. The principal also needs to figure out how it can either change the agent or redeem its interests if that proves to be necessary.

The term of a strategy could range from one or two years to infinity. The term determines the role of the various tools discussed above and below. If the term is set for a very short period of time, some of the monitoring concerns discussed above may be lessened. The longer the life of the strategy, the more care needs to be taken with respect to governance, liquidity, compensation structure, and valuation.

Once the term is agreed on, provision needs to be made for the possible termination of the agent. The strategy may well survive the agent, or it may need to be unwound by a successor agent. A fully articulated strategy and execution, a well-designed monitoring system, and productive valuation systems are grist in any decision to retain or to terminate a manager. The mere presence of the monitoring tools and the termination procedures are useful in themselves and serve as notice that expectations have been set and that a lack of correspondence between expectations and behaviors will be apparent and acted upon. For example, this type of rigor would have served CalPERS well. The most important aspect of termination procedures is not their existence, but their use. If this right is underused, the principals have only themselves to blame for the consequences.

Redemption, or reasonably secure access to liquidity (privately and publicly), almost certainly must accompany long-term strategies. This is worth paying for. Even if all is well with an agent and a strategy, a principal's needs can change. This is a most contentious area and one which is crying out for a solution. Once a solution to liquidity is found, the allocation to real estate will no longer be burdened with the high cost of repositioning. Capital will definitely respond to that.

VALUATION

Knowledge of the true mark-to-market value of each position in a portfolio is absolutely critical to managing both agents and portfolios. It is incredible that the investment community has tolerated, for so many years, the inadequacy of the methods available to assess value. And complained about the cost, to boot! The value of the investment is the single most important piece of information to the principal. Period.

The design of a better, real-time valuation assessment model is worth the effort. Part of what is stimulating interest in the public securities market is frustration with the private market's capabilities in this area. Some believe that value can be assessed more frequently (quarterly? monthly?) and with greater rigor. It is not clear that more rigor would cost more, or if the cost were greater, that it would not be well worth it. A quarterly valuation process might be possible by simply updating leases and using a mathematical construct to update the discount rate to reflect capital market conditions. Real estate valuations could actually be in line with all other financial market values. WOW! Better valuations would improve the portfolio management and allocation functions and would allow for a closer monitoring of the agent. Better agent monitoring would improve agent effectiveness. Does anyone see any downside here?

One issue associated with both compensation and valuation is that of control over the valuation system. In cases where agents are rewarded or penalized for interim unrealized values, control over the process should unambiguously not be left with the agent. However, valuation does require the cooperation of both parties so the nature of each party's role must be carefully assessed.

ECONOMICS

First, the perfect solution does not exist and, in any case, is not unique. Principals have one set of hot buttons, agents have another. So it is key to start with the motivations of each party. It is always safe and fair to assume that each party can be expected to operate and produce in accordance with its particular motivations and rewards. It is foolish to believe that either party is going to act in a manner inconsistent with the fulfillment of its own objectives. This is not bad, it is just real. Therefore, look at the strategy itself.

The compensation structure should be appropriate to the strategy. Vanilla core-type strategies do not require incentive arrangements. Figure out the cost of the service, add a reasonable profit margin, and pay it. Incentives do not necessarily create better results. For more risky strategies, fee structures that are not necessarily more complex but more performance-oriented may make some sense. If the agent is also a principal in the strategy, incentive structures are redundant. Key is getting the agent to do the right thing, including selling.

In most cases the agent's business is valued by the market at large on the basis of replicable cash flows and their expected growth over time. Thus, value for the agent is created by applying multiples to cash flows and not by performance, except insofar as performance helps grow the assets under management. The agent's employees are expensive to hire and train, and the agent is understandably reluctant to lay them off when business wanes. The agent's interest in selling must be regarded as low. An incentive fee will be hard pressed to override the basic motivations of the agent. Exotic fee structures are vain attempts to change agents from the creatures they are into other creatures, creatures like principals.

Compensation systems that require agents to co-invest with the principal are typically problematic. Most traditional institutional agents simply do not have house capital. They are not in the investment business, they are in the management business. Most agents are reasonably entrepreneurial in that they have often invested personal capital in their management companies. They chose not to act primarily as owner-operators, but as money managers. These are different businesses and no incentive structure is going to transform them from one into the other. Similarly, the mere fact that owner-operators have chosen to invest their personal and house capital in real estate assets instead of money management companies does not imply that they are more qualified or more skilled at real estate investing than are the money managers. Too much is asked of a compensation system and not enough of management systems.

Principals should look to accomplish two objectives in arriving at a proper level and structure for agent compensation. First, the compensation must be sufficient to keep the agent staffed and skilled enough to serve the needs of the principal, and second, the structure must motivate the agent to want to serve the principal! Paying the right price does not guarantee adequate service, but paying too little probably does guarantee less than the desired level of service.

Fee structures and co-investment by money managers (leaving aside significant co-investment with a like-minded principal) are vastly overrated as motivators. Economic tools must work in concert with process tools and fair compensation should be a no-brainer for fair services.

The Big Lessons, very simple really:

- clear articulation of needs and the how of execution
- redundant decision making = wasteful decision making
- simple tracking devices = useful tracking devices
- value is the most important number for all parties to know
- principals are strategists, agents are executors
- knowledge of each party's motivation is key
- good service is worth paying for

That's it, have fun and make money!

Chapter 3

Hold versus Sell Decisions

Susan Hudson-Wilson, CFA

As we move through this real estate cycle (yes, we continue to use the term "cycle"; we do not believe the good times will roll on unabated for our lifetimes or even a chunk of our lifetimes) and investors re- and newly establish positions in private and public debt and equity investments, the issue of sell discipline looms large.

The decision to sell is the mirror image of the decision to buy. Both decisions are best made within a context — what do I want my portfolio to accomplish? Will a sale move me closer and with greater certainty to a favorable result or will it move me farther away? What is the strategy of the portfolio? (The question of aiding or impeding progress is made net of the costs of the possible transaction. Costs will not be further discussed here, except to note that some sales, worthy in an absolute sense, are less attractive when the effect of the transactions net of costs is known.)

There are two primary reasons to sell an asset (let's keep this simple and assume that one is dealing with an unencumbered building): (1) the property itself has become an unconstructive means of achieving the goals of the portfolio, and/or (2) the market (defined as the property type and the urban area) within which the asset is located ceases to function as the most productive means by which to achieve the portfolio's goals. This chapter begins with a discussion of goals and then explore these two reasons in the context of the strategies. *A key part of the thinking is that there is not a right or a wrong sell discipline* — the context within which a sell decision is made is as important as the context within which a buy decision is made.

An underlying premise is that while each asset has unique characteristics that certainly influence its performance in the context of a market, it is rare for an asset to behave independently of the larger market. The market context and cycle exert a powerful influence on the performance of an asset and help define the role of the asset in the larger portfolio. If this premise is not part of your belief structure, stop reading! It is not necessary to agree on the precise degree of influence that a market exerts on an asset; there is a range of circumstances that causes an asset to be more or less of a participant in the cycle. *It is only necessary to agree that both the market and the asset contribute to the asset's behavior.*

INVESTMENT GOALS AND STRATEGY

Any investment program must be justifiable. If the investor cannot state quite simply the reason for investing, the investor should not be investing! Some simple and useful statements of goals for an investment program include:

- earning the greatest possible return,
- earning the greatest possible risk-adjusted return,
- earning an above market-index return but without taking on excessive risk,
- reducing the riskiness of the aggregate investment portfolio,
- hedging the aggregate portfolio's exposure to inflation, and
- other reasonable goals.

These directional insights are then reinforced with a plan for achieving the portfolio's goals. For example:

Earning the greatest possible return. This goal suggests that the investor is not concerned with the assumption of market or asset risk. This is a fine goal for some investors at some times and suggests the following type of implementation plan:

> Buy individual assets that are in a market which is in a deep cyclical low, and/or buy distressed assets. Make efforts designed to allow the asset to gain in occupancy and rent, and thus value (sometimes this involves nothing more sophisticated than waiting for the fundamentals to improve). Perhaps a cap rate shift could also be included in the plan to complement the NOI-induced part of value creation. When this asset has achieved its maximum combined capital value growth and NOI growth, sell it.
> Or,
> Develop assets in markets with recovering fundamentals. Capture the spread between the cost of construction and the market value of a leased and somewhat stabilized building. When the sources of value creation are mostly exhausted, sell the asset.

Reducing the riskiness of the aggregate portfolio. This goal suggests that the investor wishes to construct a portfolio that will have the least cyclical coincidence with the other major categories of assets in that portfolio (e.g., stocks, bonds, international stocks, etc.). Real estate is meant to be a volatility reducer. The investor expects that the real estate portfolio will exhibit a cycle; the cycle simply needs to be different from the other cycles embedded in the portfolio (presumably the investor does not wish to pursue risk management to the complete exclusion of return management, so there would be a floor on expected performance; below the floor, the strategy would be terminated). This is a fine goal for some investors at some times and suggests the following type of implementation plan:

Buy a collection of assets that, taken together, are expected to exhibit a particular cyclical path. Actively manage the composition of the portfolio so that this goal continues to be able to be achieved, even as particular real estate markets cycle. Happily, and in a risk-managed fashion, ride the chosen cycle.

Hedging the aggregate portfolio's exposure to inflation. This goal suggests that the investor may hold a portfolio with other assets subject to the corrosive effects of inflation (such as stocks and bonds) and so wishes to take advantage of real estate's partial hedging capability to protect against at least a portion of the effects of a possible surge in inflation. In this case, the absolute performance of the portfolio is not what is driving the investor's choices. Rather the investor is concerned with creating a pool of assets that together will respond favorably to a high inflation environment. This is a fine goal for some investors at some times and suggests the following type of implementation plan:

Identify assets and markets with characteristics that enhance the likelihood of the effective and favorable transmission of inflation. Invest in such assets and markets actively to ensure that the ability of the portfolio to provide the hedge does not suffer diminution over time.

These suggestions will suffice to make the point that there are a variety of reasonable motivations for different investors, each with different implementation implications. Each of the strategies was presented in a value-neutral way because, while they are different, they are also reasonable. *There is no "correct" way to use real estate.* It should also be noted that some of the strategies presented here may not be able to be achieved in all parts of the real estate cycle.

Now let's compare the asset-level and the market-level sell criteria with our three cases. It will be clear that there is no definitive answer to the question of when to sell. Selling is a contextual decision.

SELLING IN CONTEXT

Let's hypothesize several asset and market situations and then ask whether each of our investors would likely be sellers or holders of the asset in each case.

Asset 1. This asset was purchased at the bottom of a market cycle and the investor has managed the asset to stabilized occupancy at market rents. This is the *revitalized asset.*

Asset 2. This asset is a single-tenant building leased to a credit tenant on a long, long lease. This is the *credit asset.*

Asset 3. This asset has lost its market share because of increased competition from newer, better located assets. This is the *dwindling asset.*

Each asset is hypothesized to be located in each of three types of markets:

- a stable market with healthy fundamentals,
- a rising market, and
- a falling market.

So there are nine assets. Let's see which investor would likely sell and which would hold, and why.

The first investor is the *return maximizer.* This investor would sell the revitalized asset unless it were the one in a rising market. The lion's share of the gain from repositioning the asset would have already been achieved and so, unless the market tide was expected to continue to rise and to rise at a pretty attractive rate, this investor would be a net seller. *This investor looks to create gain from: moving rents to the market level, moving occupancy to the market level, and, possibly, realizing a pricing shift, either by selling within the private or public market, or by selling from one market into another.*

The return maximizer would also sell the credit asset, particularly if the efforts of the return maximizer had created the credit asset. Once the risk has been removed from the asset, there is no return beyond that associated with the yield on the lease. The asset exhibits bond-like behavior until the end of the lease term looms.

Finally, the return maximizer would sell the dwindling asset in the stable and falling market environments, but might hold it in a rising market environment. If there were sufficient return achievable from simply holding passively through the incoming tide, the maximizer would likely hang on, even with an asset that was clearly losing relative ground.

The second investor is the *portfolio risk reducer.* This investor uses asset allocation tools to actively manage a portfolio of specific combinations of urban areas and property types. *The risk reducer is interested in the contribution of an asset to the achievement of the mission of the portfolio.* The asset does not need to be a stellar performer; it needs to be a "market-like" performer and to be in a market whose behavior is useful for the portfolio.

If the revitalized asset were located in a rising, a stable, or a falling market *and* if that market and that property type met the investor's current allocation preferences, the investor would hold the asset. If the revitalized asset were in a market other than those identified through the asset allocation research, the investor would sell it. *The risk reducer is "saved" from holding assets in markets where the downturn is expected to be severe as the asset allocation model will select against markets where the return-risk relationship is relatively unattractive,* unless such a market has cross-correlation attributes that are truly exceptional. While it is theoretically possible for strong cross-correlations to dominate the effect of poor return-risk relationships, this never happens and the models reject the poor return-risk markets.

The portfolio risk reducer would likely never wish to hold the credit asset. *Credit assets do not participate sufficiently in the cycles of the markets in which they are located, and so do not bring the particular set of desired behaviors to the carefully designed real estate portfolio.* Even if the credit asset were located in exactly the *market* the investor most needed, the credit asset would be sold as it cannot fulfill the behavioral needs of the investor.

The dwindling asset too would be sold by the portfolio risk reducer even if it were the desired property type and were located in the desired urban area as it will clearly not perform in line with the investor's expectations and requirements for the preferred markets. *It is critical that the risk reducer be able to achieve performance at or near the market average performance.* Above-market performance is fine too, as long as the cycle of performance is still in line with the investor's expectations for the market cycle.

The *inflation hedger* would only be interested in any asset, in any of the market environments, if the asset were deemed capable of responding favorably to a bout of inflation. *The asset's performance in a non-inflationary environment is almost irrelevant* (except perhaps in the case of the dwindling asset in a falling market where performance under any inflationary or non-inflationary scenario would be unacceptable). The credit asset has potential from the hedger's perspective, depending on the structure of the lease. Certainly if the lease is a net lease, the deleterious effects of inflation on operating costs would not be an issue for the investor. If the lease were inflation indexed (fully or partially) as a very long lease might be, the inflation hedger would be very interested in holding such an asset, no matter where it was located and through any part of the market cycle.

So, out of the three assets hypothesized and the three market environments, how have the assets fared, given the perspectives of the three investors? Out of the 27 answers to the "hold or sell" question there are 13 sells, 5 holds, and 9 depends (on the inflation-hedging capability). The risk reducer and the return maximizer disagree in three cases and would agree to hold in only one case (a revitalized asset in a rising market — although the maximizer might not hold, depending on the magnitude of the expected market improvement).

The message is clear — context counts.

Chapter 4

Timing the Real Estate Market

Robert E. Hopkins Jr.

Time impacts the real estate investment decision making in a variety of ways. Many investors do not participate in the equity real estate market because they see it as a sector that is appropriate only for long-term holds of five to ten years, and many investors that do participate believe that real estate is to be held, and held. Any market timing is presumed to be impractical, counter-productive, or too expensive. The problem with these perceptions is that they are *presumptions*. And in fact, investors cannot be sure that their presumptions are correct. Everyone knows that relative to other investment sectors, real estate transactions, especially private equity ones, take a long time to consummate, have high transaction costs, and are subject to many an unknown. Investors also know that real estate will never be a daily trading asset like large-cap stocks and that even a modest market-timing strategy would be difficult to implement. Furthermore, the paucity of data on real estate returns has prevented investors from learning, even on a theoretical basis, whether a timing strategy would raise returns.

Property & Portfolio Research, Inc. developed Derived Market Returns (DMRs™) that can provide the basic data necessary for an assessment of the comparative merits of the traditional buy and hold strategy versus a market-timing strategy in real estate investment. The DMRs cover not only a broad spectrum of the market but also a long enough period of time to be indicative of past cycles. Their forecasts provide the same level of detail as the history and extend far enough into the future to be useful as a base for such timing studies. When the DMR data are combined with reasonable assumptions on transaction costs and take into account the imperfect timing of transactions, meaningful results should emerge.

And they do. Research shows that buying and selling real estate assets, and possibly buying and selling again, can make a substantial difference (in some markets) in long-term returns, even when transaction costs and reasonable delays are factored into the analysis.

METHODOLOGY

The returns to a handful of market-timing strategies were measured by calculating the internal rate of return (IRR) of an investment in any of the real estate markets covered by the DMR data when compared to the IRR of a full-period buy and hold strategy. The DMRs include income and capital value returns for each of four property types (apartment, office, retail, and warehouse) in each of 60 metropolitan areas. For comparison purposes, the overall U.S. average IRR in each property type for each strategy is also included. Thus, one can look at the results of cash flows and capital value of timing strategies in each of 244 markets. Each market was evaluated separately over the entire time period of the current DMR data series, 1982–2001. No attempt was made to combine markets.

For periods when the strategy suggests selling, proceeds from the sale were used to purchase short-term Treasury bills, which were held until a buy signal appeared. Although actual investors selling real estate in one market may buy in another market, proceeds were not allowed to be used in this manner since that could have created an enormous variety of potential income streams. For the same reason, it was required that when investors buy back into a market previously exited they must invest all of their capital plus available interest.

Transaction costs for real estate purchases *and* sales were assumed to be 2% of the asset value. Transaction costs for purchases and sales of Treasuries were assumed to be zero. No management fees were included in this analysis, which biases the results slightly in favor of trading and away from holding (since real estate management fees are greater than those on Treasuries).

Using these data, cash flows were calculated for each quarter from 1982:1 through the forecast horizon in 2001:4. The initial investment was an arbitrarily selected number ($100 million) minus 2% transaction costs. If the initial investment was made in Treasuries because real estate was not attractive at that moment, the full $100 million was put into the market. The market value of real estate assets grew (or declined) at the rate of the capital value return in the DMR data. If the real estate assets were sold (or never purchased) and reinvested in Treasuries, the capital value remained constant. Cash flow in each quarter was calculated as the income return from the DMR times the market value of the asset for real estate assets, and the current Treasury bill rate times the capital value for Treasuries. During any quarter when real estate was sold or purchased, 2% (for transaction costs) of the capital value was deducted from cash flow. The entire proceeds, less any transaction costs, were returned to the investor at the end of 2001. The IRR was calculated for each strategy in each market.

MARKET-TIMING STRATEGY

The capital value return of the DMR was used to plot the market value of a theoretical $100 million investment in real estate in each market. The plots indicated major peaks and troughs in market value. It was assumed that a sell signal was established at each peak value and a buy signal at each trough. Since value trends are not always clear, the major peaks and troughs over the 20-year span were chosen and the minor ones ignored. The length of the cycle was used to determine the difference between major and minor cycles, but the definition was not overly pre-cise. However, if the cycle was relatively long, it was defined as marking a peak and trough even if the extent of the value drop or rise was small. For markets with flat tops or bottoms (i.e., no significant change in value over a number of quar-ters), the sell signal was identified as late as possible, and the buy signal as early as possible. In markets where values declined starting in 1982, no buy occurred at all until the first buy signal went up. In some markets, properties were sold before 2001 and Treasuries were held until the end of 2001.

In the first analysis, a full 20-year buy and hold strategy was compared with this "perfect" market-timing strategy. The results demonstrate the efficacy of a tim-ing strategy that was "perfect" with 20/20 hindsight. In 216 out of 244 cases, trading IRRs were higher than holding IRRs. However, many investors would not consider such impeccable hindsight as a meaningful prescription for future behavior. And reasonably! Therefore, to enhance the usefulness of the study, five additional timing strategies were created based on those turning points used for the simulation:

1. Trade 18 months ahead of a peak. The base signals lead by 18 months. This strategy is not intended to be a good forecaster. Rather, it represents an investor that is not greedy, and likes to lock in gains while the market is still rising and active.

2. Trade 12 months after a peak. This strategy is for an investor that needs, say, six months to recognize a market turn and another six months to execute a transaction.

3. Trade 24 months after a peak. This investor is even slower at recog-nizing signals and then acting.

4. Trade with the national average peaks. This investor instantly, and with 20/20 hindsight, recognizes the market turns for each property type at the national level, but has no local knowledge to adjust the timing to account for differences between local and national mar-kets. This strategy could easily be modified to include leads and lags as previously indicated.

5. Trade at the worst possible times. This investor rode the real estate cycle down, sold in 1993, but waited until the end of 1996 to re-enter the market. In addition, this investor had no local market or property-type knowledge; all markets were handled equally badly.

Although this list is not complete, it is a reasonable set of more realistic trading behaviors. Now, what works?

SHORTCOMINGS AND CAVEATS

This study contains a number of issues that may limit its applicability for certain investors and analysts. They are:

1. The results are based on PPR's DMR data. Any errors or weaknesses in the DMR data will feed through to this analysis.
2. The returns represent metropolitan-area market averages. They are not tuned to specific properties, specific classes of assets, or even to specific submarkets. This approach may be particularly inappropriate for an investor that picks the location, asset type, and building quality appropriate for a long-term hold (assuming that such an asset exists!).
3. The analysis is limited to the period 1982 through PPR's forecast horizon in 2001. This period covers one of the nation's worst real estate crashes and, therefore, may generate more dramatic results than a more typical cycle. (What is a typical cycle? Do we know?)
4. Investors selling out of one real estate market were forced to hold short-term Treasuries, regardless of the conditions in other investment markets, including different real estate markets.
5. The study was done one market at a time. Thus, the results do not include any enhancements that could have been achieved by portfolio optimization.
6. The analysis assumes that properties held for a significant length of time maintain the market average level of quality, meaning that rents and capital values go up with the market average. Actual properties tend to fall behind the market or, in the case of trophies, outperform it.
7. The timing strategy did not consider the degree of the value change except in the case of quick reversals, where a sale was not allowed to occur. Thus, an investor may sell at a peak value that drops only modestly over several years.

The last two issues (and that of management fees) will tend to bias the results against the buy/sell strategy in favor of the buy/hold strategy. The other issues will vary in impact depending on specifics.

RESULTS

A perfect market-timing strategy would raise the overall IRR in 214 of the 240 metropolitan-area real estate markets. In 111 of the 214 cases, the IRR rose by more than 100 basis points. The optimal timing strategy would also raise the IRR of a national portfolio in *every property type* (that is, when the optimal timing was applied to the national level DMR, returns improved). At the high end, the optimal timing strategy raised the IRR in one metropolitan office market by more than 460 basis points. At the other extreme, this timing strategy lowered one apartment market IRR by nearly 100 basis points because transaction costs outweighed value declines and the generally lower return to Treasuries. (See Exhibit 1 for some examples.)

Exhibit 1: Examples from 244 Markets

Location	Property Type	Buy/Hold		Best Timing		Best Timing 18 Months Ahead		Best Timing Delayed 1 Year		Best Timing Delayed 2 Years		Best National Timing		Worst Timing	
		IRR	Rank	Gain (BP)	Rank	Gain (BP)	Rank	Gain (BP)	Rank	Gain (BP)	Rank	Gain (BP)	Rank	Gain (BP)	Rank
Dallas, TX	Office	7.1%	162	306	18	209	27	283	18	231	15	309	8	-17	63
San Antonio, TX	Apartment	5.7%	224	299	21	240	21	256	24	179	24	-68	219	-117	230
Tucson, AZ	Warehouse	8.6%	62	212	40	143	53	147	50	55	77	63	63	-78	183
Denver, CO	Retail	7.3%	149	208	42	130	60	182	36	101	46	-134	241	-91	204
U.S.	Office	6.8%	184	180	53	123	62	171	42	145	29	180	26	-23	78
San Francisco, CA	Retail	8.2%	87	5	209	-29	205	-5	203	-47	208	-34	193	-10	49
Seattle, WA	Warehouse	10.0%	16	-25	237	-41	218	-45	237	-64	223	-42	203	-23	77

The greatest timing advantages occurred in office markets. Out of the 50 markets of any property type with the greatest increase in IRR, 40 were office. Market timing in the average office market yielded nearly 250 basis points in additional return, whereas timing in the other property types produced, on average, 60–75 basis points of gain. This result was caused by the extreme value declines in office markets during the real estate crash of the early 1990s. The buy and hold strategy performed relatively poorly in most office markets.

The more realistic timing strategies obviously reduce the benefits of timing below those of the perfect timing strategy. In these imperfect scenarios markets are sold before or after the peak, and bought when markets were still falling, or had already regained some value. Nevertheless, the gains from market timing still exceeded the buy and hold strategy in more than half of the markets regardless of strategy. The one-year-delay timing strategy still resulted in 196 markets beating the buy and hold strategy, although gains were lower. Leaving money on the table by acting *early* also limited the magnitude of the gains. Even so, 174 markets gained through this active trading strategy.

The longer two-year delay in acting cut the number of markets that showed benefits to 144, and the number of basis points of gain was reduced. Even the "get-hit-in-the-head-with-a-2×4" strategy, which ignores all local market knowledge, improves returns in 141 local markets. Although local market knowledge and forecasts clearly do matter, using a national timing strategy is generally better than using no timing strategy at all.

Of course, the worst strategy (sell at the bottom, buy at the new peak) was a disaster. Investments in each of the four property types were hurt when viewed from a national DMR and local level perspective: all but 34 markets performed worse with this timing strategy. The improvement in the best of those 34 markets was limited to 48 basis points. The implication here is that while market timing is generally a good thing, wholesale bailouts well after the market has crashed are worse than holding on. Very interesting.

CONCLUSIONS

This analysis shows that real estate market timing, even if executed less than perfectly and with high transaction fees, would have raised returns in many markets over the time period studied. Conclusions are:

1. In considerably more markets than not, a reasonable market-timing strategy based on good data and forecasts would result in increased returns.
2. The closer the strategy adheres to the optimal timing, the better, but even a significant delay is generally better than holding on.
3. Local market knowledge is very useful, but a timing strategy based only on national trends would increase returns.

4. The magnitude of the office market crash dominated the results. If the next cycle is less severe, the benefits of market timing will be reduced.

5. Individual market timing varies tremendously. The sell signal occurred early in the 1980s in some markets. A repurchase signal also occurred in some of those same markets well before the recognized bottom — about a third of the way into the 1990s.

6. When local and property type markets are considered, there were always some markets available for real estate *investment* if sell signals in other markets were followed.

7. The overall internal rate of return to real estate (buy and hold) over the period studied is in the 8–10% range, not the 10–12% range often cited as conventional wisdom.

8. Once you've blown the timing of your exit, it is better to sit tight until the market recovers — bad bailouts are bad practice.

Chapter 5

Commercial Mortgage Allocation Strategies

George Pappadopoulos, CFA

A ll real estate investors are painfully aware of the detrimental effects of the last downturn, and commercial mortgage lenders are certainly no exception. Loan default losses were tremendous. According to one study, approximately 23% of the total commercial mortgages underwritten between 1984 and 1990 were restructured or foreclosed.[1] As a result of this experience, many leaders withdrew from the market, and numerous others were forced out. In fact, a major reason for many saving and loans failures were these overwhelming losses brought on by commercial loan investment.

The question naturally arises as to whether any of this damage could have been mitigated in some way. For example, were there any indexed mortgage-investment strategies that fared better than others over the entire cycle? What sort of approaches to mortgage investment would have better survived the ride, and more important, which ones did so without leaving excess returns on the table during the up cycles? After all, it is one thing to say you will only underwrite low-return 20% LTV loans, and quite another to say you could safely get a premium return for certain types of higher-LTV loans. Do you have to resign yourself to the low-LTV strategy or are there ways to safely pursue the higher-LTV and higher-return strategy?

To investigate this question several loan performance indices were constructed, and their returns compared for the period from mid-1983 through 1999. Higher- intermediate-, and lower-risk mortgage strategies were constructed based on traditional wisdom about mortgage-underwriting guidelines. A market capitalization-weighted total return index for each strategy was then created for each of four property types and across all of the property types.

Obviously, no actual performance data exist for conducting this research. Fortunately, Property & Portfolio Research, Inc.'s Derived Market Returns allowed for the needed "re-creation" of history by econometrically modeling real estate performance. Overlaying the individual investment structure then produces the pertinent results.

---

[1] Paul D. Childs, Steven H. Ott, and Timothy J. Riddiough, "The Value of Recourse and Cross-Default Clauses in Commercial mortgage Contracting," *Journal of Banking and Finance* (April 1996), pp. 511-536.

THE MODEL

The primary tool utilized for this analysis was Property & Portfolio Research Inc.'s Mortgage Model. This proprietary model links the cash flows of a mortgage portfolio directly to the cash flows of the underlying real estate and links changes in the mark-to-market value of the mortgages to changes in their loan-to-value and debt service coverage ratios. Distinct market behaviors drive real estate cash flows and valuation and, in turn, affect the borrower's default decision.

At the real estate collateral level, the model is grounded in a thorough econometric estimation of historic and future performance of real estate assets at the property type/urban area level (Derived Market Returns or DMRs™). These comprehensive forecasts of capital value and net operating income accurately capture the interactive dynamics among demand side, supply side, and capital markets variables. They provide the model with a well-researched, empirical view on what is likely to transpire, market by market, property type by property type. The benefit of this approach lies in accurately outlining the substantive differences in the underlying economic fundamentals that occur between individual real estate market and property type pairs.

The model produces a rigorous and in-depth environment for forecasting individual loan and mortgage portfolio performance. At the mortgage level, default is now viewed within the context of current, localized market pricing information, as it is based on contemporaneous pricing ratios. These factors are crucial to the borrower's own financial decision regarding the loan, and an increased understanding of this information is, therefore, crucial in the accurate assessment of value. This deterministic approach to the question of default incidence and severity represents an enormous improvement over the current industry approach, which simply hypothesizes an annual average rate of default and severity of loss and is not at all sensitive to the underlying collateral market conditions.

Additionally, the embedded DMRs allow the model to forecast critical rating ratios and thereby enable the appropriate application of time- and risk-sensitive interest rate spreads. The reward is the generation of a complete time-series forecast of mark-to-market pricing and total return for a mortgage or pool of mortgages.

CONSTRUCTION OF THE INDEX

The index of mortgage performance consists of individual loans made in each of the largest U.S. property markets (60 MSAs and four property types). The relative size of each loan is weighted by an estimate of the value of respective urban area and property types, at the time of each loan origination. In other words, the index reflects the structure of the U.S. real estate equity market at each point in history.

The index is further weighted by the gross amount of yearly commercial mortgage originations as measured by the American Council of Life Insurers (ACLI) data. Therefore, larger origination cohorts have a greater effect on the index. All loans in each cohort were assumed to be originated at the beginning of each year.

The base utilized for the index is a 10-year, call protected, bullet loan. That is, each loan is originated with a 10-year term to maturity, with equal quarterly principal and interest payments reflecting an amortization period of 30 years. The entire remaining principal balance is due at maturity, and repayment is locked out. No further term extensions or workouts were assumed to occur. Any loan that does not default is assumed to pay off in full at maturity.

Other contract terms were adjusted to reflect a range of perceived risk. Loan-to-value ratios of 50%, 70%, and 90% were used to represent our low-, mid-, and high-risk strategies. The associated debt-service coverage ratios (DSCRs) were 1.5, 1.35, and 1.2, respectively.

The contract rates applied to each set of loans were also derived from ACLI data. The average rate of ACLI originations, by quarter by property type, were used for 70% LTV loans. To account for differences in risk, contract rates were set 100 basis points lower than the respective average ACLI rate for 50% LTV loans, while contract rates for loans of 90% LTV were 100 basis points greater than the respective average ACLI rate.

RESULTS

The year-over-year total returns from 1983 through 1999 for the entire indexed portfolio are presented in Exhibit 1. This series includes all loans from all four property types, but it is broken out by strategy as differentiated by LTV and DSCRs. Overall, the three series make intuitive sense. During the early part of the period, prior to mid-1990, returns exhibit the anticipated bond-like behavior. All series move tightly together as values shift together as a result of the yield curve and spread movements. As expected, the greater the contract rate of the series, the greater the return.

Starting in mid-1990, however, we see a break in the synchronous pattern of performance. Although the effect of changing interest rates remains, all three risk strategies now exhibit differing behavior. The formerly direct LTV/return relationship becomes inverted. That is, greater LTV series now produce lower returns as defaults severely impact the riskier strategies. The portfolios are definitely impacted by the real estate downcycle. Capital values and net operating incomes are falling, and this produces greater defaults overall. Since the collateral that underlies each strategy is identical, the differences among them are driven by differences in LTV.

Many of these defaults are on loans that were originated at the peak of the market. Note that as the real estate market improves toward the end of 1994, the return behaviors revert to their former synchronized movements, and the direct LTV/return relationship is reinstated.

Exhibit 1: Year-Over-Year Total Return — All Property Types by LTV

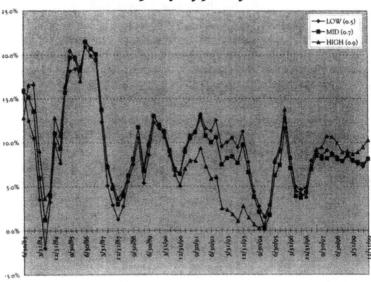

The lesson here appears to be that if you are going to seek the extra return of high-LTV originations, you must understand the position of the cycle when the loans are originated. Although interesting, none of this information is surprising. The thinking could stop here (and it has in the industry!), but it is preferable to push forward to ask a deeper question — can *safe* high-LTV mortgages be underwritten? Turning to the *property type* returns to address this, one can ask: Are there long-term benefits to underwriting only certain property types? Each of the three risk strategies for each of the property types are presented in Exhibit 2. The first thing to note is the significant differences between the four groups.

For instance, the pattern of office returns exhibits traits similar to those discussed for the total index, except that the high-LTV (90%) strategy starts suffering much earlier and suffers much more severely. As expected, it really gets hit hard in the downturn. Even the mid-LTV (70%) is impacted harshly. Overall, office exhibits much greater variance than any of the other three property types. Variance has its rewards, however, and so the more promising overall prospects for office collateral in the next three years indicate proper compensation for assuming high-LTV during the forecast period.

Perhaps more important, the other three property types appear to provide several safer alternatives. As an example, although high-LTV warehouse is also negatively impacted by the downturn, both the mid and low strategies are substantially less affected. In this case, mid-risk returns are always at least equal to those of the low-risk strategy and, therefore, mid-risk loans outperform the low-risk loans over the long term, including the forecast risk.

Exhibit 2: Year-Over-Year Total Returns by LTV
Apartments

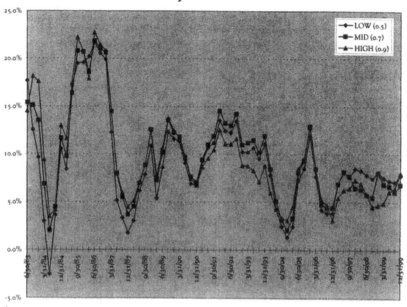

Office

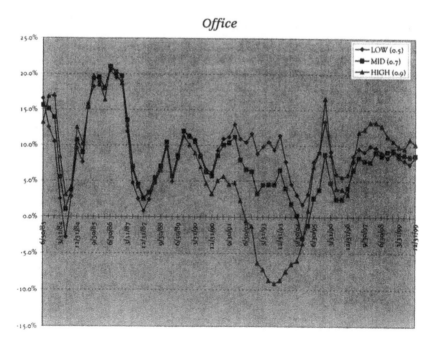

Exhibit 2 (Continued)
Retail

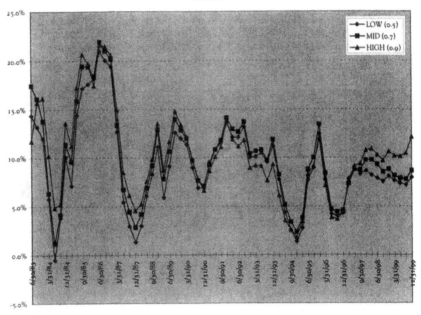

Warehouse

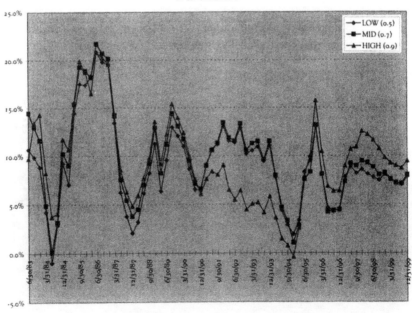

The differences between the three apartment series are visibly less severe. The high-LTV loans are still impacted enough to reduce returns through the downcycle, but the mid-risk level returns outperform the low-LTV loans throughout the entire cycle. It is important to note, however, that this is not the expected scenario over the shorter forecast period.

Finally, retail sector loans appear to have behaved quite similarly to those underlying the apartment index. Once again, the high-LTV loans take a smaller hit during the downturn, while the mid-risk strategy outperforms the low-risk strategy throughout the cycle. An important difference lies in the forecast period. The outlook is for a fairly general rebound in retail and, therefore, the riskier strategies get properly compensated.

CONCLUSIONS

The intent of this analysis is not necessarily to show exactly what happened to commercial loans from mid-1983 through 1999. Instead, it is more of an attempt to uncover and better understand the long-term behavioral differences that may exist between loan portfolios underwritten at various levels of risk, at various times in the cycle, and on various property types.

The index constructed here illustrates the general behavior of a very broadly, albeit naively, diversified portfolio. Not surprisingly, the results expose substantial differences across conventional lines of risk (LTV), and it is readily apparent that if an investor seeks the extra return of a higher-risk mortgage, accurate knowledge of the specific market cycle in which the loan is to be underwritten is imperative.

The analysis reveals significant behavioral differences across property types. The research has shown that it is indeed possible to safely obtain a premium return for certain types of high-risk loan portfolios. Excluding originations of certain property types and/or watching the cycle like a hawk can significantly reduce the downside exposure of higher-risk loan pools. Higher spreads can be obtained without necessarily taking on more risk. This result occurs because loan underwriting standards are overly general and dogmatic. This is good news for a thinking underwriter who carefully anticipates cycles.

This analysis has not even considered the extra benefits to be gained from explicit market timing of particular market origination and sales with the ups and downs of that particular market's individual cycle; a broadly indexed portfolio was constructed, but the model works at the MSA level as well. It is, therefore, possible not only to understand the overall cycle, but also to predict particular market cycles. Rather than naively diversify, once can actively allocate and obtain the most efficient and productive group of investments. Then one may truly profit from the ride, and not merely attempt to survive it.

Chapter 6

Appraised Value versus Sale Price

Jeffrey Fisher, Ph.D.

A popular maxim is that appraised values used to calculate appraisal-based indices such as the NCREIF Index lag the transaction prices and the "true" market values for the same property. The implication is that appraised values are lower than transaction prices in a rising market and higher than transaction prices in a declining market. This belief is based on popular mythology, appraiser-bashing, and very limited evidence from studies that have used the NCREIF Index to compare the transaction price and appraised value for properties which were sold by firms that had been contributing quarterly appraised values and other property information to the index.

As an example of the evidence for this lagging phenomenon, Brian Webb[1] pointed out that during the declining market periods of 1987 through 1990 appraised values exceeded sale prices by about 3.3% for all the properties in the NCREIF Index (see Exhibit 1). In contrast, during the rising market of 1986 to 1987 the sale price exceeded the appraised value by an average of 2.3% and similarly, in the generally improving market from 1976 to 1986 sale prices exceeded appraised values by an average of 7.8% for all properties.

An attempt to verify and update the above research compared the sale price and appraised value of properties sold from the NCREIF Index.[2] The data were analyzed in a different manner, however, than in previous studies such as the study cited by Webb.

Exhibit 1: (Price-Appraised Value)/Appraised Value Mean-Equal Weighted

	Pre-1986	1986:1 Through 1987:3	1987:4 Through 1990:4	All Years
All	0.078	0.023	−0.033	0.016
Office	0.060	0.001	−0.067	−0.022
Retail	0.030	0.005	−0.027	0.005
Industrial	0.105	0.049	−0.013	0.040

[1] Brian Webb, "On the Reliability of Commercial Appraisals: An Analysis of Properties Sold from the Russell-NCREIF Index (1978–1992)," *Real Estate Finance* (Spring 1994).

[2] Jeffrey Fisher (with David Geltner), "Real Estate Portfolio Management and Strategy," prepared for the National Council of Real Estate Investment Fiduciaries (NCREIF), 1996.

Exhibit 2: Transactions Price versus Appraised Value
Price/Earnings Ratios

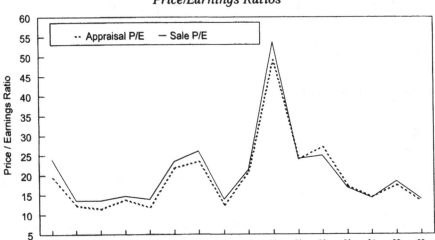

The characteristics of properties being sold are not constant over time, e.g., there may be changes in average size, age, location, etc. Thus, prices and appraised values may increase or decrease because the characteristics of the properties change. The amount of information about the characteristics of each property in the NCREIF database is too limited to statistically control effectively for these differences.

It is common, however, for appraisers to look at comparable sales in terms of ratios of the price to the net operating income (NOI) of the properties. This ratio partially controls for the existence of meaningful changes in the nature of an asset or a pool of assets. It can be determined either by dividing the price by the NOI analogous to the price/earnings ratio calculated for stocks, or by dividing the NOI by the sale price, creating a capitalization rate.

The 1996 study calculated both of these ratios in the following fashion. For every year from the inception of the NCREIF Index in 1978, both of these ratios were calculated for each property sold. The ratios were calculated based on both the actual sale price and on the appraised value of the property during the preceding quarter.[3] The ratios were averaged for all the properties sold during the year. Note that the NOI used was the actual trailing four-quarter NOI — not the anticipated NOI for the following year.

Exhibit 2 shows the comparison of sale price and appraised value based on price/earnings ratios. Several things stand out in this exhibit. First, note that price/earnings ratios for the properties reached about 55 in 1987 before markets crashed! Clearly, price/earnings in this range are not sustainable for real estate

---

[3] It is necessary to lag the appraised value by one quarter in these kinds of studies because the appraised value in the quarter in which the property was sold is generally reported to NCREIF as the sale price.

income property. Second, note that the sale price P/E was greater than the appraised value P/E during almost the entire history of the NCREIF Index. The sole exception was from 1989 to 1991 — only three out of the 16 years of history shown in the exhibit. With the exception of this time period, the sale price exceeded the appraised value whether P/E ratios were increasing or decreasing.

Exhibit 3 shows the comparison of sale price and appraised value based on capitalization rates. Note that this exhibit is not simply a mirror image of Exhibit 2 as might first be expected. This is because P/E ratios are much more influenced by properties with low earnings than are capitalization rates.[4]

Exhibit 3 certainly does not suggest that appraised values lag sale prices. In this case capitalization rates are lower when based on the appraised value than on the sale price for the same three years (1989–1991) and appraisal P/E ratios are higher than sale P/E ratios. Thus, both indicate appraised values exceeded sale prices during this brief time period. Note, however, that the appraisal cap rate was also lower than the sale cap rate during two additional years, 1984 and 1986. During the remaining 11 years, appraisal cap rates exceeded sale cap rates — which suggests that appraised values were lower than sale prices.[5]

This exhibit also highlights the gradual repricing of real estate captured by generally rising capitalization rates over the entire time period, especially after 1988.

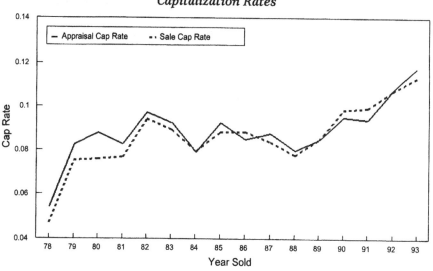

Exhibit 3: Sale Price versus Appraised Value
Capitalization Rates

---

[4] P/E ratios approach infinity as earnings approach zero, whereas cap rates approach zero as earnings approach zero. Only properties with positive P/E ratios were included in the averages calculated in this study.

[5] Higher capitalization rates imply lower appraised values.

CONCLUSIONS

This study, done as part of the preparation of a portfolio management and strategy seminar for NCREIF, contradicts the traditional wisdom that appraised values lag transaction prices. Of course, one should not generalize too much from these limited data and from these of prior studies using the same NCREIF database (but with fewer sales). Looking at the data in terms of average P/E ratios and average capitalization rates for both appraised values and transactions prices does provide some interesting insights not previously discussed in the literature concerning the behavior of real estate appraised values and transactions prices. The evidence here shows that the P/E ratio based on the actual sale price exceeded the P/E ratio based on the appraised value in 13 of the 16 years examined. The average amount by which the sale P/E exceeded the appraisal P/E for all 16 years was 6.53%.

Cap rates based on appraised values exceeded cap rates based on transaction prices in 11 of the 16 years examined, implying that appraised values were less than transaction prices. For all 16 years, the appraisal cap rate exceeded the sale price cap rate by an average of 27 basis points.

From both P/E ratios and cap rates, it is clear that during this 16-year time period appraised values, on average, were less than sale prices. This conclusion contrasts with that of previous studies, which concluded that appraised values systematically lagged transaction prices. Real estate values rose fairly steadily from 1978 until peaking in about 1985 and fell thereafter. Thus, according to conventional wisdom, appraised values should have been less than sale prices until at least 1985. This does not appear to be the case based on the analysis shown in this study. Clearly, more work needs to be done on this issue because it has important implications for the interpretation of appraised values. We hope NCREIF's database can be used to update our analysis and confirm or disprove our theory — because real estate markets have recovered so much and so quickly since the time this study was done.

Chapter 7

Real Estate and Stock Market Linkage

Susan Hudson-Wilson, CFA

B eginning early in October 1997 stock markets throughout the world, and increasingly in tandem, fell, and fell some more before stabilizing at a new lower price level.[1] Following a long and pleasant ride the roiling stock market has created a need to rethink comfortable attitudes toward the risk of stock equity and the relationship between stocks and the real estate markets. Four issues loom large:

1. On the basis of the U.S. stock market's behavior through the late summer and early fall a new appreciation for the true volatility of the stock equity markets has been established. On 32% of 1997's trading days, the S&P 500 closed up or down by 1% or more from the preceding day's close — twice as volatile as 1996, more than three times as volatile as 1995.[2] This new awareness will renew investor interest in discovering and exploiting *truly* less volatile ways to operate the portfolio.

2. For investors using international allocations to reduce the risk of their portfolios, the risk mitigation benefits are now manifestly less. Not only because we know that stock equity is riskier than we have recently been lulled into believing, but also because the market shift occurred with an unpleasant degree of synchronization. The search for substantive ways to reduce the risk of the portfolio will be renewed.

3. The debate on whether REITs and other publicly traded real estate securities are or are not "real estate" is again open for discussion — new and extremely volatile data created through the market gyration allow and encourage rethinking to occur.

4. Finally, the rough ride in the stock market forces us to consider a more subtle and less discernible response — the shift of capital from public financial to private real assets and the shift from equity to debt as the boomers age. Surely even a small shift in the flows would cause private

---

[1] Peak values in the U.S. stock market were achieved on August 6, 1997, when the Dow Jones reached 8259.31. The trough was found on October 27, at an index value of 7161.15, for a 13.3% decline in total value. *The Wall Street Journal* (January 2, 1998), pp. R2, R14-15.

[2] *The New York Times* (January 5, 1998), p. D33.

and public, and equity and debt asset values to change meaningfully, both domestically and internationally.

So there are four "side effects" worth exploring in the wake of this "correction" in the market. Each will be examined with an eye toward their implication for real estate investments.

STOCK EQUITY VOLATILITY

From 1871 until 1982, the earnings/price (E/P) ratio *always* was greater than the bond yield. That's 100 years of history; and it must taken fairly seriously. *But* since 1982, the bond yield has been *greater* than the E/P. It appears that the risk has risen for debt and diminished for equity. There has been such a long run of actual attractive stock-equity behavior that this anomaly has not been reversed. The recent turmoil, however, is a reminder that the pricing in today's stock market might, in fact, be a bit aggressive and that perhaps the roiling is an attempt to reestablish "normal" debt/equity return and risk relationships. Given that equity is unambiguously exposed first to any gyrations in the value of any asset, it cannot be true that debt would require a greater risk premium than equity for any sustainable period of time. (The only exception to this might be in a period of very high inflationary expectations, where debt would be regarded as more "at risk" than equity. However, one must remember that the flipping occurred after the high-inflation early seventies, not during it.)

Here is a hypothesis: The rise in the value of stocks, which has caused the decline in yields, has been triggered by the flow of baby-boomer savings into the market, and by the disproportionate flow into stocks at the expense of bonds. Why has this flow been disproportionate? Because the boomers, who have in recent years accelerated their savings rate (this version of savings is not reflected in government statistics as it is taking place outside of the categories the government counts as savings), regard themselves as "young" and, therefore, are inclined to invest in "risky" investments because they have time in their favor. (In fact, the government's definitions of what constitutes savings are quite sensible. It distinguishes savings from investing. Investing is a risky activity, savings should not be. Since the boomers have a warped view of the true riskiness of the stock market, they see it as a reasonable place to "save.") But the flow has not created the effect the boomers were hoping for. Instead of investing in volatile but high-growth assets over a prolonged period of time, they have invested in short-term high growth (not fueled by intrinsic sources — selling more widgets — but by capital flows — not good) and now are investing in ridiculously low-yielding assets with *diminished* longer-term growth potential. The boomers bid the values up ahead of the companies' ability to generate commensurate earnings! (This has happened in real estate. It always "resolves" itself!)

In fact, movement in the bond yields is not the source of the flip in the "normal" relationship between stock and bond yields. The flip occurred because of the shift in the stock market. So, while bond flows have been proceeding in a normal fashion — not too heavy, not too slow — stock flows have created a *temporary* shift in the normal relationship. Why temporary?

Because as the boomers age they, and their financial counselors (including asset allocation models available on the Internet), will gradually shift their risk profile toward debt and away from equity. This is logical since as investors get closer to retirement, and stop growing their capital and start preserving what they have grown, there will be a natural shift to the logically less risky asset — debt. What happens then?

The true volatility of equity will reestablish itself, capital will flow out of equity and into debt, and the natural order of things will reassert itself. The yield on equity will again be greater than the yield on debt. Of course, this will happen because the value of equity will fall and the value of bonds will get bid up! This is not to imply any shifts whatsoever in the fundamental earning power of any asset. This whole correction has nothing to do with earnings fundamentals; it has everything to do with capital flows. Life isn't going to be painless for those caught in the flow.

It has been established that stock equity volatility is only seemingly lower, not actually lower. Further support for this position is found in a paper written by Laurence Siegel in 1993.[3] He argues that if we use U.S. history to reveal anything about the true volatility of the stock market, we may delude ourselves. The history represents only one possible outcome (and a pretty good one) but it is not necessarily representative of what will happen in the future. So yesterday's performance understates risk; true risk is higher. This is consistent with how people are pricing stocks today — as if yesterday's estimates of risk are correct.

What are the implications here for real estate? Simple. Investors will again understand risk reduction and the need for it. There will be a backlash of demand for assets that are true risk reducers and real estate is the largest and most widespread class of risk reducer known to the investment community.

There are, of course, many additional implications for individuals managing their own retirement funds, but the general direction is clear.

INTERNATIONAL ASSET ALLOCATION

Why did prudent investors originally seek to place capital in nondomestic stock and bond markets? Simply for the diversification benefits. Stephen Lofthouse argues that the idea of diversification (not the math, the idea) has been understood by investors and businessmen *forever*.[4] He actually said "100 years" — close enough.

---

[3] Laurence B. Siegel, "Are Stocks Risky: Two Lessons," *Journal of Portfolio Management*, vol. 23, no. 3 (Spring 1993).

[4] Stephen Lofthouse, "International Diversification," *Journal of Portfolio Management*, vol. 24, no. 1 (Fall 1997).

A study by Wellington Management Company found that the diversification benefit is modest but consistent.[5] The study looked at a 26-year period (1970 to 1996) and at a portfolio that used a 20% allocation to international investments within an overall allocation of 70/30 stocks/bonds. The foreign countries that contribute the most to risk reduction are Austria, New Zealand, Denmark, and Spain; the least contributions come from Singapore, Hong Kong, and the United Kingdom.

So, the idea that international assets are a worthwhile addition to portfolio choices (net of costs, including currency risk) is well established and useful.

However, Michaud, Bergstrom, Frashure, and Wolahan found that there are shifts in the nature of the diversification benefit over time.[6] Data from 1959 to 1975 compared with data from 1975 to 1995 suggest that there is little relationship between these two subperiods. The average correlation between the U.S. and a wide range of foreign markets was 0.30 in the first period and 0.38 in the more recent period. One wonders has even more changed, even more recently? What if Michaud et al. had examined rolling correlations throughout the most recent 20 years? Are the correlations growing? Are the diversification benefits diminishing?

Richard Bookstaber notes that "During major market events, correlations change markedly."[7] Usually the correlations *rise* during wild swings! When risk management matters the most! Bookstaber also notes that "Compounding this is that large market moves are contagious."

Thus, the long-run averages describing the advantageous use of cross-border stock equity investing may not hold when you need them the most.

What is the implication for real estate? Simple. There is a need for good diversifiers and real estate is one that is more effective than global stock and bond diversification. Timing is important, however: move before, not during, contagion.

ARE REITS REAL ESTATE?

Giliberto and Mengden have done a piece of very important work in which they replicated the pricing of the public market in the private market and the private market in the public market.[8] Their finding is very clear: the cash flows of REITs and private equity are highly correlated; the stark differences in performance patterns come from the manner in which each market *prices* the cash flows. So, are REITs real estate? By this measure, definitely yes, and definitely no. Let's look at the market roiling and see whether REITs behaved in line with, or contrary to, the stock market.

---

[5] Wellington Management Company, "International Investing: Conventional Wisdom Revisited" (1996).

[6] Richard O. Michaud, Gary L. Bergstrom, Ronald D. Frashure, and Brian K. Wolahan, "Twenty Years of International Equity Investing," *Journal of Portfolio Management*, vol. 23, no. 1 (Fall 1996).

[7] Richard Bookstaber, "Global Risk Management: Are We Missing the Point?" *Journal of Portfolio Management*, vol. 23, no. 3 (Spring 1997).

[8] Michael Giliberto and Anne Mengden, "REITs and Real Estate: Two Markets Reexamined," *Real Estate Finance* (Spring 1996).

During the last week in October 1997 the overall stock market fell 6.9%, but REITs fell only 3.2%.[9] That's a beta of about 0.5. Feels different. *But* there were some wild deviations from the REIT average. For example, Vornado fell 10%, Cali 8%, and Patriot American 8%. *Barron's* pointed out that prior to the crunch the S&P was up 27.1% while the Morgan Stanley REIT Index was up only 15.6%. Perhaps this was only a case of what goes up more comes down more. Are REITs defensive? Are REITs stocks or real estate? One really can't tell from this "evidence"/experience.

The implication for real estate is less simple. The REIT is not a substitute for private equity, but it is not necessarily a lock step part of the overall stock market. Thus, one should probably remain open-minded about the role of REITs as risk managers and as useful substitutes for private equity.

On the international diversification front there does appear to be compelling news about the role of public real estate equity versus the role of general stock equity or general bonds as diversifiers. Piet Eichholtz[10] and, separately, Hartzell, Watkins, and Laposa,[11] found that real estate securities display more diverse characteristics across international borders than do the same countries' general stock and bond markets. So, in the search for better diversifiers, we may wish to look more carefully at the real estate subsector of an overall public market than at the public market as a whole. Specialized real estate funds investing in the public markets could be quite useful to investors interested in risk mitigation. (Of course, it is also important to pay attention to the composition of a country's stock market. For example, the Hang Seng is dominated by real estate stocks!)

CAPITAL FLOWS AND REAL ASSET VALUE

As the riskiness of the stock market is better understood and the search for risk mitigators expands again, as the linkage of cross-border stock markets is understood to have increased, and as the baby boomers' awareness of true market risk improves and their personal investment risk profiles downshift, there will be moves away from stock equity and toward bonds and real estate and perhaps other lower-risk and risk-mitigation investments. Again, none of these shifts requires any change in the underlying cash flow patterns or the prospects of any of the classes of investment. The pure motion of the capital flows will create the conditions in which the theory will be borne out. As capital shifts from stock equity to other investments, the performance of stock equity will suffer. As the capital flows into the alternatives (bonds and real estate), their performance will improve. Risk mitigation will be ratified. The world and its financial market relationships will be right-side up again.

---

[9] "The Ground Floor," *Barron's* (November 3, 1997).

[10] Piet Eichholtz, "Does International Diversification Work Better for Real Estate than for Stocks and Bonds?" *Financial Analysts Journal*, vol. 52, no. 1 (1996).

[11] David Hartzell, David Watkins, and Steven Laposa, "Performance Characteristics of Global Securities," paper presented at the 1997 AREUEA Meeting, New Orleans (December 1996).

An interesting twist on this otherwise straightforward view of the prospective flows is the source of the "Asian Flu." To a large extent, the inflated pricing in the Asian real estate markets, readily financed by banks, created the "bubble" that had to burst. Banks found themselves overleveraged and exposed to the realities of the cash flow potential of underlying real estate and other asset values. Speculation in real estate contributed to speculation in the stocks of real estate and other companies. Suddenly investor confidence collapsed, and the great repricing began. In contrast, capital flows in the U.S. are largely attributable to the baby-boomer savings craze, while the run up in Asian markets was caused more by even greater, and widespread, "irrational exuberance." But no matter how the bounce began, once started it must self-moderate and in the process remind investors of how the world really works.

CONCLUSIONS

To summarize briefly:

- Stock risk will reassert itself;
- Risk management is as relevant as ever;
- Real estate is a proven diversifier and will be valued for that role again;
- The role of international investment as a diversification weapon is diminished, further enhancing the need for true sustainable diversifiers;
- The mix of stock-like and real estate-like behaviors in REITs is still muddy, but the use of cross-border real estate stocks is more efficacious than the use of cross-border general stocks or bonds; and
- The gyrations, the shifting risk tolerance of the baby boomers, and the level of cross-border stock market linkage will cause a new and improved awareness of the need for a shift away from stock equities and toward debt and real estate, pushing returns on stocks down and the returns to real estate and bonds up, reestablishing the "normal" risk-reward relationships in the global and financial markets.

How long will all of this take? Quite a while. Evolution, not revolution. But in the meantime it means that:

- The capital flows support for real estate is growing and sustainable;
- The capital flows support for bonds is sustainable; and
- There is weakening capital markets support for stock equities.

And all without consideration of the cash flow generating powers of any of these assets! Capital flows are very, very powerful.

Chapter 8

Leverage in a Private Equity Real Estate Portfolio

Susan Hudson-Wilson, CFA

Whenever interest rates fall and positive leverage conditions hold, the subject of the use of leverage in a portfolio of real estate inevitably comes up. When the cost of debt falls below the income yield on an asset or portfolio of assets, there is positive leverage and it can be used to raise the return on the asset(s). While using leverage seems trivial (how can positive leverage be a "bad" thing?), it is, in fact, quite complex and raises some philosophical and operational issues for the investor. Here the many aspects of the leverage decision are explored and a recommendation is offered. Throughout the discussion it is assumed that leverage can be applied, creating a positive spread, at least initially. The use of very aggressive leverage as an opportunistic strategy is not discussed; leverage is considered only in the context of a base real estate portfolio strategy.

REAL ESTATE LEVERAGE

Real estate leverage, in concept, is no different than any other type of leverage: it is borrowing against the collateral of an asset or portfolio of assets. The borrower may want to do so for a variety of reasons (see below), and the lender may be interested in earning a rate of return that is considered attractive on a risk-adjusted basis. While at times the provision of debt is a method used by lenders to make equity investments, and at times it becomes a de facto equity investment, typically the lender expects to receive the principal and not the property at the end of the term of the loan. In general, the lender regards itself as a fixed-income investor and the borrower behaves like the equity holder. In the discussion below it is assumed that the lender's motivations are typical.

There is one very interesting difference between some commercial real estate debt and most other kinds of debt, including residential real estate debt — the use of nonrecourse terms. Nonrecourse debt allows the lender access only to the collateral in the case of a default or other violation of the terms of the mortgage and not to the borrower or the borrower's other assets. This anomaly continues even though lenders have experienced firsthand the effects of this factor on

61

their ability to recoup value lost on their mortgage investments. This term is very useful to the borrower when times are tough since it essentially renders the mortgage a put option from the borrower to the lender. When the borrower borrows on a nonrecourse basis, it is short selling the asset: the borrower takes money out of the asset, reducing its exposure to it, and can walk away from the asset when and if it chooses to. The lender cannot force the borrower to continue the relationship with the asset or to compensate the lender for any loss of principal. In the price of the loan it is not clear what the borrower is actually paying for this option. Certainly in very low-interest-rate or in very competitive environments the borrower is not paying much, if at all, for this useful option. But it is an important consideration to an investor in determining whether or not to use leverage, and in determining the type of leverage preferred.

Mortgages may be structured as single asset, multiasset, cross-collateralized, noncrossed, recourse, or nonrecourse vehicles. The interest rate will reflect more or less appropriately, depending on the conditions in the overall debt and equity markets, the relative bargaining power of both the lender and the borrower. Loans may be interest only, amortizing or nonamortizing, short- or long-term, fixed- or floating-rate, participating or nonparticipating, and at high or low loan-to-value ratios.

Interestingly, lenders do not currently give much consideration to the true riskiness of the market within which a particular mortgage is underwritten. They tend to develop a general set of terms (rate, term, amortization, ratios) and then to apply these terms pretty evenly across all markets and, in a slightly less dogmatic fashion, to all property types. An understanding of the actual differences in market risks can be very helpful to a borrower that can essentially cherry pick its portfolio and can place debt (with the embedded put option) on its riskier assets. It can reduce its exposure to the assets more likely to present problems through the cycle.

Given the many faces of leverage, it is very important to think through the reason for using leverage (or for not using it) since the reason for using it greatly influences the type of leverage chosen.

LEVERAGE IN A REAL ESTATE PORTFOLIO

There are six principal reasons for using leverage:

1. increase the total return of the leveraged portfolio,
2. hedge the downside risk of an investment,
3. enable a certain fixed amount of funds to be spread over more individual investments,
4. increase the yield and the cash flow generated from a fixed pool of capital,

5. reduce exposure to an asset or pool of assets as a way of reducing the allocation to a class of investments (an alternative to a disposition), and
6. enhance the diversification role of real estate in the context of the overall portfolio.

Each of these reasons is discussed in turn.

Leverage, assuming that there is positive spread and assuming that the value of the collateral does not fall below the principal balance, will increase the total return on an investment. The two assumptions cited are, however, important. If those assumptions fail to hold, leverage will enhance the degree of loss on an investment in the same fashion that it enhances the degree of gain. Leverage is a two-edged sword, and so it must be used carefully and with a great deal of consideration of at what point in the cycle it is used, on what it is used, how it is structured, and at what cost. Under proper circumstances leverage will improve the performance of an asset or pool of assets, so the concept of using leverage as a return enhancer is legitimate although it is not a tool for all parts of the real estate or interest rate cycles.

Leverage is a partial sale of an investment. However, it is a sale which the borrower can essentially revoke by paying the loan off, or can choose to consummate in the case of a loss of asset value sufficient to cause the borrower to prefer to put the asset to the lender rather than pay off the loan. Alternatively, the borrower can simply keep the leverage in place, replacing it when the end of the term occurs, in order to continue the "partially sold" strategy. This partial sale aspect of leverage can be used to hedge the possible downside movement in the value of an asset (a stop loss). For example, at the top of a market cycle an investor has three choices. It can hold the asset even though there is more downside risk than upside potential, it can sell the asset in its entirety and so book the value accumulated in the asset, or it can place a mortgage on the asset and so partially book the value of the asset while leaving a portion of the value exposed to the market cycle. If the asset's value does indeed decline (below the mortgage balance), the severity of loss to the borrower will be lessened. The investor will have also lost its remaining equity, but will have hedged its exposure to the full impact of the asset's decline in value. The placing of a mortgage can be far less expensive in terms of direct and indirect costs (such as time) than a sale of the asset. Further, if the market cycle proves to be less egregious than was anticipated, the borrower still holds the asset as the market recovers and so does not have to "rebuy" the asset in order to participate in the market cycle and does not have to bear search or acquisition costs. This can be a very savvy way to time markets.

Along the same lines of using leverage on a portfolio as a hedge, is the third use of leverage: to enable the same total volume of invested dollars to be spread over more individual investments. In this way leverage is a method to increase the diversification of the portfolio (assuming that this diversification effort is effectively executed), which, in turn, reduces both the idiosyncratic and market cycle risks of the portfolio. The use of leverage increases the riskiness of the portfolio, but the enhanced diversification can readily mitigate some of that risk. One can quantitatively assess the proper amount of leverage to apply to ensure that total portfolio risk is not increased. Using leverage to increase the number and type of assets in the portfolio also allows the average value of each asset to remain at an "institutional" level and does not force the investor to enhance diversification by acquiring smaller individual assets.

The fourth way that leverage can be used is to increase the cash flow and the yield generated from a fixed pool of capital. As the capital raised from putting a mortgage on an asset is redeployed into another asset and then that asset is leveraged and the proceeds are redeployed, etc., the cash flow generated off the original pool of capital grows, as does the yield. This happens only when positive leverage exists. If the asset's yield and the cost of debt are the same, the yield does not rise and the borrower has to work very hard to even regain the level of its original unleveraged cash flow.

The fifth way that leverage can be used by an investor is to adjust, at the margin and cost effectively, the aggregate portfolio's exposure to real estate as a class of investment. When there is concern that the relative performance of the real estate portfolio might suffer (or that other assets might perform relatively better), there is a desire to reduce the allocation to real estate. One of three strategies may achieve this. The investor can liquidate certain assets within the portfolio until the real estate exposure has been pared down, can apply leverage to the total real estate portfolio and redeploy the proceeds to other classes of investment, or can apply leverage to selected assets and then redeploy the proceeds to other classes of investment. The first approach bears the cost of commissions and execution time and could upset the balance of the portfolio across market risks. The second bears fewer costs and preserves the balance of the portfolio across the markets (assuming that the portfolio was initially thoughtfully allocated across the various market cycles). The third approach allows the portfolio manager to simultaneously alter the mix and the size of the portfolio.

The final use of leverage applied to a real estate portfolio is to "short out" the debt-like behavior from the real estate portfolio and so more closely capture the pure equity-like behavior of real estate. When this is done, the leveraged equity behaves in a more complementary fashion relative to the stock and bond portions of the portfolio than does unleveraged real estate. Thus, the diversification benefits of real estate, already very useful, are strengthened. Leverage improves the correlation relationships among the assets in the portfolio, because unleveraged real estate asset behavior is comprised of greater and lesser degrees of bond-like behavior (derived from the cash flows from the leases) and equity-like behavior (derived from the marking-to-market of the residual equity value of the property). When leverage essentially removes bond-like behavior from the asset (the debt service on the leverage is "paid" from the cash flows derived from the lease payments), the leveraged asset's behavior is primarily driven by the effect of the real estate cycle on the asset — the asset is fully exposed to the incremental performance of the real estate equity market and so its value is more closely aligned with the market cycle. Thus, if the investor sees real estate's diversification benefits to be very valuable, leverage is an important means for amplifying these benefits.

LEVERAGE AND RISK

Leverage increases the risk (measured as the volatility of the return stream) of any investment to which it is applied. Period. A leveraged asset's performance will be greater as a market cycles up and lesser as a market cycles down than the performance of an unleveraged asset. This is a fact, but should not necessarily discourage the use of leverage.

In fact, it is often the case that one can apply leverage to low-risk investments and so boost their volatility, but not to a level above the volatility of a different unleveraged investment. In other words, while it is true that leverage increases the volatility of any return stream, the mere application of leverage does not mean that the volatility of an investment's return stream rises to a level above an acceptable one. It is possible to apply leverage selectively — only to assets whose volatility is generally lower than average — and judiciously. In this way the total volatility of the real estate portfolio does not need to rise above the investor's tolerance for risk.

It is also important to think about the part of the market cycle in which leverage should be applied. Leverage applied at the bottom of a cycle carries theoretical downside risk, but the likelihood of its deleterious effects is not substantial. Leverage applied as a cycle is peaking carries a substantial hazard (as does continuing to hold an unleveraged asset). Thus, the risk of leverage can be managed if one is respectful of cycles and takes a stance on cycles, market by market. If one does not believe that cycles can reasonably be predicted, the use of leverage must be regarded as simply adding risk.

MORTGAGE STRUCTURE AND LEVERAGE

Assuming that markets cycle and so introduce volatility to an unleveraged real estate investment, and assuming that leverage increases this volatility, how can the structure of a mortgage mitigate one's exposure to the negative effects of leverage? Here it is also assumed that one cannot anticipate market cycles with any degree of accuracy (a debatable assumption, but a conservative one) and so one would simply place debt on an asset or a portfolio and then ride out the cycle.

Property & Portfolio Research, Inc. has simulated the effect of different mortgage structures on the same market. One example used a typical asset in the highly volatile Phoenix office market from 1982 to 1996. A mortgage with a 70% loan-to-value ratio was compared with a mortgage with a 60% loan-to-value ratio.

All other terms were the same. The 70% mortgage went into default when the Phoenix market went south while the 60% mortgage stayed in place. This is because property values fell by more than 30% and less than 40%. In other words, the 60% borrower was able to use the good effects of the mortgage even through a deep cycle and was not forced to put the asset to the lender. The borrower certainly lost value through the cycle, as did every investor — leveraged and unleveraged. This loss of value represented a very high percentage of the borrower's equity in the asset, because the borrower had essentially executed a partial sale by placing leverage on the asset. Because the value of the asset never fell below the principal balance of the mortgage, the owner of the asset held through the cycle and was still trying to recoup some of the loss when the market turned. As market values rose again the borrower experienced a very high positive return on the remaining equity, essentially mitigating, or at least partially mitigating, the prior losses. A more highly leveraged borrower would have lost the asset and would not have been able to offset large percentage losses with large percentage gains.

Thus, the structure of a mortgage can influence the effect of a cycle on the borrower's position in the asset and on the borrower's ability to recoup a loss. Unleveraged holdings clearly allow the owner to recoup losses, but sometimes even the seemingly "safe" unleveraged owner can never make up what has been lost. The most productive leverage is perhaps that which allows the owner to ride through some downside of a cycle while acting as a stop loss through really damaging cycles. In other words, perhaps low leverage offers the owner the best of both worlds.

LEVERAGE IN A BROAD INSTITUTIONAL PORTFOLIO

There are three important factors in thinking about real estate leverage in the context of an overall portfolio. One, the enhancement of the diversification role of real estate that was discussed previously, is briefly restated below. The issues of whether an investor should ever lend and borrow at the same time, and the practicalities of institutional money management are fully discussed in this section.

As mentioned before, cross-correlations among real estate, stocks, bonds, and other assets improve when real estate returns are measured as leveraged returns. That is, leveraged real estate is a better diversifier than unleveraged real estate. If an important goal of the real estate portion of the portfolio is to reduce the riskiness of the overall portfolio, a portfolio of leveraged real estate will accomplish this objective more effectively than a portfolio of unleveraged real estate.

The second factor is that leverage is a borrowing by the investor and so begs the following question: Should an investor be borrowing in one part of the portfolio and lending (i.e., holding Treasury securities, private debt, and corporate debt securities) in another part? In particular, should an investor be lending at a lower rate than the one at which it is borrowing? (The same question might be asked with respect to the purchase of stock equities, which are typically leveraged. In the case of stock equity the investor does not borrow, the corporate entity does, but the issue is analogous. In response, stock equity portfolio managers cite the fact that they cannot purchase unleveraged company securities, so whether the question is begged or not is somewhat moot.)

If the investor is lending in the fixed-income portfolio, should the fund consider borrowing in the real estate portfolio? Or, would these two investment strategies essentially neutralize one another while incurring transaction costs? If there is an opportunity to exploit a spread sufficient to more than cover the transaction costs in the marketplace, and if it is possible to exploit the spread without incurring an unacceptable degree of risk, it would seem useful to exploit the spread. If the investor can borrow at a lower rate than the one at which it lends on a similar credit, it probably should consider doing so. Given that there is typically a positive spread between same-credit mortgages and corporate securities, traditional mortgage debt will probably not meet this standard. Portfolio-level debt, or other nontraditional approaches to real estate debt might, however, allow this type of credit spread investing.

An additional consideration is the availability of nonrecourse debt in the real estate market. The fixed-income portfolio will likely consist of recourse loans while traditional mortgages may be executed on a nonrecourse basis. This useful characteristic might be sufficient to mitigate the fact that the rate at which the borrowing would be done would likely be greater than the rate at which the lending would be done for the same credit. It may be possible to create an ideal situation where the fund could borrow nonrecourse and lend recourse. Few investors other than insurance companies and pension funds can actually execute such a strategy.

Could the debt side of an investor ever lend to the real estate side of that investor? The debt side could earn the mortgage spread over corporates that has long characterized the mortgage market. The return of the debt portfolio would rise and the return of the real estate portfolio would rise — as long as the market cycle were not too egregious. Unfortunately, if the cycle were less well behaved, the debt side would be in the difficult position of needing to negotiate a workout on the mortgage with the real estate side. Not a very practical scenario. If all went well, the borrowing and the lending would be productive. If less than well, the complexities and the conflicts would be untenable.

The final issue with respect to the context of the aggregate investor portfolio concerns an important practicality for most institutional investors — the level at which performance is measured, and the manner in which the aggregate portfolio and each asset class are managed. Typically the chief investment officer (CIO) is responsible for looking across the entire pool of assets for opportunities to create value while each asset's portfolio manager is responsible for performance within the borders of the asset. The real estate portfolio manager is certainly motivated to use, where appropriate, every portfolio management tool available. Wisely employed leverage, as has been shown, constitutes a very useful portfolio management tool. On the other hand, the CIO is concerned with the effects of the use of various tools on the performance of the aggregate portfolio. Whether the real estate and other asset portfolio managers are, or are not, granted the latitude to employ the tools available depends on how the CIO manages the portfolio. Is the portfolio managed as the sum of the individual asset pools, or is it managed in a fully integrated asset management endeavor?

In the former case a portfolio manager is expected to accomplish the objectives of his or her part of the portfolio as effectively as possible. The total portfolio's performance is the sum of these individual efforts. The CIO will be concerned with setting the objectives for each portfolio manager and with asset allocation decisions. The objectives for each asset portfolio will include guidelines for the expected return of the asset class and likely set limits on the degree of risk to be assumed to achieve the return objectives. Each portfolio manager executes strategy within these guidelines, trying to do the best possible job.

As an alternative to this approach it is theoretically possible to simultaneously manage each asset class in a fully integrated fashion. The noted portfolio strategist Bill Sharpe calls this approach "integrated asset allocation." With this approach all decisions throughout the portfolio are made with an eye to their effect at the aggregate portfolio level. This is a theoretical model because, while it is clearly a conceptually superior approach, there are numerous practical problems with its implementation. Thus, most investors use the disaggregated approach and simply set some global rules to guide each portfolio manager's actions.

It is possible that the CIO might set some constraints on the types of portfolio management tools each portfolio manager would be permitted to use, but it is more practical to simply set the required return and the permissible risk. If each portfolio manager achieves his or her bogey, the sum of the parts will create a coherent whole.

So three observations seem relevant with respect to the issue of leverage in the aggregate portfolio: (1) leveraged real estate is a better diversifier than unleveraged real estate, (2) investors can be both borrowers and lenders as long as the borrowing is done via third parties, the spread is favorable, and/or the stop loss use of leverage constitutes the reason for borrowing, and (3) there are practical issues in the management of the overall portfolio that suggest that each asset class should simply strive to best achieve its return and risk objectives as set forth by the CIO because the concepts of fully integrated asset allocation and portfolio management are very difficult to implement.

CONTEXT

Leverage constitutes a partial sale and so must be regarded as a way to raise capital, not to use capital. Before using leverage it is important to consider the need to raise additional investment capital. If an investor is not invested up to the level that has been approved for real estate, the notion of adding to the cash available for investment is a questionable one. Can additional capital be beneficially and efficiently put to use? Can the existing staff manage the incremental investments in addition to the already approved volume of investments? It may be that an investor would choose to allow the use of leverage, but only after the total existing allocation is fully employed and only if the most constructive type of leverage can be executed.

If an investor chooses to allow the use of leverage, the type of leverage used must be consistent with the return and risk requirements for the real estate portfolio, and care must be taken that the allocation of the leveraged portfolio over the various real estate investment behaviors is at least as thoughtful as the allocation of the now unleveraged portfolio. If sufficient care is not taken, the riskiness of the portfolio could very well rise beyond an acceptable level.

EXECUTION

If an investor decides that leverage is a tool that should be available to the real estate portfolio manager, several threshold questions need to be addressed before deciding on the desired approach to the problem:

- What is (are) the purpose(s) of the leverage?
- Is the stop loss useful (i.e., is nonrecourse leverage preferred to recourse)?
- Is the leverage to be placed at the asset level and/or at the portfolio level?
- What is the preferred structure of the leverage (term, prepayment, public, or private)?
- Does the cost of the leverage relative to the fixed-income side of the portfolio matter?
- Who will be responsible for placing and managing the leverage?

Investors have many options from which to choose. A few examples will be presented below, but none is intended to represent a recommendation. Before delving further into the practical questions raised above, the threshold question of the use of leverage in the real estate portfolio must be addressed.

Let's assume that an investor wishes to use leverage for the purpose of raising the prospective return of the real estate portfolio, but does not wish to raise the riskiness of the portfolio to an unacceptable level. It could evaluate the current portfolio's riskiness and then set a level of increased risk that would be acceptable. The portfolio could then be analyzed to determine which assets(s) could benefit from the application of leverage, the portfolio diversification effect of placing the leverage and deploying the proceeds, and the effect of the leverage and the incremental investments on the return of the portfolio. It is conceivable that if this were very carefully thought through in advance, the portfolio's return could be raised without adding any incremental portfolio-level risk.

Then let's assume that the investor is concerned that some of the markets in which it has investments may have reached the peak of their cycles. Rather than execute a sale in these markets, it might choose to leverage the assets in these markets as a way of placing a stop loss to ensure that if the markets were to cycle down, its gains would be preserved. In this case the analysis to select the appropriate markets would involve the identification of markets which are highly volatile and where research suggests that values may be at, or near, a cyclical peak. High loan-to-value, nonrecourse mortgages would be placed on these assets and the proceeds would be used to invest in new assets chosen to ensure that the real estate portfolio's composition is still efficient and productive.

A third approach might be to apply low loan-to-value portfolio-level leverage to the entire existing portfolio. This would preserve the current allocations across property types and geographies and would permit incremental investments to be made that would further enhance the diversification of the portfolio. Such leverage could be in the form of a securitization that could be executed either privately or publicly at quite a low interest rate.

Of course, an investor could combine various aspects of these concepts to best manage the return and the risk of the overall real estate portfolio. One very important part of the process of managing the leverage policy through time would be a frequent reevaluation of the utility of leverage for the portfolio. As discussed earlier, leverage is not appropriate for all parts of the market cycle.

BENCHMARKING

Portfolio managers who are allowed to use leverage in execution of their investment strategy should be judged on whether they used the tool effectively. Thus, benchmarking and performance attribution should be designed to evaluate the portfolio managers' performance given what they did, and then compared with what they could have done. The performance of the real estate portfolio would be the sum of the effects of asset allocation within the real estate portfolio, asset selection within the chosen property types and geographies, property management, and the chosen financial structure of the assets and the portfolio. Probably some tracking error around an appropriate benchmark would be tolerated.

It is important for the portfolio manager to get credit for the appropriate use of leverage and to not receive credit for using leverage instead of productive unleveraged strategies. In other words, the focus of the portfolio manager's attention must remain on the management of the real estate and not on the management of the capital markets.

CONCLUSIONS

If a pension fund can agree that it is reasonable and practical to be both a borrower and a lender within the overall portfolio, the real estate portfolio manager (and others) should probably be granted the latitude to use leverage in a careful and accountable fashion. It is reasonable for an investor to be both a borrower and a lender for several reasons:

1. Positive spread lending and borrowing across a credit category are productive;
2. Nonrecourse borrowing has an additional use as a stop loss, and lending recourse while borrowing nonrecourse is certainly advantageous;
3. The increase in risk that is possibly generated for the investor using leverage is possibly mitigated by both the enhanced diversification provided by a portfolio of leveraged versus nonleveraged real estate, and by the ability to use the proceeds from leverage to improve and proactively manage the diversification of the real estate portfolio;
4. Leverage is already in use within every institutional portfolio that invests in stock equities; and
5. The management of the overall portfolio must sometimes yield theoretical high ground to practical high ground, and so is likely to better produce the overall returns that it requires at the risk level it is willing to tolerate by allowing each asset type to operate somewhat independently, and as intelligently as possible.

Therefore, the real estate portfolio manager should be allowed to use conservative and thoughtful leverage as a tool for improved portfolio management of the real estate portfolio when the spread is positive and if risk management tools are carefully and empirically used. Furthermore, a system of performance measurement and attribution should be designed that can be used to ensure that portfolio managers are fully accountable for their choices, and that further study be done to determine the most effective way to design and execute a leverage strategy.

Part II

Public and Private Equity

Part I

Public and Private Equity

Chapter 9

The U.S. Office Market

Stephen M. Coyle

In spite of the U.S. office market's strong recovery, we should not forget that office investments have performed both splendidly and horribly over the years. The volatility of U.S. office returns (from 1982 to 1998) was more than 35% higher than for retail, and 60% greater than for apartments and warehouse (see Exhibit 1). Because the creation of office supply takes more time to plan, finance, and construct, office usually enters the construction cycle later than other product types. However, entering the construction cycle later does not protect office, since it also pulls back later from the development process. The magnitude of the office cycle is very high on the upside and very low on the downside. Therefore, one must carefully assess a market's underlying fundamentals and its position in the real estate cycle prior to making an investment decision.

As of the fall of 1999, most office markets have begun to enter the over-building cycle. Very few markets still enjoy vastly improving market fundamentals (rising occupancies, recovering rents, and increasing values). At the U.S. level, demand outstripped supply from mid-1992 through the first quarter of 1999, creating falling vacancies (see Exhibit 2). As capital flows to office have increased pushing prices, rents have risen, net operating incomes (NOIs) have strengthened, and total returns at the U.S. level have recovered rapidly. After bottoming out below negative 10% in 1991, total returns increased to more than 16% by year-end 1998. Volatility at its best! But we should remember the downside of volatility. Total returns plummeted from 15% in 1984 to negative 10% in 1991. The level of volatility varies widely across office markets. Virtually all office markets are more volatile than the corresponding markets for the other three major property types.

WHAT DOES VOLATILITY MEAN TO RETURNS?

Unlike previous cycles, when almost all markets were on the same cycle (the mid- to late 1980s come to mind), there are many different cycles occurring simultaneously in the U.S. office market today. While we can generalize and state that,

Reprinted with revisions with permission from *Mortgage Banking* Magazine, September 1998, pp. 42-48, published by the Mortgage Bankers Association of America.

the U.S. office market is now transitioning from a recovery into a peak, some markets still recovering, while others are turning down (e.g., Hartford is just beginning to recover, while Atlanta's total returns peaked in 1996 and are declining). Thus, we must look at each market's position in its relevant market cycle.

The timing of volatility is just as important as the level of volatility. When considering an office investment, we must carefully consider the following question: "Is the expected timing and magnitude of volatility more likely to generate a good surprise or a bad surprise?" In markets that are well into the recovery cycle, where construction has already begun to overwhelm demand (e.g., Atlanta, Columbus, Dallas, Phoenix, Portland, and Salt Lake City), the surprise will likely be an unpleasant one. In markets such as northern New Jersey, Philadelphia, and Los Angeles, where construction remains low and capital flows are limited, volatility may prove to be constructive.

THE U.S. OFFICE MARKET TODAY

The swing in office returns is largely due to the longer construction cycles and the lumpy capital flows that follow office investments. When markets heat up and capital flows increase, office responds with rapid price increases and very strong returns.

Exhibit 1: PPR60 Office versus Apartment, Retail, and Warehouse Derived Market Return

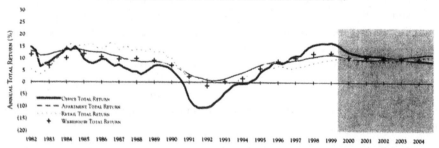

Exhibit 2: Office Market Trends

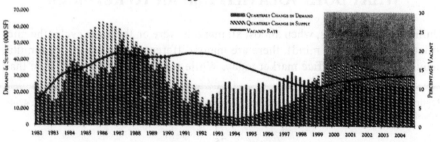

Exhibit 3: Individual Market Investment Cycle

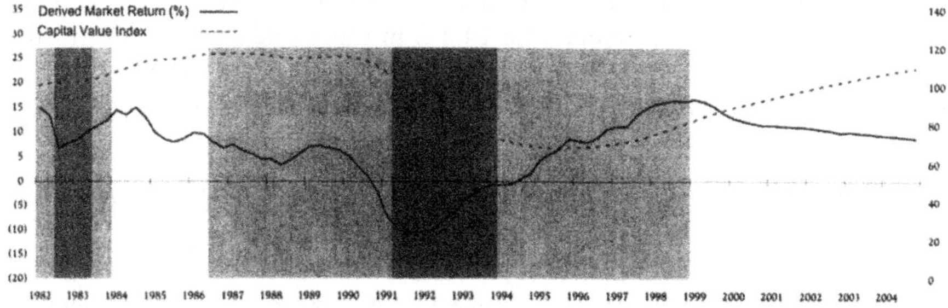

However, total returns at the national level have peaked (see Exhibit 3). U.S. office returns should slow gradually over the next few years as more markets begin to overbuild. In many suburban submarkets, rents have already risen to the level supporting new development. Most of the new development consists of utilitarian "Class A for a Day" space, justified by current rents and demanded by tenants. Submarkets such as Scottsdale, Tempe, and Chandler in Phoenix, North/Far North Dallas, and suburban Boston are building vast amounts of new space as developers seek to realize high current returns. Surging suburban construction will limit both the scope and the location of future development. We are unlikely to see widespread development of the ultra high finish "Cathedrals to Commerce" in most markets, as we did in the 1980s, since rent growth will generally be capped off by the early entrance of Class A for a Day buildings. While a few vibrant downtowns may witness significant construction (Minneapolis, Portland, Chicago, and Seattle/Bellevue, for example), other, less vibrant Central Business Districts (CBDs) will suffer as excessive suburban construction limits their recoveries.

DOES THE TYPE AND LOCATION OF CONSTRUCTION MATTER?

Let's look at Dallas as an example. Downtown Dallas began to post a moderate recovery during 1996 and early 1997 as vacancy rates at the Metropolitan Statistical Area (MSA) level plunged below 15% and shortages of large blocks of contiguous space emerged. Because of limited availability of such large blocks at the suburban level and low rents in the CBD, large users such as Blockbuster chose to locate downtown. However, over the past several years, as the level of new development has increased dramatically in the suburbs, CBD absorption has slowed and vacancy rates downtown have stabilized near an unfortunate 28% to 30%. Dallas now has more than 10.5 million square feet under development, with most of this new space located in Las Colinas and north/far north Dallas. Most of the new space is Class A for a Day space with rents in the low to mid-$20s. Since new supply is expected to outpace demand through most of the forecast period,

Dallas' future recovery and the recovery of its CBD will be severely limited. Whereas the Dallas MSA's office vacancies fell below 10% during the last cycle, vacancies bottomed-out at more than 14.5% in this cycle (late 1997). In some other markets, like Atlanta, early construction of suburban buildings has occurred at such a rapid pace that the downtowns have seen even less of a recovery.

WHAT ABOUT BUYING BELOW REPLACEMENT COSTS?

Being able to buy buildings below replacement cost is not a sufficient reason to invest in office buildings. The relevant question is, "What is the replacement cost of a competitive asset?" In Dallas and Atlanta, for example, a competitive asset for many tenants is a $120–$140 glass curtain wall building in the northern suburbs with minimal finishes and surface parking. Simply buying below the (much higher) replacement cost of a granite- and marble-clad building in the CBD can often equate to a purchase price in excess of the suburban building, despite higher CBD Class A vacancies and weaker net effective rents. Thus, the implications of investing in downtown Dallas have shifted dramatically as the development cycle has changed. Investing in downtown Dallas or downtown Atlanta could still be a good idea, if the asset, which must be defined to include suburban Class A for a Day space, can be acquired at a cheap enough price/relative to its true competitive set.

ARE DOWNTOWNS DEAD?

There still are a number of vibrant downtown markets. In cities like Boston, New York, Fort Lauderdale, Minneapolis, Orlando, Portland, San Francisco, and Seattle, the vacancy rate downtown is lower than that in the suburbs. While some CBDs, such as Minneapolis, Orlando, Portland, and Seattle, have responded with significant construction (e.g., downtown Minneapolis with six towers under construction), development remains constrained in other vibrant downtowns. In markets such as downtown Boston and midtown New York, rents generally remain below the level needed to justify new Class A towers. However, as the prices paid for existing buildings begin to exceed development costs, construction will occur. This is truly scary construction, as it is justified by capital flows, not by market fundamentals. (Can anyone construct a new tower in Midtown for less than $500+/SF — We think so! Thank you, Mr. Trump! How about in Boston for $375? Sure, a tip o' the hat to the Reichmans!) (Should anyone take these prices as signals to build? No!)

IS THIS THE 1980S ALL OVER AGAIN?

Today's U.S. office cycle is unlikely to be a repeat of the mammoth events of the 1980s. However, this observation contains both good and bad news. Unlike that of the 1980s when incredible growth was overwhelmed by unprecedented supply, the cycle of 1999–2004 will be defined by more moderate supply and demand growth. This does not mean that the U.S. office market is immune from cycles. In fact, as has been shown, the office market is, by its very nature, cyclical.

In the 1980s, we witnessed record growth in the labor force because of demographic events such as the entrance of the baby boomers into the workforce and women's increased participation. During the 1990s, however, demographic trends have limited growth in the workforce. With U.S. unemployment at a very low 4.1% (a 28-year low) and all the baby boomers already in the workforce, it will be increasingly difficult to add workers. There are simply not enough unemployed bodies to support growth at the current levels. The rate of growth in the working-age population is expected to slow continuously through the next 10 to 15 years. Since it is pointless to add new office space without new workers, slower growth in employment will translate into weaker absorption of office space (this is even more true as the cost of workers and space rise together). Office employment should grow at a fairly slow 1.8% annual rate during 1999–2004, versus the 3.2% rate of the 1980s and the 2.7% rate of 1990–1998.

This is happening just as rents are approaching the levels needed to support new construction and as capital has begun to flood the office market. Development is increasing in response to tightening market conditions. While the scope of development is different in this cycle (Class A for a Day), the level of demand is also different. (After all, it will be harder to fill huge downtown towers in this cycle, given the market's muted demand story.) However, construction is increasing just as we are at or beyond full employment. Rising supply and falling demand will translate into overbuilding.

While the rate of overbuilding is unlikely to reach the level of the 1980s, U.S. office vacancies have already bottomed out in this cycle at 10%, versus less than 5% during the last cycle. This has serious implications for the markets. First, at a micro level, not all submarkets will recover to the levels attained in the last cycle. Second, values are unlikely to reach their peak 1980s' levels except in a few markets. Third, less supply will be needed to push vacancies up to rent flattening levels in this cycle. So, rents will probably not rise as far as they did during the previous cycle. Vacancies at the national level are projected to increase gradually through 2004 as demand slows and new supply increases. However, vacancies are projected to approach 14%, versus their 1980s' peak near 19%. You can see, some good news, some less good news.

WHERE IS THE OFFICE MARKET GOING?

Going forward, growth in values is expected to drive total returns. Although NOIs are expected to grow by 1% to 2% annually over the next few years, the rate of growth in NOIs will substantially slow from its current level. Much of the gain in NOIs has already occurred. During the past few years, the gain in NOIs was driven by second- and third-tier markets that witnessed rents rising and vacancies falling from near 30% to the low teens. While NOIs have some room to grow, in most markets they will not be driven by rising occupancy levels. Rather, they will be primarily driven by rising rents, which will temporarily offset increasing vacancy rates. Then, the tenants will figure out what's going on.

Capital values are expected to increase by more than 15% as investors continue to seek well-located office properties. However, rapidly rising sales prices that are increasingly nearing or exceeding replacement costs (i.e., $300/SF for the Lincoln Place in the Washington, D.C. suburb of Arlington, $371/SF for 100 Wilshire in Los Angeles, and $500/SF for the GM building in Manhattan) indicate that pricing has gotten well ahead of market fundamentals. If pricing is, indeed, far ahead of market fundamentals, this may be occurring at the expense of future value growth. After all, investors are looking further ahead in this cycle. Therefore, as NOIs slow because of falling occupancies, values may peak prematurely.

Nevertheless, office space is still an attractive investment. While the rate of growth in capital values and NOIs will slow in most markets, growth will generally remain positive over the next two to three years. The rate of return for office investments will slow going forward as we get further into the cycle, but the returns will continue to be attractive in many markets. Not all markets will overbuild. Some MSAs, such as Miami, Bergen County, Stamford, Los Angeles, and Chicago, are expected to witness fairly balanced supply and demand growth over most of the forecast period. For these markets, this should translate into steady returns, with moderate risk.

WHAT TO WATCH OUT FOR

At this point in the office cycle, PPR is most worried about those markets that are prone to overbuilding. Demand should remain strong at the national and regional levels. While there are a few markets to watch from a demand standpoint (e.g., is Hartford in the midst of a long, secular decline? What does the Asian financial crisis mean to Honolulu, long term?), most markets will continue to absorb space. As the office markets continue to recover, rents will rise and further approach replacement costs. This will spur developers to begin construction, consistent with normal cyclical behavior. Therefore, except for an unforeseen national recession, the shock that the office market is most likely to see would be increased supply.

What markets especially concern us? Atlanta, Dallas, Orlando, Minneapolis, Phoenix, Portland, and Charlotte continue to overbuild. At a national level, new supply has already begun to outpace demand. Many markets that have been relatively slow to build, such as Seattle, San Francisco, Washington, and San Diego, are now witnessing rapidly rising construction levels. Across virtually all markets, development continues to increase even as the U.S. economy has begun to slow its expansion.

Exhibit 4: Office Market Trends

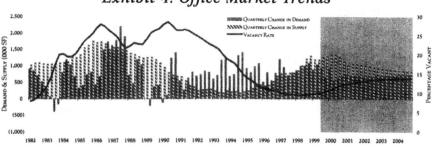

Let's look in closer detail at the Phoenix office market. Phoenix continues to enjoy a rapidly expanding economy that is growing at a pace more than twice the U.S. average. Although net in-migration totaled more than 60,000 new residents during 1998, unemployment remains very low at 3.2%. Unemployment has begun to limit the growth in Phoenix's red hot economy. While job growth expanded at more than a 7% rate in 1995 and 1996, it slowed to near 5.5% in 1997 and 1998. Employment growth is expected to further moderate as migration flows have continued to ease and as unemployment has fallen. Phoenix is expected to continue to outpace the U.S. average, expanding at almost a 4% rate but growth will continue to slow as labor availability and slower national growth impede demand. Phoenix has high current exposure to Asian demand because of its reliance on high-tech exports. Demand is expected to re-strengthen over the longer term, as Asian producers begin to demand chips for their finished goods.

The Phoenix office market has posted a strong recovery since late 1992 (see Exhibit 4). Demand exceeded net new supply during 1991–1997 by a ratio of 2.5 to one. Strengthening market fundamentals translated into stabilizing values, and by 1995, values and NOIs were increasing rapidly. Attracted by a large and relatively inexpensive labor pool, back-offices have flocked to submarkets near the airport and in the southeast. Vacancies declined from near 29% in 1990 to near 9.5% in 1998.

Extremely low vacancy rates, solid rent growth, and impressive high returns have stimulated a strong wave of office development in Phoenix. As rents have risen significantly, especially in southeast and northeast Phoenix, developers have returned with a vengeance, adding almost 4 million square feet during 1998, half of which was located in the Scottsdale market. Additionally, almost 2 million square feet of space have come online during the first half of 1999, and there are more than 4 million SF under construction. Most of the new space is concentrated in the Camelback Corridor and the rapid growth markets of Scottsdale and Tempe. Large downtown corporate tenants, such as Dial and Finova, have recently announced relocations to newer, more utilitarian space in Scottsdale/ Tempe. Most development consists of these Class A for a Day utilitarian buildings. However, as the development cycle has matured, new construction has begun to include towers in the Camelback Corridor. The list of developers includes many national forces, such as CarrAmerica, Opus, Hines, Koll, Trammell Crow, and the Ryan Companies. Construction shows no signs of slowing. In fact, more than 4.2 million square feet are actively proposed, and construction has begun on a new CBD tower with Bank America as the lead tenant (which is 50% pre-leased — translation: still 50% vacant — as of mid-1999)!

Unfortunately new supply is rising to its highest levels of the 1990s just as demand is beginning to slow. While demand will likely remain well ahead of the U.S. average and supply will be much less than it was during the 1980s, over-supply will still occur. (After all, vacancies rise when relative supply is higher than relative demand.) It is very unlikely that demand will be able to keep up with supply. In fact, given our current supply expectations, even if demand remained at its current level, vacancies would still rise. PPR projects that vacancies will increase to near 14% by 2003-2004.

Sources of capital are plentiful, and many investors are trying to buy into the "Phoenix growth story." (This is, in part, why we have seen prices in the Camel-back Corridor shoot past $200/SF.) PPR interprets these signals as the beginning of the end. This does not mean that the bottom will fall out of the Phoenix office market immediately (unless, of course, we really have "learned from the past" and new supply comes to a screeching halt!), but rather, that the market is weakening from this point forward. It is likely that rents and values will continue to increase for a while, but their rates of increase will slow. Values are projected to peak over the next two to three years, and then flatten. As values peak and total returns decline, the market will begin to enter a downturn, and capital flows to Phoenix will likely ease. If construction continues, rents will eventually slow, making construction harder to justify and bringing on the next part of the cycle — the recovery.

WHERE TO GO?

What office markets do we like? We like those markets where there is a strong demand story *relative* to supply. Those markets where the fundamentals are continuing to move in the right direction and returns are rising. Which come to mind? Los Angeles, Miami, Bergen County New Jersey, and Suburban Chicago. While many of these markets have rising supply levels, new construction remains well below the level of demand. Rents continue to rise as the market fundamentals strengthen, and widespread development does not yet make sense. With a few submarket exceptions (West L.A. and the Tri-Cities), the capital markets are not too far ahead of the recovery.

CONCLUSIONS

The easy money has been made in the U.S. office market. We have completed the recovery and are nearing the peak. While values and NOIs will continue to increase in the near future, they will do so at a much slower rate. Construction has reappeared and threatens to limit many markets' future expansions. Market selection and hard-edged, objective analysis are key. A number of good office investment opportunities continue to exist, as not all markets are at their peak. There are a number of different cycles co-existing in the market today. However, exposure to downside volatility continues to increase as the cycles mature. Do your homework and choose your markets and cycles well!

Chapter 10

The Market for Multifamily Housing

Susan Hudson-Wilson, CFA

Joanna M. Stimpson

Although multifamily housing has been exhaustively studied by housing economists, the relationship between multifamily market fundamentals and investment performance has seldom been examined. Similarly, little attention has been paid to the importance of allocation among different property types (warehouse, office, retail, and apartment) in a real estate portfolio containing multiple property types. This chapter shows that multifamily investments are underrepresented relative to a "market neutral" weight in current institutional portfolios. The percentage allocated to multifamily properties is less than would be called for by a naïve diversification strategy. A change in allocation policy might enhance achievement of some investors' return and risk objectives.

The supply and demand sides of the multifamily housing market are examined, and then these fundamentals are linked to asset performance, both in absolute terms and in the context of a real estate portfolio containing multiple property types.

The multifamily investment market has two critical dimensions: the space (physical) market and the investment market. The two markets interact, with various leads and lags, to produce supply, demand, and investment returns.[1] The demand side of the space market is developed first. The discussion considers traditional sources of demand as well as the changing face of today's renter household. The forces causing the number of renters to rise have reversed themselves and are now producing the opposite effect. Next, the supply side of the space market is analyzed. Supply is observed in the aggregate. Demand and supply are contrasted and past, current, and prospective conditions of market fundamentals are assessed. It then becomes clear that neither absolute supply nor absolute demand are sufficient to determine the performance of a market — each must be evaluated in the context of the other, market by market.

---

[1] For a detailed discussion on this topic, see Jeffrey D. Fisher, Susan Hudson-Wilson, and Charles H. Wurtzebach, "Equilibrium in Commercial Real Estate Markets: Linking Space and Capital Markets," *Journal of Portfolio Management* (Summer 1993).

Next, the investment environment is studied and the past performance of the multifamily sector is examined, first on its own merits and then relative to other major property types. Of interest are the factors motivating performance. Total returns, net operating incomes, cash flows, and capital appreciation and expenditures are examined. We follow with a discussion of the portfolio context within which an investment in the multifamily asset might be held in order to understand the role of multifamily investments as a return enhancer or risk reducer. Both naïve and more technical asset allocation rationales are described. Investor interest in multifamily investments is conditioned by the specific objectives of each individual real estate portfolio; some possible motivations are examined.[2] The conclusion examines the investment policy implications for institutional investors.

THE SPACE MARKET: DEMAND

There is a perception that because the U.S. is well into the period characterized as the "baby bust," demand for multifamily housing must be declining in absolute terms. Conventional wisdom holds that multifamily tenure is purely the province of the young. Patterns of the past show that as the population moves through the life cycle, aging households achieve growing levels of income. Since housing is a "normal" good that is consumed in greater quantity as income rises, more housing is purchased as households age. Part of the improvement in the level of housing is the size of the dwelling, and part is in the nature of the unit itself: single-family detached units are preferred over attached; owner-occupancy is preferred over rental.[3] Thus, if indeed the population is aging, and the patterns of behavior that have characterized the preceding generations still hold true, the percentage of owner-occupied households should be increasing and that of renter households decreasing.

Through the 1970s and the early 1980s, as the 81.8 million members of the baby boom cohort began to set up independent households, the demand side of the multifamily housing market was widely and properly understood to be booming. Household formation reached unprecedented levels and these new young households were choosing to rent rather than own.[4] This segment of the population was very mobile, and often earned too little income to consider purchasing a home. This group was also incented to be mobile as the fortunes of various geographies varied widely. If the prospects for employment were weak in one region, the young workers would simply move to another, more attractive region.

---

[2] For further discussion, see Mark Coleman, Susan Hudson-Wilson, and James R. Webb, "Real Estate in the Multiasset Portfolio," in Susan Hudson-Wilson and Charles H. Wurtzebach (eds.), *Managing Real Estate Portfolios* (Burr Ridge, Ill: Irwin, 1994), pp. 98–123.

[3] See Richard L. Cooperstein, "Quantifying the Decision to become a First-Time Home Buyer," *Urban Studies* (April 1989).

[4] For further discussion, see F. Modigliani, "Life Cycle, Individual Thrift, and the Wealth of Nations," *American Economic Review*, vol. 76, pp. 297–313.

Traditional perceptions of tenure choice are based on the reasoning that as the population ages and the age of household heads rises, the growth rate of households slows, the average tendency to rent falls (because older people own at disproportionate rates), and, therefore, the *growth* of the renter population should slow. In theory, if the aging of the population were substantial enough, the absolute number of renter households could actually decline over time.

The median age of the population has been rising since the 1970s, and this trend is expected to continue. This aging trend, along with other factors, has caused the rate of household growth to slow. The baby boom cohort that has long dominated trends in the U.S. is inexorably growing older and causing the median age of the population to rise sharply to levels never before experienced.[5]

There is also a growing "echo boom" comprised of children of the boomers that is not yet a factor in the rental market but will be in future years. Interestingly, there is increasing evidence that the echo boom, also previously called the "boomlet," will perhaps become as large as the original baby boom (perhaps it should be called the "boom-boom"!). Delayed marriages and childbirth created the impression that the baby boom would not quite replace itself. It is now becoming apparent that this will not be the case, although the composition of the echo is turning out to differ from that of the original boom. These shifts in composition will have repercussions for the housing market 20 years hence.[6]

As a result, there are now relatively fewer younger and more older heads of households. In 1990, 27% of the households were headed by persons less than 35 years old; in 2000, that share will drop to 21%. In 1990, 28% of the households were headed by people between the ages of 45 and 64; in 2000, that share will rise to 34%.[7] The 1990s represent the last time period when there was a fairly even distribution of household headship rates over the age groups. Given the new insights about the boom-boom, a more even distribution might be expected to reappear in 15 to 20 years when the boom-boom cohort comes of age and forms households.

Along with the aging of the population, the rate of new household formation is falling gradually and is forecasted to rest at a prospective level of approximately 1.1 to 1.2 million new households per year.[8] There is typically a cycle in the rate of household formations that is determined not solely by demographics but also by changing economic fortunes and societal norms.[9] The recession of 1982 dampened household growth, as did the economic slump in 1990. The rate

---

[5] For a comprehensive discussion on trends in home ownership and rental housing, see William Apgar, Jr., George Masnick, and Nancy McArdle, "Housing in America: 1970–2000," Joint Center for Housing Studies of Harvard University, 1991.

[6] An article of interest on the echo boom is "A Generation's Heritage: After the Boom, a Boomlet," by Trip Gabriel, *The New York Times*, February 12, 1995.

[7] U.S. Bureau of the Census, *Current Population Reports*, Series P-20, no. 1129 (1997).

[8] U.S. Bureau of the Census, *Current Population Reports: Household and Family Composition* (March 1997).

[9] For a discussion on household formation, see J. Doling, "The Family Life Cycle and Housing Choice," *Urban Studies*, vol. 13, no. 1 (February 1976).

of household formation, like the rate of consumption of any economic good, is created both by the *desire* and the *ability* to consume. In a recessionary period, multiple factors cause a decline in the rate of household formation. Among the most significant are the loss of economic purchasing power and of job security produced by layoffs and prolonged job searches. Between January 1993 and December 1995, 4.2 million workers who had been employed in a specific position for at least three years were displaced because of less work, plant closings, or the abolition of their positions or work shifts.[10] Unemployment duration over the last decade has ranged from an average low of 11.9 weeks in 1989 (the same as in 1980) to 16.7 weeks in 1996.[11] Of course, the tide resoundingly turned with the ongoing multi-year economic expansion. Corporate downsizings are decreasing steadily and consumer confidence, while slightly off its peak level, is still very high. These events cause household formation to reinvigorate, somewhat mitigating the downdraft created by demographics.

It is often difficult to separate the effects of economic factors, such as employment, from societal factors. For example, in the late '80s and early '90s more 20- to 30-year-olds resumed residence in their childhood home, returning either from higher education or a brief stint away from the family.[12] The initial motivation may well have been economic, but such behavior had become socially acceptable and so the trend may have increased beyond the level explained by economics alone.

This said, the U.S. population is still growing and households are still forming. In fact, as the economy continues to improve, there is an increasing propensity to form households, *partially* countermanding the effects of the baby bust.

Thus far, three facts have been established: (1) the population is aging, (2) the average age of the head of the household is rising, and (3) although there is still positive growth in the total number of households, the rate of growth is slowing. If past assumptions about the preference to rent of households along with the first two characteristics still hold true, the average propensity of all households to rent must be falling. The slowdown in the rate of household formation causes additional downward pressure on the propensity to rent although the health of the economy causes household growth to improve. It would seem to be a logical conclusion that the number of renter households is declining. Not so!

This presumption had been accurate because there were other demographic and economic factors influencing the propensity to rent. For example, the median age of a first-time homebuyer was 28.3 years in 1980 and rose to 32.4 years in 1996.[13] This delay in first-time buying behavior was evident in all but the

---

[10] U.S. Department of Labor, Bureau of Labor Statistics, News, USDL 96-446.

[11] *Statistical Abstract of the United States 1997* and Bureau of Labor Statistics, *Employment and Earnings*, vol. 45, no.1 (January 1998).

[12] For a discussion on youth and housing, see Donald Haurin, Patric Hendershott, and Dongwook Kim, "Housing Decisions of American Youth," *Journal of Urban Economics*, vol. 35 (1994), pp. 28–45; see also, U.S. Bureau of the Census, *Current Population Reports*, Series P-20, nos. 433 and 445 (1997).

[13] *Statistical Abstract of the United States 1997*. Section 25: Construction and Housing.

very oldest cohort of households. The average propensity to rent is actually rising over time. Of particular interest is the behavior of the baby boomer cohort, since it is by far the largest group.

When the rental propensity of each of these age groups is weighted by the size of the cohort and then summed, one has the total percentage of renter households. From 1975 to 1980, the percentage of renters dropped precipitously, but beginning with the recession of 1981–82 the tendency to rent began to grow. It settled at a rate of about 36% until 1994, when it began to decline (Exhibit 1).

The increase in the tendency to rent had indeed caused the absolute number of renter households to grow. If the propensity to rent had remained stable and did not rise any further, there would have been positive growth in the number of renter households. However, this trend did not last. Instead the rate of home ownership has risen to historical highs. Thirty-year lows in mortgage interest rates and record high levels of consumer confidence have contributed greatly to the growth in home ownership.

This shift toward renter households and then toward home ownership, over the past decade, is important to understand.

There were many reasons causing an increased tendency to rent rather than to own. Among the economic factors are regional and macroeconomics pressures on job security and real incomes, and the volatility of interest rates and house prices. There are also socio-demographic influences on the size of the household such as marriage, divorce, and childbearing rates, and immigration.

Economic Pressures

The macroeconomy had been putting pressure on wage rates, real incomes, interest rates, housing prices, and the number and mix of jobs. Each macroeconomic event is exaggerated when viewed in the context of certain regional economies. As the rolling recessions proceeded, the events discussed below affected one region or another in turn.

Exhibit 1: Percentage of Renter Households, 1975–1998

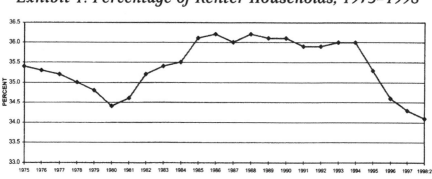

Source: U.S. Bureau of the Census

The U.S. economy has steadily transformed its base from manufacturing to services. This transformation is occurring at different times across the cities of the nation. Manufacturing's share of employment has been falling while the service sector's share has increased in both large and small cities in varying geographical areas.

This transformation in the structure of the U.S. economy has had two important results. First, many workers were dislocated. The sectors where they earned their livelihoods have in many cases simply disappeared from the economic landscape. The textile industry is a classic example of this shift. Even textile manufacturers that initially relocated to less costly parts of the United States have now shifted to even lower-cost production sites in other countries.[14] The workers displaced by this kind of industry relocation are not trained for alternative occupations, nor are they typically living in areas where the emerging service employment is located. There are very real costs associated with retraining and relocating, which many find difficult to afford. Even if new employment is eventually found, there is often a considerable diminution in the wealth the household has managed to accumulate. This clearly influences the ability to own a home.

Once this shift has had its effects, the repercussions cease. The displaced workers either settle into a less affluent lifestyle and stay where they are, or they move to another part of the country where opportunity seems better. The economy is now well through the really savage part of this transformation and, in general, the economy is far healthier; so the detrimental impact on home ownership is largely behind us.

The second result of the transformation is that the wages in the service sector, while very attractive for certain well-trained professionals, are less attractive for some blue-collar workers. In 1997, workers in manufacturing industries earned an average of $13.17 per hour, while many in the service sector earned an average of $12.28 per hour.[15] Assuming that a displaced worker was living in an area where service sector firms were located, and assuming that he or she obtained the training to qualify for a position in a service industry, it is very likely that the new position would pay less in salary and benefits than the original job. The diminution of benefits alone means that salary must be diverted from consumer goods, including housing, to provide the household with the same medical and other benefits. Also, the cost of education is rising faster than the rate of inflation. Data available from the Consumer Price Index for All Urban Consumers (1982–84 = 100) indicate that in 1996 the index for All Items combined stood at 156.9, compared to 279.8 for College Tuition.[16] Clearly, the cost of becoming one of the lucky minority able to get a high-paying position in the new economy is increasingly dear.

---

[14] Bureau of Labor Statistics, *Employment and Earnings*, vol. 45, no. 1 (January 1998).

[15] *Statistical Abstract of the United States 1997.*

[16] For further discussion about baby boomers and the labor market, see P. Levine and O. Mitchell, "Expected Changes in the Workforce and Implications for Labor Markets," in Rappaport and Schreiber (eds.), *Demography and Retirement: The 21st Century*, Pension Research Council, 1993, pp. 76–96.

Exhibit 2: Growth Rate of Working-Age Population

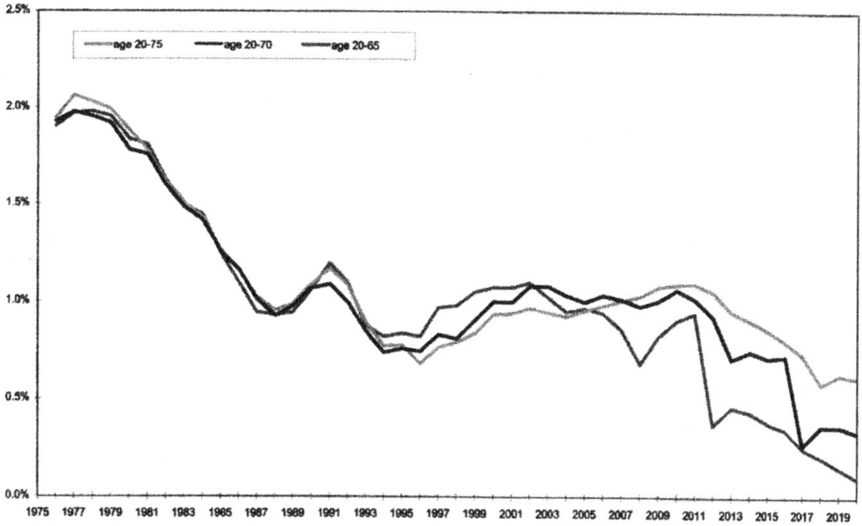

Source: U.S. Bureau of the Census

Furthermore, the service economy is not as unionized as the manufacturing sector. Everyone looking for work must negotiate a position and salary as best he can, in the face of a baby boom–heavy, highly competitive job market.[17] Even members of the lucky minority who are able to get the education necessary to obtain a position with a decent salary and benefits package are finding that as they age and rise through the ranks, there are fewer top-level positions available and very stiff competition for each job. Thus, original expectations for lifetime earnings are adjusted downward, as are consumption of housing and other consumer durables.

There have also been sharp cutbacks by the formerly most secure and attractive sectors of the service and manufacturing economies. A position at a leading bank, a Baby Bell, Ma Bell, or IBM is no longer a guarantee of lifetime job security. Successful businesses have learned to manage their bottom lines rigorously to match the growth of the national economy. More recently this extreme pressure on earnings and profits has significantly eased and companies are downsizing considerably less. The baby bust has another key ramification — a great decline in the growth rate of the labor force (Exhibit 2) and thus the unemployment rate. Workers, in such excess just a few short years ago, are now scarce, very scarce. Job security has risen, and worker and consumer confidence have risen with it.

This trend of increasing labor scarcity can only produce one of several equally unappealing results: the growth rate of the economy can suffer and/or wage inflation can rise and prompt the Federal Reserve Bank to respond. In any

---

[17] U.S. Bureau of Economic Analysis, *National Income and Product Accounts of the United States*, vol. 2, 1959–88, and *Survey of Current Businesses*, July 1992, August 1993, and March 1994.

event, consumer confidence is likely to suffer, dampening both household formation and home ownership.

The above risk and the difficulty of maintaining a steady income caused
many households to both deplete their savings in times of economic distress and
to find accumulating savings difficult even in times of less distress. The national
savings rate was abysmally low, as was the accumulated wealth of the average
household. In 1980 personal saving comprised 7.9% of disposable personal
income; by 1993 that figure was a low 4.0%.[18] By 1996 the rate had risen some, to
4.9%.[19] Again, a rising savings rate and the accumulation of wealth are two
events that the life-cycle hypothesis would predict, given the current demographic
configuration of the U.S. These trends bode well for home ownership rates.

On top of the difficulties of maintaining a steady paycheck, additional risks
have been introduced into the housing markets. Interest rates had proven volatile,
and it had also become clear that house prices can fall as well as rise. High rates
clearly chill enthusiasm for purchasing a home, as they price a large segment of buyers out of the market. Even if potential buyers have accumulated a down payment,
they cannot always meet the income requirement and so cannot qualify for a loan.[20]

The volatility of interest rates causes many to worry about the risks of variable rate mortgages and their ability to sell a home in the future if rates rise.[21] From
peak (1981) to trough (1998), rates fell more than 58% and from trough (1978) to
peak (1981), rates rose 70%. Translating this into payment terms, interest rate volatility produces a range of possible total interest payments on a $100,000 mortgage,
assuming no amortization and a 30-year term, of from $219,900 to $499,200!

We are clearly operating in an entirely different economic environment as of
this writing. The Fed has successfully dampened inflation and has radically reduced
the volatility of inflation. Inflation is low, and interest rates are low, but asset prices
are raging, along with an increasing likelihood that inflation, caused by rising wages
given the low unemployment rates, will again be an issue. Certainly the Fed will
respond to this long-term and sustaining pressure and may again send the economy
back to the difficult years of the last recession (if Asia and Moscow don't do it first!).

Thus, while interest rates were driving an increase in renters through the
early '90s, they are now sponsoring an increase in home ownership. We live in
volatile global times and so a reversal of today's good fortune can readily happen.

---

[18] *Statistical Abstract of the United States 1997*, U.S. Bureau of Economic Analysis, "National Income and Product Accounts of the United States," 1929–94, forthcoming, and *Survey of Current Business*, May 1997.

[19] Ibid., p. 12.

[20] For additional discussion, see Peter Linneman and Susan Wachter, "The Impacts of Borrowing Con-straints on Homeownership," *American Real Estate and Urban Economics Association Journal*, vol. 17, no. 4 (1989), pp. 389–402; Peter Zorn, "Mobility-Tenure Decisions and Financial Credit: Do Mortgage Qualification Requirements Constrain Homeownership?" *American Real Estate and Urban Economics Association Journal*, vol. 17, no. 4 (1989), pp. 1–16.

[21] For further discussion about the impact of interest rates and inflation on housing demand, see William Wheaton, "Life Cycle Theory, Inflation, and the Demand for Housing," *Journal of Urban Economics*, vol. 18 (1985), pp. 161–179.

An additional, and heretofore unusual, risk has been added to the home ownership decision criteria. It is now well established that houses can actually lose value, and are not necessarily a secure store of wealth. In Boston and Los Angeles, for example, people were effectively locked into their houses as values fell below the mortgage balances. In Boston, average house prices fell more than 12% from the peak to the trough, and in Los Angeles the erosion in value was 25%. This means that in the case of a typical 75% loan-to-value mortgage the Boston owner lost 50% of his equity, and the Los Angeles owner lost 100% and possibly more.[22]

This scenario was repeated in virtually every city in the nation. Householders found their mobility restricted as they were forced to write a check to the bank in order to extricate themselves from their homes. Families had to declare bankruptcy and suffer real losses of equity they had never contemplated. Again in recent years some of these losses have been regained. Certainly in Boston, home prices are above their prior peaks. But the householder has learned that this too can change.

For the average American, this experience with macroeconomic pressures, diminished then reestablished economic security, and interest rate and house price volatility is very real and certainly influences thinking and behavior. As these risks have subsided, there has been a return to historic renter and owner trends. From 1994 to 1997, four million new householders became home owners. There is, however, evidence to suggest that risks to consumers' confidence can re-emerge. The very hint of economic stress might be enough to chill the increase in home ownership, and perhaps initiate its decline.

Demographic and Sociological Factors

In addition to economic trends, there are some very real demographic and sociological factors that can push households toward a greater propensity to rent. Among the most important of these are delayed marriage accompanied by delayed childbirth; more single-parent, single-person, and other nontraditional households; and immigration. An additional "soft" influence is the increasing scarcity of time.

These demographic and social phenomena have produced smaller households. In 1980, the average household size was 2.75, and in 1997, it was 2.64.[23] This number is expected to continue to fall slowly over the next 5 to 10 years and possibly speed up its downward drift as the baby boom ages. In the early phases of aging, the children of the boomers will leave home. In the later phase of the

---

[22] For further discussion, see Karl Case, "The Real Estate Cycle and the Economy: Consequences of the Massachusetts Boom of 1984–87," *New England Economic Review*, (September/October 1991), pp. 37–46; Karl Case and L. Cook, "The Distributional Effects of Housing Price Booms: Winners and Losers in Boston, 1980–89," *New England Economic Review* (March/April 1989); Karl Case and Robert Shiller, "The Behavior of Home Buyers in Boom and Post-Boom Markets," *New England Economic Review* (November/December 1988), pp. 29–46; Patric Hendershott and Yunhi Won, "Introducing Risky Housing and Endogenous Tenure Choice into a Portfolio-Based General Equilibrium Model," *Journal of Public Economics*, vol. 48, no. 3 (August 1992), pp. 293–316.

[23] U.S. Bureau of the Census, *Current Population Reports: Household and Family Composition,* March 1997.

aging process, one of the spouses or partners in a married or nontraditional household will die. Once the baby boom effect is past, average household size may rise
again, but not for quite some time.

Smaller households have reduced space requirements and those households comprised of single parents and nontraditional groups have fewer economic
resources with which to purchase a home. Single-parent and nontraditional households are also typically less stable and so are less willing to lock themselves into
a home, particularly now that the risks are better understood.[24]

An important demographic and social issue worthy of mention is the
immigrant population. Recent immigrants comprise (generally) an equal size or
even larger group than the group that entered in all the years prior to 1980. The
share of each major gateway city's population that is comprised of immigrants is
growing. Immigration is likely to increase with the global free trade initiatives
and as the domestic labor force continues to decline, and so this population will
materially shape housing demand.

It is interesting to look at the age distribution of the immigrant population
compared with that of the native-born population. Exhibit 3 makes it clear that
immigrants are young. Young people still rent in higher proportions than older people. In the case of the immigrant population, the tendency to rent is quite extreme so
that, in fact, this group's overall tendency to rent is a very high 75%. Among the
younger cohorts and the more recently arrived immigrants the propensity is virtually 100%.[25] It is anticipated that immigration will continue and perhaps even
increase. In fact, as the impact of the slowing growth rate of the working-age population is duly noted in falling unemployment rates, a shift in immigration policy is
highly likely. This trend will certainly contribute to the stock of renter households.

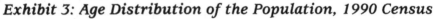

Exhibit 3: Age Distribution of the Population, 1990 Census

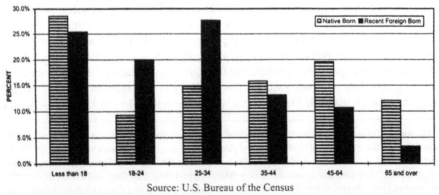

Source: U.S. Bureau of the Census

[24] Discussion of household composition trends can be found in "The State of the Nation's Housing, 1997,"
Joint Center for Housing Studies of Harvard University.
[25] Nancy McArdle and Kelly S. Mikelson, "The New Immigrants: Demographic and Housing Characteristics," Joint Center for Housing Studies of Harvard University, Working Paper W94-1.

A less measurable, but nevertheless influential, societal factor is the increasing scarcity of free time.[26] Americans are working longer hours, and, on average, the typical workweek is now up to 39.3 hours from the 1970 level of 38.3 hours.[27] There are now many two-worker households and so the time available for the routines of everyday living has become progressively a scarcer resource. In 1960, 37.7% of all women aged 16 and over were participants in the workforce. By 1996, female participation had risen to 59.3%.[28] If the household dwells in a rental unit, many of the services associated with running the household (trash and snow removal, building and grounds upkeep, etc.) are included in the rent. Owning a home is unconditionally more time-consuming than renting, since at least some portion of the routine services must be provided by the owner. At a minimum, the owner must take the time to make some provision for the delivery of these services. As a lifestyle choice some households are expressing a preference for renting, not only to conserve time, but financial resources as well. It is typical for a household, as it ages and begins to plan for retirement, to become more interested in financial investments and less interested in housing market investments. A household's risk premium rises as its retirement savings objective increases in importance, and if home ownership is perceived to embody risks, older households may shift wealth out of housing and into financial assets.[29]

One counterforce to the desire to gain time by renting rather than owning is the magnitude of the tax benefit associated with home ownership. The desire for an easier lifestyle must overwhelm this obvious and great tax shelter. It may very well do so in some, but probably not in a large number of cases.

The Trend

From all the hard and soft evidence presented above it seems likely that while the propensity to rent will continue to be low, the rate of household formation and the shift in the nature of the households will continue to evolve. Net-net will the total number of renters rise or fall? The number will rise, but how fast?

THE SPACE MARKET: SUPPLY

The discussion of demand is only interesting or relevant to an investor in the context of supply. Will either a favorable or less favorable demand scenario be undermined by an inappropriate degree of supply? Here historical and current supply are examined. Then the availability of capital to the multifamily construction market will be assessed in order to make some observations about prospective supply.

---

[26] For a discussion of this topic, see Eric Solberg, "Family Time Use: Leisure, Home Production, Market Work, and Work Related Travel," *Journal of Human Resources* vol. 27, no. 3 (Summer 1992), pp. 485–510.

[27] U.S. Bureau of Labor Statistics, *Employment and Earnings*, January issues.

[28] Bulletin 2307.

[29] See Gurdip Bakshi and Zhiwu Chen, "Baby Boom, Population Aging, and Capital Markets," *Journal of Business*, vol. 67, no. 2 (1994).

Exhibit 4: U.S. Apartment Market Trends

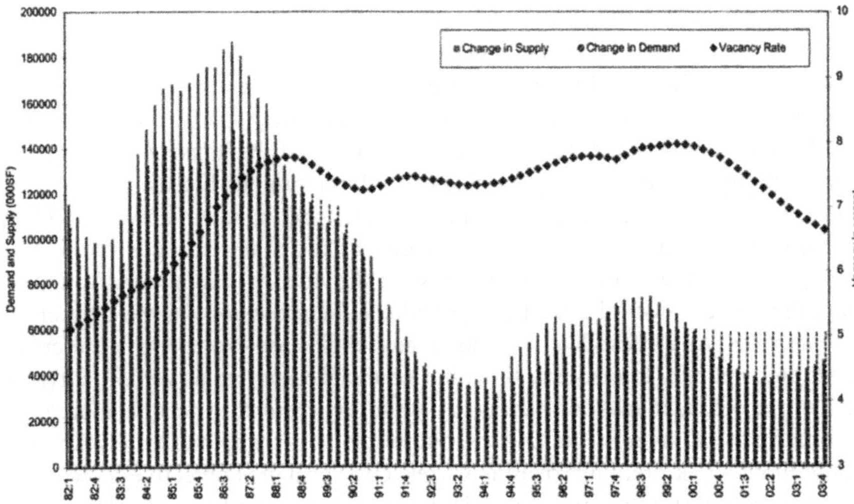

Source: Property & Portfolio Research, Inc.

Construction of multifamily units in buildings with five or more units has been highly cyclical over time.[30] From the peak of construction in 1985 to the trough in 1993, multifamily starts fell more than 83%. The tax benefit-induced peak of 1985 produced an unambiguous oversupply of rental housing, even though the peak coincided with a demand spike in household formations. Here was a case where the demand picture was fully favorable but was rendered fully useless by the supply side of the market! The supply correction occurred in the manner of most construction corrections, with a vengeance. In 1997, approximately 296,000 units were started, a rate 62% below the former peak. Construction has not even yet regained the levels that preceded the peak. It is not expected that the levels of the mid-1980s will ever recur (Exhibit 4).

On a flow basis there have been some years since 1990 where additions to demand have exceeded additions to supply, but by far the reverse has been true and supply has outstripped demand. At the end of the 1990s the market looked to be in balance overall.

Rental rates continued to rise beyond the period of excess construction. Such pricing inefficiencies occur because both landlords and tenants have imperfect information about housing supply and demand. Furthermore, rents are "sticky" because tenants need to initiate a search and incur the costs of moving in order to take advantage of changes in the general price level.

---

[30] For additional discussion on cyclicality of real estate markets in general, see Joseph Gyourko and Richard Voith, "Leasing as a Lottery: Implications for Rational Building Surges and Increasing Vacancies," *Journal of American Real Estate and Urban Economics Association*, vol. 21 (1993), pp. 83–106.

Exhibit 5: New Construction by Segment 1975–1997
(Apartments in Buildings with 5+ Units)

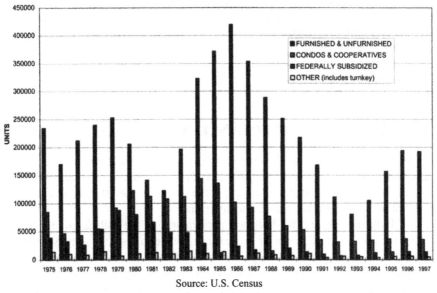

Source: U.S. Census

Furthermore, landlords do not adjust their rents downward until the turn-over in a property rises to a certain level and occupancy may have begun to erode. However, multifamily rents are less sticky than office rents as perseverance in a loose market environment leads to a reduction in total revenues as above-market rental rates are offset by below-market occupancies.[31]

Nominal rents stabilized as vacancy rates began to drift downward in 1991.[32] Landlords became aware of the tightening conditions and were able to increase rents without suffering a diminution of occupancy and total revenue. Tenants recognized that the assumption of search costs would not produce a more favorable rent. As hypothesized, vacancy rates drifted downward, and were below the level experienced during the period of excess construction. In the late 1990s construction reemerged (Exhibit 5), but at a disciplined pace overall. On average rental rates are fairly stable across the U.S. markets.

The great excess supply of the 1980s was mainly attributable to the overly generous tax code.[33] The tax inducements were part of a general stimulus program. There is virtually no possibility that such a tax benefit would be enacted again. The great rush of legitimate 1980s demand was met by a great rush of legitimate supply, which was then abetted by the tax code. The environment of

---

[31] For further discussion, see Randall Eberts and Timothy Gronberg, "Wage Gradients, Rent Gradients, and the Price Elasticity of Demand for Housing: An Empirical Investigation," *Journal of Urban Economics*, vol. 12 (1982), pp. 168–176.

[32] Housing Vacancy Survey — first quarter 1998.

slow-moving demand and commensurate supply should be sustainable on average with some exceptions in some urban areas at some times. Typically this occurs in the highest growth urban areas and is always followed by drastic reversals. Such boom-bust cycles are both predictable and avoidable. Even the REITs figure out that excess supply does not serve either themselves or their shareholders and so eventually turn off the spigot. Thus it is fair to plan on experiencing generally unexciting, but stable, multifamily fundamentals. Sometimes "unexciting" beats the heck out of the alternatives!

INVESTMENT PERFORMANCE: MULTIFAMILY SECTOR

This section focuses on the absolute and relative investment performance of the aggregate multifamily asset class. Multifamily's exposure to loss, return characteristics, and reward relative to risk are compared with the other asset categories available to private market real estate investors.

Exhibit 6 presents the historical performance of the multifamily investment sector relative to the other major property type categories. Property & Portfolio Research's forecast of the future performance of each sector is presented. Based upon the supply and demand fundamentals as well as the capital market environment discussed above, multifamily investments should slightly underperform the office and retail sectors and very slightly outperform the industrial sector through 2003.[34]

Exhibit 6: NCREIF and PPR Derived Market Returns by Property Type

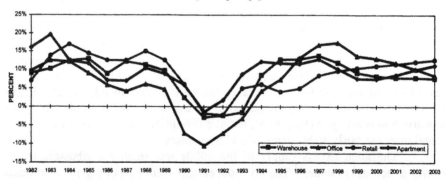

Sources: National Council of Real Estate Investment Fiduciaries and Property & Portfolio Research, Inc.

[33] For additional discussion, see Denise DiPasquale and William Wheaton, "The Cost of Capital, Tax Reform, and the Future of the Rental Housing Market," *Journal of Urban Economics*, vol. 31 (1992), pp. 337–359; and James Follain, Donald Leavens, and Orawin Velz, "Identifying the Effects of Tax Reform on Multifamily Rental Housing," *Journal of Urban Economics*, vol. 34 (1993), pp. 275–298.

[34] Similar analysis is conducted for each of the other property type categories in order to derive expectations of their performance.

Exhibit 7: Average, Maximum, and Minimum Two-Year Rolling Returns, 1982:1-1997:4

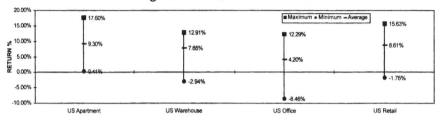

Sources: National Council of Real Estate Investment Fiduciaries and Property & Portfolio Research, Inc.

Exhibit 8: Average, Maximum, and Minimum 5-Year Rolling Returns, 1982:1-1997:4

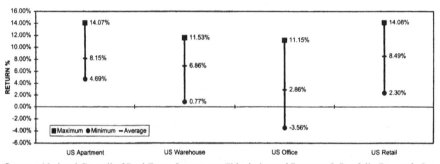

Sources: National Council of Real Estate Investment Fiduciaries and Property & Portfolio Research, Inc.

Perhaps more insightful than the standard line plot of historical returns are the two-year and five-year rolling returns for each property type presented in Exhibits 7 and 8. These plots depict the maximum gain, maximum loss, and average performance experienced over rolling two- and five-year holding periods. The message of the two holding periods is virtually the same — multifamily investments achieved higher or equal maximum returns, better average returns, and less severe maximum losses than any of the other sectors. This indicates that the return per unit of risk is quite favorable for multifamily investments.

In addition to the basic facts regarding the overall performance of multifamily investments versus other property types, it is interesting to observe the composition of returns. Investors typically prefer to know how their return will be delivered to them: as booked, but possibly not realized, net operating income (NOI); as received cash; or as booked, but possibly not realized, capital. Exhibit 9 presents annual NOI returns by property type and shows that, although the industrial sector has experienced the greatest NOI returns, it has also experienced the widest swings in the level of NOI. The level of multifamily NOI almost always dominates the levels of the industrial and retail NOI. In the forecast period retail NOIs are expected to recover nicely after a prolonged period of underperformance.

Exhibit 9: NOI Returns by Property Type, 1982–2003

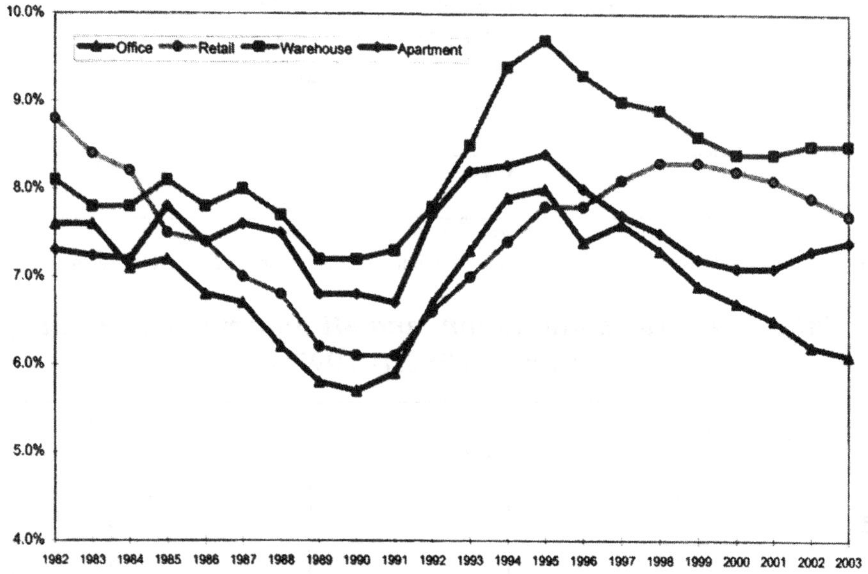

Sources: National Council of Real Estate Investment Fiduciaries and Property & Portfolio Research, Inc.

Multifamily exhibits the lowest absolute level of capital expenditures and so more NOI is received by the investor than from any other property type. NOI is an accounting concept, which may or may not be suggestive of realized returns. When capital expenditures are examined and subtracted from NOI to obtain a view of realized cash flows — a concept analogous to the dividend on a stock — the comparison changes. Exhibits 10 and 11 capture the effects of capital expenditures on NOI and cash flows. An investor with a preference for returns paid out in cash will have an interest in the multifamily sector as it is the source of the bulk of the return.

Multifamily cash flows provide a low-volatility source of return because of the lease and tenant characteristics of multifamily properties. There are many tenants occupying each property so that some aspects of credit risk are mitigated. Because lease terms are typically short, occupancy can be managed through frequent adjustments to rental rates as driven by market forces. To the extent that turnover can be minimized, capital expenditures can be further suppressed. The cost of turnover is real in the operation of multifamily assets and progress in reducing its velocity moves cash directly to the bottom line.

Because such a large portion of the return to a multifamily asset is derived from known cash flows, the pricing of multifamily properties tends to be more stable than for other property types. Less of the present value hinges on an uncertain residual value and more reliance is placed on current and understandable cash flows.

Exhibit 10: Average Cash Flow and Capital Expenditure as a Percentage of NOI, 1982-1997

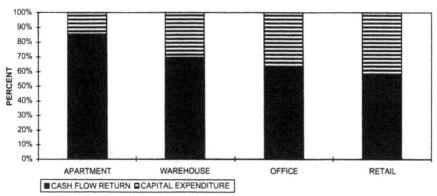

Sources: National Council of Real Estate Investment Fiduciaries and Property & Portfolio Research, Inc.

Exhibit 11: Cash Flow Returns by Property Type, 1982-2003

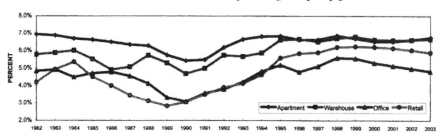

Sources: National Council of Real Estate Investment Fiduciaries and Property & Portfolio Research, Inc.

Thus, on a stand-alone basis, multifamily investments exhibit relatively stable aggregate performance over time, attractive relative performance in terms of the maximum, minimum, and average return experiences over different holding periods, and derive the bulk of their performance from cash flow rather than capital growth. Multifamily assets may not be exciting, but they are reliable and some investors require exactly this temperament in an investment.

INVESTMENT PERFORMANCE: PORTFOLIO CONTEXT

This section describes the role of the multifamily asset within the context of a portfolio of private market real estate investments, and shows that the multifamily asset has a long-term, "evergreen" role within a portfolio as a risk reducer. Multifamily investments are, in fact, the most powerful risk reducers available to real estate investors.

Exhibit 12: PPR Estimates of Value — 1998
(For the 60 Largest Urban Areas)

	Dollar Value Billions	% Share
Retail	$0.999	35.35%
Office	$0.979	34.65%
Residential	$0.611	21.62%
Warehouse	$0.237	8.38%
Total	$2.827	100.0%

Exhibit 13: NCREIF Weights — 1998

Residential	15.2%
Retail	29.1%
Office	37.2%
Warehouse	12.7%
Other	5.7%

Two ways to start thinking about the role of the multifamily asset are to look at its place in the market index and in a typical pension fund portfolio. How large is the asset type and how are tax-exempt investors actually using the asset? Property & Portfolio Research, Inc. has estimated the value of the four primary property types. Estimates of their absolute and relative values for 1998 are presented in Exhibit 12.

These estimates are largely consistent with the findings of past studies and are certainly acceptable as a starting point. Investors who wish to bring the simple systematic behavior of real estate to bear on the return and risk of the aggregate portfolio would allocate their real estate portfolios in line with these weights.[35] This approach would constitute a naive, or passive, investment strategy.

A reference point with respect to the actual behavior of U.S. pension funds is the allocation over property types as captured by the combined index of the NCREIF property performance database that appears in Exhibit 13.

NCREIF data place a greater weight on office and retail investments and lesser than market weights on industrial and multifamily property types. Thus, it is clear that institutional investors are currently underweighted, versus the market or naïve benchmark, in the multifamily sector. It is, therefore, apparent that investors are bringing something other than the systematic behavior of the real estate asset to the aggregate portfolio. Is this underweighting deliberate? Is it the result of an objective and calculated desire to capture a different real estate investment behavior?

---

[35] For an in-depth discussion, see Chapter 6: "Real Estate Portfolio Management" in Susan Hudson-Wilson and Charles Wurtzebach (eds.) *Managing Real Estate Portfolios*.

In order to address these questions, a more rigorous framework is employed for assessing the role of the multifamily asset in the overall real estate portfolio. This framework applies the mathematics of mean variance analysis used in *modern portfolio theory* to the asset allocation problem within the real estate asset portfolio. Two efficient frontiers, calculated across two time periods, illuminate the role of multifamily investments.[36] These frontiers are calculated using the inputs of expected or average historical return, standard deviation, and correlations. The model asks how the performance, the risk, and the relative behavior of each asset come together to suggest a role for each asset in an investor's portfolio. The analysis allows for the examination of the portfolios that lie exactly on the frontier; these are the "mean-variance efficient" portfolios and represent the best portfolio one could hold at each level of risk.

Four major property types were included in this analysis: multifamily, office, warehouse, and retail. The analysis is conducted over the following time periods:

Full historical — 1982 through 1997, and
Full forecast — 1999 through 2003.

The analysis uses the time period specific average returns to capture "expected" return and the full historical time period estimates of standard deviation and correlation.

Exhibit 14 presents the full, historical efficient frontier. A couple of points may be made. First, the frontier is quite short, suggesting that investors would have been wise to focus their attention on a fairly narrow set of investment candidates. Second, the frontier is quite high, suggesting that, if the investors were smart about what they did, they would be well rewarded for assuming risk. The portfolios falling right on the frontier are strongly dominated by allocations to the apartment sector, nicely complemented by investments in retail. Office investments do not even enter the realm of preferred investments as the return *over the entire period* was not attractive relative to the risk. Office investments are volatile and require very careful, year-by-year use. Third, the portfolio actually held by the pension fund community as a whole does not even come close to replicating this efficient set of allocations and so was not even in the ballpark of being efficient. A final observation is that while the model prefers multifamily over warehouse investments, in fact, they are fairly close substitutes with multifamily just edging out warehouse and so one might use them both rather than focus on multifamily to the exclusion of warehouse.

---

[36] For a description of mean-variance analysis, see Edwin J. Elton and Martin J. Gruber, *Modern Portfolio Theory and Investment Analysis*, 3rd ed. (New York: John Wiley & Sons, Inc., 1987).

Exhibit 14: Efficient Frontier and Allocations, 1982–1997

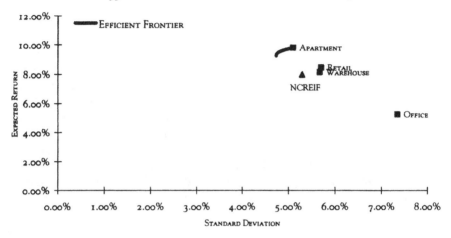

Source: Property & Portfolio Research, Inc.

Efficient Frontier Allocation

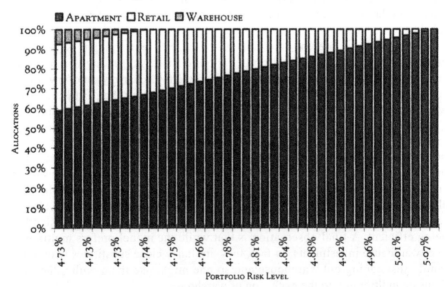

Source: Property & Portfolio Research, Inc.

So how could an investor have used this insight to invest through the last cycle? An investor might have created a base portfolio of retail and multifamily holdings. Over the early part of the cycle this investor might have added, very carefully, some of the better performing office and warehouse markets to raise returns while assuming more, but adequately rewarded, risk. As the market cycle deteriorated the investor would have moved out of all high-risk, and now less-well-rewarded, assets and retreated to a smaller core position consisting of retail and multifamily holdings. The investor could have captured the benefits of the market cycle while evading the deleterious aspects of volatility. The investor could have maintained a position in real estate through the entire cycle, but would have assumed a more defensive posture during the downturn. This is precisely what portfolio managers in other asset classes try to do.

Over the forecast period one sees a major difference in the shape of the efficient frontier and in the composition of the portfolios along the frontier (Exhibit 15). The forecast suggests that office investments do have a role in a risk-managed portfolio, but that the role is at the high-risk end of the frontier. At the very right end of the frontier the portfolio consists of 100% office investments.

Along the moderate and less risky portions of the frontier the efficient portfolios are comprised of a mix of multifamily and retail (as was so over history) with the same caveat concerning warehouse — it really is somewhat of a substitute for multifamily with multifamily just edging it out. Interestingly, as one moves from left to right, the allocation to retail stays about constant while the multifamily allocation yields to the office allocation.

The pattern of the use of the four property types in efficient private market portfolios suggests that the key role of the multifamily asset is to reduce real estate portfolio risk. There are two reasons why the multifamily asset is such a useful risk reducer. First, the standard deviation of the returns of the multifamily asset is low. Second, and perhaps more important in the context of a portfolio, is that the correlations between multifamily and the other property types are low. So when multifamily is added to a portfolio, a powerful risk reduction benefit is realized. The timing of the multifamily cycle is just sufficiently "off" the timing of the other cycles to render the asset most helpful.

Now it is possible to look back to the current allocation of pension fund capital as evidenced by the NCREIF data and assess the implications. The multifamily weight is definitely below that suggested by either of the mean-variance analyses and is below the weight implied by a naïve diversification strategy. This implies that the institutions represented in the NCREIF data set either have a secret cache of multifamily they are not sharing with NCREIF or that their tolerance for real estate risk is quite high, or, most likely, that they lack an understanding of the risk-reducing characteristics of multifamily investments.

All of this analysis is time-sensitive. As the markets continue to cycle, the relationships among the four property types will shift and the exact implied portfolio allocations will change. The time periods examined suggest that all four property types have a role in a well-managed real estate portfolio. The exact role depends on when, and on the investor's need for return and tolerance for risk.

Exhibit 15: Efficient Frontier and Allocations, 1999–2003

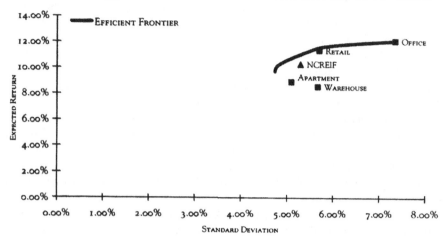

Source: Property & Portfolio Research, Inc.

Efficient Frontier Allocation

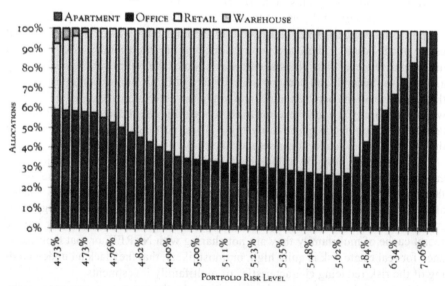

Source: Property & Portfolio Research, Inc.

CONCLUSIONS

In this chapter we have examined the fundamental drivers of multifamily investment performance and reviewed the historical and prospective behavior of the property type both alone and in the context of the portfolio. It is clear that the past is not necessarily a prelude to the future. The conditions in the multifamily sector shift greatly as the demographic and economic influences shift.

Both the demand and the supply side of the market have changed. On the demand side there are some different behaviors governing a household's decision to rent. The propensity to rent rose radically through the 1980s and has since settled back down. The supply excesses of the '80s have been steadily reduced. The balance between supply and demand is on the mend and any future overbuilding is likely to be localized and avoidable. The great wave of supply that occurred in the '80s is very unlikely to recur as it was a creation of the tax code, a government-sponsored response to a healthy demand picture.

The investment performance of the multifamily asset is constructive both in absolute and portfolio terms. The asset is a powerful risk manager, and any investor with a moderate to low tolerance for risk in his real estate portfolio will be interested in the multifamily sector. The return-maximizing, high-risk-tolerant investor will have less of an interest, except in the context of the periodic and drastic reversals in the office sector.

Chapter 11

Real Estate and Retailing

Stephen M. Coyle

U.S. retailing's fortunes rise and fall with consumer confidence levels and the rate of personal income growth. Demographics likewise play a significant role with retail sales strongly impacted by the number of consumers reaching their peak spending years.

In the late 1990s these factors combined to produce an impressive surge in retail sales that has helped promote a recovery in the retail real estate sector and piqued the interest of investors. Yet not all retailers and retail formats have shared equally in sales growth, and therefore not all retail real estate properties are necessarily prudent investments.

This chapter explores the primary drivers of retail sales performance, projecting their impacts through 2003. The analysis then turns to the prospects for the different retail formats and how their ups and downs will carry over into real estate investment performance, concluding with implications for investors.

THE DRIVERS

U.S. consumers have remained extremely confident, despite earlier international economic turmoil. The stock market has become very important to the average consumer's confidence level. Because of the ubiquity of 401(k) plans and mutual funds, more people look to the stock market as a source of current and future wealth than ever before. In fact, many households view stocks as an alternative to savings accounts.

The consumer confidence index remains very high relative to its expansionary average of 100. A confident consumer is great news for the retail industry. Consumers have been so confident that RFA has even described them as "spendthrift." The extremely low unemployment rate also fosters high consumer confidence (Exhibit 1). Furthermore, as the Asian crisis unfolded, the price of imports decreased, creating cheaper consumer goods. Cheap goods, rising incomes, and lower costs of borrowing have all contributed to the strongest real growth in consumer spending since the mid-1980s. However, many question whether this trend could continue.

As of February 2000, this economic expansion was the longest since World War II. While very tight unemployment translates into high consumer confidence and increased retail spending, it limits the opportunity for future growth. Barring any major, unforeseen downturn, the major question now is, "How do you expand the economy without workers?" While low unemployment is troublesome for the office market (after all, it is very hard to add office space without new workers), it may be a boon to the retail market. Tighter labor markets usually translate into rising wages. Despite much of the rhetoric about increased technology holding wages down in this cycle, personal incomes grew more than 5% in 1999, driven primarily by higher wages. As the labor market remains extremely tight, wage pressures continue to increase. This is good news for retailers, because higher incomes almost always translate into higher sales.

As consumers typically exhibit maximum spending habits at age 46, another major source of retail sales growth is the rising number of 46-year-olds, which will peak in 2003. Demographics, therefore, suggest that retail spending will continue to increase for four or five more years. Interestingly, the last two major recessions both coincided with dips in the number of 46-year-olds. The number of 46-year-olds will, however, decline dramatically from 2008 through 2020 (Exhibit 2).

The only major short-term threats to retail spending and personal incomes are: (1) an unforeseen economic downturn, (2) a very low savings rate by U.S. consumers, and (3) a major correction in the stock market. The U.S. appears able to weather the global economic crises that unfolded in Asia and Brazil. However, there is always the threat of a recession, during which spending declines precipitously as people lose their jobs. Since the U.S. savings rate continues to stay at a very low level, consumers would be unlikely to use savings for retail spending during a recession. The most likely scenario for the U.S. economy is that job and GDP growth will eventually slow, as full employment creates an economic slowdown.

Exhibit 1: Consumer Confidence Index, 1985–1998

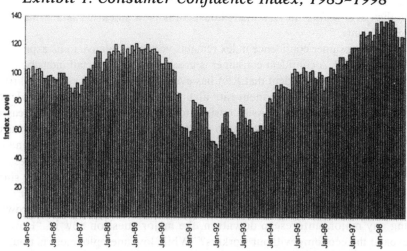

Sources: Regional Financial Associates and The Conference Board

Exhibit 2: Number of Prime Consumers — 46-Year-Olds, 1955–2030

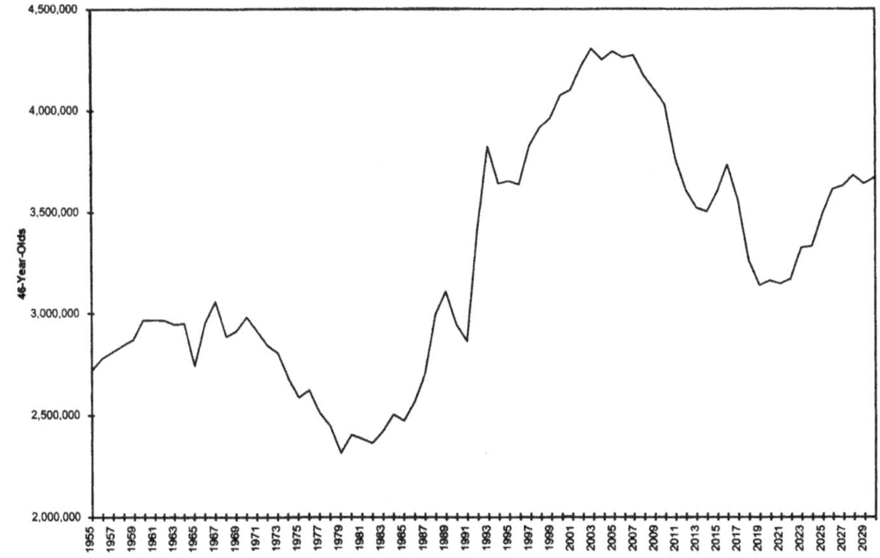

The Dow's correction in the third quarter of 1998 provided a clear example of how the stock market shapes U.S. consumers' views, and could threaten retail sales. As the Dow dipped from 9400 in July to near 7600 in September, consumer confidence fell from June's historic peak of 138 to 119 by October. Stock performance is now critical to consumer attitudes and, therefore, to retail sales!

THE RETAILERS

While many retailers are making hay of the giant increase in sales, others are continuing to wither on the vine and/or disappear. Certainly, Wal-Mart is a clear example of a winner, while losers include Sears, JC Penney, Toys "R" Us and CompUSA, with same store sales declining over the important holiday periods. Many have closed weak stores and laid off employees. Toys "R" Us, the world's largest toy retailer, closed 9 U.S., 50 European, and 31 Kids "R" Us stores, stating that declining sales and market share prompted the closures. Retailers that disappeared or declared bankruptcy in the late 1990s include: Venator Group's Kinney Shoes unit, Boston Market, and Venture stores.

Why some retailers enjoy rising sales and profitability while others suffer depends in part on different approaches to retailing. Wal-Mart epitomizes the superefficient approach to retailing and market domination as a pioneer of widespread computerized inventory management. Its systems use bar codes, scanners, and readers from direct receipt of inventories through the point of sale.

Exhibit 3: The Superefficient Retailer

The Superefficient Retailer

By tracking goods all the way from the suppliers to the register, Wal-Mart is able to determine: (1) how long various goods sit on store shelves, (2) whether goods "disappear" from the store at an above-average rate, (3) how many goods are damaged, and (4) what types of stores sell different combinations of goods. Wal-Mart then uses these data to order and restock inventory that moves fastest, and no longer orders poor sellers or goods that sit on the shelf for most of the year, only to be sold during a few weeks. Wal-Mart also uses a more flexible approach to its sales floor. In contrast to the industry standard of having dedicated seasonal sales aisles, seasonal aisles vary in size and number, according to how goods sell during that particular season. The type of goods offered varies according to store location and consumers' historical buying patterns. Strict inventory management combined with careful statistical analysis allows Wal-Mart and other superefficient retailers to increase both sales and profitability. As sales and profitability increase, retailers then lower prices to the consumer, capturing further market share.

Superefficient retailers use these increased sales, profitability, and shorter inventory hold periods to bargain for better rates with their factors, who lend them money to purchase large inventories of goods. The factors' rates vary according to the retailers' credit quality, the amount borrowed, and the time that it takes to repay the loan. The more efficient and profitable a retailer is, the better the rate. As retailers gain strength and market share, they use these lower borrowing rates to further increase profitability and decrease prices. The falling price of goods translates into an even greater increase in market share (Exhibit 3).

Bargaining power with factors is a very important step in the creation of a superefficient retailer; however, it is not the only one. Since superefficient retailers increase their sales at the expense of held inventories, the retailers negotiate better rates with their suppliers. And some very large superefficient retailers, like Wal-Mart, discovered that they could order directly from some manufacturers, allowing for further decreases in the cost of goods to consumers and even larger gains in market share.

The Big-Box Retailers

The evolution of the superefficient retailer helped create big-box retailing as we know it today. As retailers witnessed the successes of stores like Wal-Mart and Home Depot, many decided that bigger was always better, and jumped into the big-box arena. However, many of these new entrants did not have the same inventory management systems or approach to retailing. Some retailers, like Toys "R" Us, confused large store sizes with increased sales per square foot and better margins.

Certainly Toys "R" Us is a very successful big-box retailer. Toys "R" Us emerged in the 1980s and 1990s to become the world's largest toy seller. Its stores are more than five times the size of a typical toy store, and its clothing stores, Kids "R" Us, are five to ten times the size of most children's clothing stores, giving consumers wide selection at moderate prices. However, while its prices are below those of specialty toy and clothing stores, it does not approach the rock bottom pricing of retailers like Wal-Mart or Target. Furthermore, Toys "R" Us had a long-standing policy of carrying a large inventory of toys throughout the year, and distinguished itself from its competitors based on selection, not price. Unfortunately, since toy sales are very seasonal, it has been difficult for it to compete in the new era of value shopping. Inventories are expensive to carry, necessitating higher prices. Indeed, high prices appear to have hurt Toys "R" Us, which remains a major big-box retailer, albeit one with increasing problems.

There are also many examples of traditional retailers that attempted to enter the big-box arena without success. As an example, Tandy, owner of Radio Shack, saw the emergence of big-box/value as a new retail paradigm that could launch it into the twenty-first century. Tandy's first entrance into the big-box arena was its Incredible Universe stores, an answer to flagging sales in the traditional 1,500- to 3,000-square-foot Radio Shack stores. Unlike Radio Shack, Incredible Universe outlets did not just stock Radio Shack and Tandy brands, but also computers and electronics goods from most of the major manufacturers. Unfortunately, Incredible Universe stores were large ... very large. In fact, the stores ranged from 125,000 to a whopping 180,000 square feet. Consumers found them excessively large, and their prices noncompelling. The result was the eventual closure of every Incredible Universe store.

Tandy's next foray into the world of big-box retailing was its Computer City stores. Like Incredible Universe, Computer City stores sold computers, peripherals, and software from many different distributors and manufacturers. Unlike Incredible Universe, Computer City stores sold only computer-related equipment and were "only" 25,000 square feet, on average. While Computer City fared significantly better than Incredible Universe, Tandy finally sold all its stores to CompUSA, its largest competitor. Once again, Tandy had failed at big-box retailing.

Tandy helps illustrate the point that bigger is not always better. However, some retailers have taken advantage of big-box retailing to improve their draw and market share. For example, The Gap has broadened its reach to younger and less affluent customers with its larger Old Navy Clothing stores, whose growth has been largely responsible for The Gap's sales increases.

Big-box/value retailing is here to stay. The efficiencies created by larger/better managed retailers help create savings for consumers and increased profitability that are hard to beat. However, one must question how many big-box retailers can survive in any given category. The shake-out in big-box retailing is only in part because of ill-fated concepts, like Incredible Universe. Most big-box tenants have disappeared because there were simply too many large retailers. The nation does not need four or five or six big-box electronics or home improvement chains. As a result, the retail landscape has been littered with victims, including: Nobody Beats the Wiz, Lechmere, Handy Andy, Grossman's, and Builders Square. In most cases, the best managed and most efficient big-box retailers have survived. Going forward, there will probably be fewer big-box closings. There will also be fewer new big-box entrants, because it is very difficult and expensive to replicate the inventory management systems and efficiencies of most of the big-box retailers.

The Value Retailers

Prior to the early 1990s, value retailing was confined to nonregional mall retailers. Goods at most major department stores were seldom on sale. In fact, 90% of the time, less than 10% of the goods in a store were on sale. Stores usually confined sales to the end of the summer and after-Christmas seasons. Today, with the advent of big-box, discount, value-oriented, and outlet retailing, 90% of the time the department stores have more than 10% of their goods on sale! To some degree, every retailer (except for a few very upscale specialty stores) must offer value to its customers. A result has been consolidation among department store chains. An example is Birmingham-based Proffitt's acquisition of Saks Fifth Avenue, which promises to help increase Proffitt's high-end draw, and also allow it to compete in the highly competitive California, New York, and Boston markets. Additionally, the sale included Saks' Off-Fifth stores, which cater to higher-end value-oriented shoppers.

In another highly publicized department store merger, Dillard's acquired Mercantile Stores, which were also sought by Proffitt's and the May company. Prior to the closing, however, Dillard's sold 15 Mercantile stores to Proffitt's and 11 stores to May. Another big department-store merger was Ames' $30 million acquisition of Hills Stores, enabling Ames to enter Ohio and Indiana and become the nation's fourth largest discounter after Wal-Mart, Kmart, and Target.

Most of the major department stores witnessed moderate sales growth during the late 1990s holiday seasons, but weak apparel sales constrained overall performance. Since most traditional department stores are primarily fashion apparel retailers, there was limited upside for growth.

Sears and JC Penney suffer from weak, mid-market apparel offerings. While both have put major efforts into revitalizing their soft goods, neither has been successful. Perhaps one of the major problems confronting both Sears and JC Penney is the stratification of U.S. incomes. As the rich get richer and the poor get poorer, the middle class, a mainstay of these two venerable retailers, has shrunk, leading to a decline in sales. While upscale retailers like Neiman Marcus, Saks, and Federated have profited from rising apparel sales, so too have low-end department stores and discounters. Ames, for example, has seen significant increases in same store holiday sales, its resurgence partially because of better inventory management systems as well as a renewed focus on low-priced goods.

THE BIG RETAIL MERGERS

Supermarkets

While the big-box struggle for market dominance may be entering its final act, the grocery fight is still unfolding. Grocers actively competed with one another to control markets. In the late 1990s, Kroger was the nation's largest grocer, but Albertson's briefly jumped into the number one position with its plans to merge with American Stores in a $11.7 billion deal, creating a 2,470 chain store with more than $34 billion in annual sales. Kroger soon struck back and merged with Portland, Oregon–based Fred Meyer, to form the largest supermarket chain in the country with $43 billion in annual sales.

Much of the supermarket merger frenzy was the indirect result of the entrance of discounters into the grocery business. While Kroger, Albertson's, and Safeway rank as the number one, two, and three food sellers in the country, respectively; Wal-Mart, Costco, and Sam's Club, a Wal-Mart subsidiary, rank next. Even after its Giant Food, Stop & Shop, and Bi Lo acquisitions, Royal Ahold ranked a lowly seventh.

Wal-Mart did not rest on its laurels, opening three prototype Wal-Mart Neighborhood Market stores. The new stores are 40,000 square feet and compete with traditional supermarkets. The Neighborhood Market will not replace the Wal-Mart Supercenter, but rather, service the people who live between existing Super-centers. All the Neighborhood Market stores feature drive-through pharmacies as well as traditional supermarket and drugstore products. In 1999, Wal-Mart planned to open 40 new discount stores and 150 new Supercenters. Wal-Mart will roll out more Neighborhood Market stores if the prototypes are successful. Interestingly, food purchases account for nearly half of Wal-Mart's Supercenter sales.

Kmart, also a player in the grocery wars, announced renovations of 2,000 stores to include grocery sections. Additionally, Kmart has explored merging with a number of major supermarket chains in order to remain competitive.

As the supermarket wars have heated up, the number of independent gro-cers declined dramatically, and weaker, smaller chains suffered. Great Atlantic &

Pacific Tea Company, owner of the A&P chain, announced that, because of flagging sales, it was closing 127 stores. Once the largest in the nation, A&P fell to tenth in sales. Similarly, the Independent Grocers Alliance, I.G.A., saw membership decline from 2,700 grocers to only 2,000 between 1988 and 1998.

This supermarket competition comes just as the Internet is changing the way we shop for groceries. Entrants, such as Peapod and NetGrocer, promise to deliver groceries less than 48 hours after an order is placed. All consumers need is a two-hour window available for delivery, a computer, and a fax modem. So far, Internet grocers have not performed well, with the earliest entrant, OnCart, now out of business. OnCart's problems were largely because it did not have its own food warehouses and wholesale suppliers. However, both Peapod and NetGrocer have also failed to meet analysts' expectations, and their futures remain uncertain. While online supermarkets make sense, it is increasingly harder for startups to access the major food distributors. Larger mainstream grocery chains translate into fewer, stronger relationships for distributors. In fact, the number of full-line food wholesalers nationwide fell from 300 in 1987 to fewer than 100 by the end of 1999; 12 account for 80% of the dollar volume sold. While it is difficult for a new online supermarket entrant to establish relationships with distributors, it will be interesting to see if one of the major supermarkets enters the virtual world as a new way to capture market share. While Hannaford's has entered the online market with its HomeRuns service, it remains in its early stages. One should closely watch HomeRuns to see how it fares in the grocery wars.

Traditional grocers continue to experiment with various store sizes and formats, including new, upscale supermarkets that cater to high-income households. Most are smaller (35,000 to 40,000 square feet) and carry a wider variety of prepared foods. While most grocers have abandoned the extremely large, 80,000- to 90,000-square-foot stores of the mid-1990s, the average new supermarket is approximately 65,000 square feet and carries a variety of food and nonfood goods. Grocers seek and receive exclusives for everything from drugs/health and beauty aids to bakeries, photo developing, florists, and even banks.

Drugstores

As the supermarkets have grown in size and their offerings have increased to include health and beauty aids and prescription drugs, traditional drug retailers have had to re-invent themselves. Like their archrivals, the supermarkets, major drug retailers have also embarked on an aggressive consolidation wave. In 1997, CVS purchased Revco, and JC Penney, owner of Thrift Drug stores, purchased Eckerd. Penney/Eckerd continued their growth strategy by acquiring the 141 stores of New York–based Genovese drug in November 1998. Industry leader Walgreens has chosen to expand via internal growth rather than acquisitions.

The drugstores are moving out of the shopping centers because of increased competition from supermarkets and to better compete with discounters like Wal-Mart and Target. Through exclusive sales clauses in their leases, supermarkets are increasingly pushing the drugstores out of their traditional home in the neighborhood center. In an effort to compete with discount giants and the supermarkets, many drugstores have made the preemptive move to stand-alone stores with drive-in pharmacies. By stressing convenience, short lines, and quick service, drug retailers are attempting to hold onto market share against their price competitive rivals.

Is this formula succeeding? It is too early to tell. However, traditional drugstores must differentiate themselves from the supermarkets and discounters if they are to survive. Unfortunately, because of their lower volumes, drugstores cannot compete on price.

THE INTERNET

Internet sales have increased dramatically. The Senate helped boost sales when it passed the Internet Tax Freedom Act, creating a three-year tax moratorium on Internet sales. Jupiter Communications, a high-tech consulting firm, estimates that "e-tailing" will increase from $2 billion in 1997 to $37 billion in 2002. However, this estimate appears very aggressive. In fact, all total nonstore sales (including the Internet, catalogs, and home shopping) totaled less than $130 billion in 1997. This is an important number to watch, because Internet sales typically compete most directly with home shopping and catalogs.

Fewer than 25% of Americans use the Internet regularly, and many have security concerns regarding Internet shopping. However, commodity goods and better-known products are well positioned to compete on the Internet. Goods that are less well known, or where color or texture matter, do not sell well. For example, Saks Fifth Avenue closed its Internet site after less than a year, because of poor sales. Saks customers largely avoided the site because it lacked the store's ambiance, attentive sales people, and overall shopping experience.

Additionally, it is expensive to market items on the Internet. Online marketing costs average $26 per order, versus the average retail store's budget of $2.50 per sale. In order to be successful, Internet shopping needs to be convenient and easy. However, the time to download images of products is often excessive, and many potential shoppers simply surf away.

Internet shopping is here to stay, and it will likely increase over the next several years. However, it still is not yet ready for prime time, and has a long way to go before it begins to threaten traditional retail sales in a meaningful way.

REAL ESTATE AND RETAILING

In 1996 we boldly said that the U.S. retail real estate market had turned the corner. We continue to stand by this statement and believe that retail real estate is still in a prolonged recovery. NCREIF returns finally substantiated this point, as total returns rose very quickly during 1998 and values turned the corner! Strong growth in retail sales and slower construction levels led to better-performing real estate and lower economic vacancies.[1]

Retail demand's recovery from the recession of the early 1990s began as early as 1992. Negative sales growth and heavy big-box construction during 1990–91 created high economic vacancies, which peaked at 20%. During late 1992 through 1994, vacancies recovered. As construction ramped up and sales growth slowed somewhat during 1995–96, vacancies stagnated, but extremely strong sales growth resumed by mid-1996, and vacancies plummeted once again. The market continued to tighten, and economic vacancies approached 15% at the U.S. level.

As the market tightened further in 1998, PPR's value index finally turned the corner and began increasing. Falling vacancies and firming rents created rising NOIs, which grew 4.3% last year, while values grew an estimated 3.5%, the first increase since 1990. Capital markets woke up to the retail recovery! Since the office, apartment and warehouse recoveries are yesterday's news, retail remains the only sector with significant upside.

The growth in retail sales should slow as the national economic expansion moderates and the savings rate increases slightly. Because of significant construction of new grocery-anchored neighborhood centers, new supply may remain near its present level in the year 2000; however, supply growth should slow longer term. In fact, new retail construction starts have fallen, indicating that a future slowdown in new supply will occur. While vacancies at the U.S. level will likely increase over 1999-2000, they should remain well below the levels of the early 1990s, and rents should continue to grow (Exhibit 4). However, not all markets are equally exposed to increasing construction levels. Many markets, such as Chicago, Boston, and Miami, will post declining new supply levels and strong demand.

Exhibit 4: U.S. Retail Market
Retail Market Trends

Local versus U.S. Derived Market Returns

---

[1] Economic vacancy represents retail space unsupported by retail sales.

Retail returns are projected to remain quite healthy, averaging near 11% at the U.S. level, with values and NOIs increasing throughout the forecast. Values should grow faster than NOIs, as capital flows to retail real estate continue to increase. PPR projects that NOIs at the U.S. level will increase at an annual average rate of near 1% through 2003, while values should grow at a 3.2% annual pace. Although U.S. retail total returns are underperforming apartments, warehouse, and office, they are forecast to remain fairly stable going forward, while the other sectors are expected to dip. In fact, retail should outperform the other sectors by as early as December 2001.

OUTLOOK FOR THE DIFFERENT RETAIL VENUES

Venue is less important today than ever before. For the first time in history, many retailers now compete in a variety of venues. The Gap, for example, competes in regional malls, power centers, community centers, anchorless strips, outlet malls, and high streets. Similarly, Barnes & Noble has stores in regional malls, neighborhood centers, community centers, power centers, and high streets. These retailers realize that they can access bodies and dollars with a variety of formats. Sometimes, as in the case of The Gap, the store format and inventory need to shift slightly (The Gap versus Old Navy versus The Gap Outlet), in order to capture the highest possible sales dollars. However, the retailer's goal and identity remain intact. By competing in a number of different venues, many retailers can increase their market penetration.

Granted, venue still matters and is important to some retailers; however, the mindless, single-venue focus of many retailers has disappeared. Instead, most retailers examine how they can best compete in today's marketplace. If the best way for that retailer is to compete in a variety of real estate venues, the retailer usually will. Retailers are only concerned with sales dollars. Those strategies that maximize revenues will succeed, while the others will disappear.

The Regional Mall

Regional centers allow up-and-coming retailers to establish a national identity. However, once that identity is established and the retailer is well known, then it only "needs" to be in the regional mall so long as its profit margins exceed those available in other venues. Certainly, The Gap and The Limited are two retailers that achieved a national identity propelling them beyond the mall. For a small, up-and-coming retailer, however, the mall often remains critical to creating a large national presence.

Historically, the regional mall has also allowed the retailer to gain the greatest exposure to the benefits of cross-shopping. By locating near very successful national retailers, mall tenants often increase their sales volumes. However, as the regional mall has evolved into a fashion center, with virtually no other lines of goods, the competition for sales dollars within the mall has actually increased, with tenants competing against one another. Thus, the power of the mall (from the retailers' perspective) is weakening somewhat.

The face of the American mall is changing as well. While there have been only a handful of regional malls under construction in the U.S., development of value center/entertainment malls continues to increase. Mills Corp., for example, has projects in Charlotte, Orange County, Nashville, San Francisco, New Jersey, and Toronto. Additionally, Mills has actively planned other projects in suburban Maryland, Atlanta, and Tampa. While these projects primarily attract outlet stores, many of the goods (and the retailers) are also found in a typical regional mall. In fact, like a regional mall, they have primarily fashion-oriented tenants.

While the Mills concept also stresses entertainment, most retailers have not jumped on the entertainment bandwagon. Real estate developers have sold the entertainment center as the next great wave in retailing. However, this is a real estate–driven concept, not a retailer-driven concept, and most retailers remain somewhat skeptical. Entertainment will compete with retail for the same pool of sales dollars. Entertainment often creates flow problems within a mall that can distract shoppers. The primary purpose of the Mills centers is selling fashion-oriented goods, and, therefore, those centers compete closely with the outlet and the regional malls.

The Neighborhood Center

Many investors have focused on neighborhood centers as one of the few growth and development opportunities, and real estate folks love growth and development stories. (Unfortunately, it is development or the sudden disappearance of growth that usually hurts us most!) Competition among grocers is driving the expansion of the neighborhood centers, as supermarkets enter new markets at a very rapid pace. New supermarkets mean new neighborhood centers, as developers almost always build new centers with an anchor tenant in hand. Many of the grocers (and the developers that follow them) are chasing population growth. So most of the new development has occurred in hot growth markets like Phoenix, Atlanta, Las Vegas, and Portland. In an effort to capitalize on population growth, some have even built neighborhood centers in expectation of future population growth, and this is a very risky strategy!

As discussed earlier, the supermarket wars will yield both winners and losers, and as the grocers continue to offer a greater selection of items, they demand more exclusive sales conditions as part of their leases. More powerful grocers exert more control over the lease negotiation process, demanding and receiving exclusives on items ranging from drugs to health and beauty aids, bakery goods, floral arrangements, photo developing, and banking! This translates into fewer opportunities to attract tenants to new neighborhood centers, which are evolving into grocery stores with a few service-oriented retailers next door. The movement of the drugstores into stand-alone sites has further decreased the number of credit tenants within a center.

As the average work week of the American consumer continues to increase, the demand for service goods increases, a boon to neighborhood centers, which offer easy access to supermarkets and service-oriented tenants. However, U.S. population growth is slowing; RFA expects U.S. population growth to average only 0.8% annually through 2003. Regardless, neighborhood centers continue to grow well beyond the pace of the population. Demographics do not suggest that we will have a sudden burst in the level of participation of the working–age population in the work force; thus, it is unlikely that our population will suddenly demand even more service-oriented items. While the growth rate in the "prime" consumer (age 46) will expand through 2003, this will not create a significant boost in demand for grocery or service-oriented goods.

Neighborhood centers do offer investment opportunities, the best ones in markets where limited development exists and projected sales growth is moderate to strong. In markets with significant development of new neighborhood centers, investors should carefully examine the level of new supply relative to demand.

The Community Center

The community center is a retail venue struggling for an identity, somewhere between a very large neighborhood center with a few big-box tenants and a power center with a grocery store and noncredit retailers. Community centers mix credit and noncredit tenants, often containing a grocery store, large national retailers, and local mom-and-pop retailers. From the real estate investor's standpoint, this venue mixes more stable cash flows from national retailers with upside possibility from mom and pops, but is often difficult to analyze. First, it covers many different trade areas. For example, a local jewelry store may have a trade area of two or three miles, whereas a national home improvement chain (like Home Depot) may draw from as far away as 15 or 20 miles. Second, community centers face competition from many other retail venues, including neighborhood centers, power centers, and anchorless strips.

So why invest in a community center? Unlike neighborhood centers, community centers usually have more than one credit tenant other than the grocer. (This may prove helpful in the age of the supermarket wars!) Second, unlike power centers, not all their leases are long-term, and there is upside from the mom and pops. Community centers can be successful if they are carefully managed and if their locations attract the right mix of shoppers. It is difficult to combine groceries, destination retailers, and small shops; however, a few retail locations (in the right markets!) can pull this off. Of course, layout and parking are very important factors in drawing shoppers.

Power Centers

The long, painful shake-out among the big-box retailers is nearing an end, as a few strong retailers remain and most of the weak have disappeared. The disappearance of many of the big-box retailers has led many investors to question the role of the power center. In the early 1990s, developers sold power centers as retail bonds. By the mid-1990s, many investors likened power centers to junk bonds, as vacancies skyrocketed and tenant defaults became commonplace. However, out of this mayhem, a few dominant power centers have emerged.

In spite of strong discount-merchandising fundamentals, there were just too many discount retailers during the early 1990s, not all of whom were equipped to play the value/discount game (remember Tandy?). Those who are well equipped to play (Wal-Mart, Home Depot, Circuit City, Best Buy, TJX) will continue to increase their sales volume and gain market share. As they have gained strength, many have focused on locations with the best access and visibility to shoppers. Thus, a few "must have" power center locations have emerged.

Do we need new power centers? No! There are still too many. However, weakness throughout the power center category is negatively affecting the price of almost all power centers, and this is unnecessary. The best locations will attract the best retailers. While power centers were sold as having destination tenants with few cross-shopping benefits, most retailers have discovered that the best locations work well for the other big-box tenants as well. Thus, there may be limited cross-shopping, but a critical retail mass does matter. Power centers with excellent locations, a strong draw, and the right tenants are a great investment, especially given the current bias against this venue!

CONCLUSIONS

The retail industry continues to change, and its changing nature will impact all of us. The fundamentals remain very strong, and there is continued opportunity for growth in both the retail industry and the real estate that it supports. Real estate investors should realize strong returns through 2004. Strong real estate fundamentals will combine with the healthy retail industry to create rising values and NOIs. The time is still ripe for searching for real estate investments. However, as capital flows increase, the best opportunities will be snapped up. Choose your investments well and they will help support healthy returns with moderate volatility.

Chapter 12

Modeling Office Returns at the Regional Level

Ruijue Peng, Ph.D.

Susan Hudson-Wilson, CFA

Oral Capps, Ph.D.

Investors have two problems using the National Council of Real Estate Investment Fiduciaries (NCREIF) data to make decisions. The first is that every day they are making bets based on what *will* happen, not what *has already* happened. Although the future of real estate is influenced by its past, performance in the future will not be the same. The second problem is the obvious fact that different economies and real estate markets across the country perform differently during the course of the business cycle. A national index misses those differences.

The solution would seem to be the creation of good forecasts of returns at a subnational level, if quality subnational data were available. For years, NCREIF has been publishing property investment returns at a regional level so it is possible to obtain, say, summarized office returns for unlevered, institutional-grade properties for fairly broad regions of the country. These data are published in the quarterly NCREIF reports and are available from its data service. Of course, NCREIF also summarizes returns at the national level.

It would appear, therefore, that it is possible to create models of property type returns at a regional level. Are such forecasts feasible and reliable? Do they yield any interesting insights into the influences on real estate markets that cannot be gleaned from equivalent national forecasts? As part of a continual effort to investigate new ways of improving forecasting methodology, Property & Portfolio Research created return models and forecasts for the office markets in the eight NCREIF regions. The results show that these models can offer some interesting conclusions about the differences among and similarities across real estate markets.

A WORD ABOUT NCREIF RETURNS

The NCREIF return data come from a fairly large sample of individual property returns submitted by institutional investors. Because the database entries are at the individual property level, they could, theoretically, be aggregated to any level of geographic and property type detail. Unfortunately, reality rears its ugly head. The

NCREIF database, while substantial at \$65 billion in more than 2,300 properties, is not large enough to provide details about all property types in all local real estate markets. With 60 major markets in the country and four major property types, the NCREIF database is not big enough to have even 10 properties in each market cell. Returns on the average of 10 properties are too easily influenced by idiosyncratic events, management, and luck to be modelable. Moreover, the NCREIF database is not distributed evenly across all the markets. NCREIF members, in total, own many more than 10 properties in Chicago, Washington, Los Angeles, and Atlanta, for example. As a result, there must be fewer than 10 in some property types in many other metropolitan areas. In fact, in the latest NCREIF report, there are only 27 metropolitan area/property type combinations with more than 20 properties in the database, and 68 with more than 10. Since the database has grown over time, the level of coverage deteriorates for older data. Therefore, a comprehensive model of property type returns at the metropolitan area level cannot be created directly from NCREIF data. Even at the state level, the database contains 20 or more properties in only 30 state/property type combinations with 35 states not represented at all.

The lowest practicable level for the direct regional modeling of NCREIF returns is the NCREIF "divisions." These are broad regions of the contiguous geography that are, not coincidentally, quite similar to what the Census Bureau uses for its divisions. Exhibit 1 shows how these regions are defined by NCREIF. The returns in the NCREIF index are calculated for these geographical definitions by property type by summarizing all the properties in the database according to the different cells. The latest quarter's data are available for 31 of the 32 region/ property type cells. However, 10 years ago, only 22 of the combinations could be supported by the database at NCREIF's 20 property per cell standards. This limitation on the available data would impinge on the ability to extend the methodology of this study to property types beyond office.

THE REGIONAL OFFICE MODEL

The goal of this study is to model the return to real estate in the regional office markets. Before the details about the regional nature of the data are discussed, the return concepts at the heart of the model must be clarified.

Total return consists of two components: (1) asset value or capital appreciation return, and (2) income return, also called yield or cap rate.[1] In plain terms, appreciation return is the simple growth rate calculation from last quarter's value to this quarter's value.[2] Income return is the ratio of the net operating income in this quarter to the value at the end of the last quarter. Conventional real estate modeling practices would favor modeling the *income* (in dollars) and the income *return* and

---

[1] Cap rate has many variations that create distinctions in the details but in this context the nuances are unimportant.

[2] Again, this is a general description. The NCREIF return formulas contain more complex ratios.

using the two to calculate the implicit capital value.[3] The change in this calculated value becomes the appreciation return. However, modeling income *return* directly may not be the best approach because a slight error in the estimate can result in a large swing in the asset value for a given level of income. Since the movement of value accounts for most of the variation in the total return, a small forecasting error in income return can produce an unacceptable error in the forecasts of total return.

Exhibit 1: NCREIF Divisions

Northeast (NE)	East North Central (EN)
Connecticut	Illinois
Maine	Indiana
Massachusetts	Kentucky
New Hampshire	Michigan
New Jersey	Ohio
New York	Wisconsin
Pennsylvania	
Rhode Island	**West North Central (WN)**
Vermont	Iowa
	Kansas
Mideast (ME)	Minnesota
Delaware	Missouri
Maryland	Nebraska
North Carolina	North Dakota
South Carolina	South Dakota
Virginia	
Washington, D.C.	**Mountain (M)**
West Virginia	Arizona
	Colorado
Southeast (SE)	Idaho
Alabama	Montana
Arkansas	Nevada
Florida	New Mexico
Georgia	Utah
Mississippi	Wyoming
Tennessee	
	Pacific (P)
Southwest (SW)	Alaska
Louisiana	California
Oklahoma	Hawaii
Texas	Oregon
	Washington

---

[3] Econometric models, such as the ones being built in this study, generally consist of structural equations and "identities." The structural equations contain statistically estimated coefficients. Identities are equations that do not need any statistical estimates because the relationship to other variables are definitional, not statistical. As an analogy, one can measure a ball's diameter with calipers and then calculate its circumference by multiplying by pi. Alternatively, one could measure its circumference with a tape measure and calculate its diameter. Either way there is one parameter that must be measured (estimated) and one that is calculated.

Consequently, the approach in this regional office model is to estimate equations for value and net operating income separately, with the income return determined implicitly as the ratio of the two. The rationale is that the movement of both asset value and NOI is determined by similar factors such as demand, supply, and capital market conditions, leading to partially synchronized movements through time. The differences between the two concepts are primarily in their response, both in time and in amplitude, to changes in these factors. The fact that income return moves in a relatively narrow range is a final empirical argument in favor of this approach. Also incorporated into the model is the common observation that forecasting equations perform better in *growth rate* form than in *absolute level* form.

Thus, the structural model consists of two key equations: asset value appreciation and income growth. Asset value and income level determine income return. Total return is simply the summation of income return and value appreciation or depreciation.

The first step in creating a forecast is to estimate the parameters of the model through a statistical analysis of the historical data. The second step is running (simulating) the model to produce forecasts. Of course, even with the statistically estimated parameters, one cannot simulate the model without having forecasts of the outside variables that interact with those parameters. For real estate modeling, it is practical to obtain forecasts of general economic variables, such as employment and inflation, from a reputable general forecasting company. Economic forecasts from Regional Financial Associates (RFA) are used.

The model also requires a forecast of new office supply since returns clearly depend on the amount of office space. But supply also depends on returns[4] since developers are economically motivated beings. Even if one could obtain a good supply forecast from RFA, it would not be usable in this model. Therefore, a third equation was developed pertaining to new office supply. A detailed discussion of this supply equation is beyond the scope of this chapter, but the capital appreciation and income equations are described briefly below.

NCREIF REGIONAL RETURNS

The total returns for office properties by region over the period 1983:1 to 1997:4 are presented in Exhibit 2. Total returns were negative across all regions from 1991:2 to 1993:2. Not until 1995:1 did all total returns become positive. From 1996:4 to 1997:4, total returns were at double-digit levels. There is a great variation in the level and volatility across regions. Exhibit 3 displays the summary sta-

---

[4] Returns and supply are simultaneously determined and must be endogenous to the model. The simulation software must be able to handle the fact that one answer depends on the other answer, which depends on the first. It does so by iterating around results until both equations are satisfied. This is why econometric models cannot be simulated in Excel spreadsheets.

tistics of the returns for the historical period. The average of total return varies from −29% (Southwest) to 7.23% (Mideast), and the standard deviation varies from 6.2% (Mideast) to 10.4% (Northeast). Exhibits 4 and 5 present the two components of total return — capital value appreciation and income return. As shown, most of the variation in total return is attributed to capital appreciation. Income return varies in a relatively narrow range across both regions and time.

THE CAPITAL VALUE APPRECIATION EQUATION

The capital value appreciation equation should be a function of several factors relating to the use and availability of office space in the market. The equation tests the following drivers:

• the relationship between demand and supply in each regional office market,
• regional economic growth,
• changes in income generation in the market, and
• aggregate conditions in the national financial markets, including interest rates and inflation.

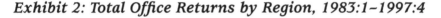

Exhibit 2: Total Office Returns by Region, 1983:1–1997:4

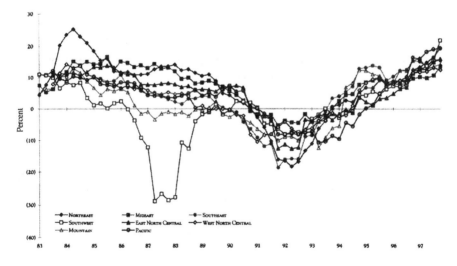

Exhibit 3: Summary Statistics of Total Office Return and Associated Components, 1983:1-1997:4

	Northeast	Mideast	Southeast	Southwest	East North Central	West North Central	Pacific	Mountain
TOTAL RETURN (%)								
Mean	6.87	7.23	2.97	−0.29	4.85	3.42	4.25	2.64
Median	9.15	8.35	3.89	0.33	6.72	4.95	5.65	0.80
Std-dev	10.43	6.21	9.07	9.97	7.04	6.72	7.52	7.57
Min	−17.79	−4.88	−18.13	−28.41	−12.38	−9.90	−10.13	−11.97
Max	25.05	16.66	15.98	21.87	16.08	14.23	19.50	16.28
VALUE APPRECIATION (%)								
Mean	−1.17	−0.72	−4.46	−6.52	−2.70	−4.55	−2.52	−4.86
Median	0.22	0.24	−2.75	−4.77	0.23	−2.07	−0.73	−4.54
Std-dev	10.14	6.07	8.44	9.64	7.11	6.76	7.72	7.02
Min	−25.70	−12.54	−25.31	−32.99	−20.08	−17.72	−17.60	−20.18
Max	17.52	9.28	6.38	12.23	6.51	7.29	13.90	7.46
INCOME RETURN (%)								
Mean	8.05	8.03	7.90	6.90	7.87	8.30	7.38	7.64
Median	7.74	7.60	7.26	6.64	7.63	7.93	7.11	7.15
Std-dev	1.06	0.98	1.31	1.74	1.17	1.35	1.21	0.97
Min	6.50	6.63	6.19	4.56	6.02	6.55	5.70	6.59
Max	9.67	9.68	9.83	9.64	10.04	10.65	9.93	9.48
NOI GROWTH (%)								
Mean	−0.94	1.72	−3.05	−5.39	−1.23	−1.83	−1.93	−4.06
Median	−3.08	0.30	−3.72	−7.09	−2.21	−1.07	−2.74	−4.37
Std-dev	6.80	6.49	7.62	14.43	7.94	8.89	5.92	6.62
Min	−12.13	−10.91	−19.60	−34.74	−18.42	−21.32	−12.15	−17.52
Max	14.07	17.74	15.31	24.23	19.38	18.08	21.01	9.41

Exhibit 4: Capital Appreciation Return by Division, 1983:1-1997:4

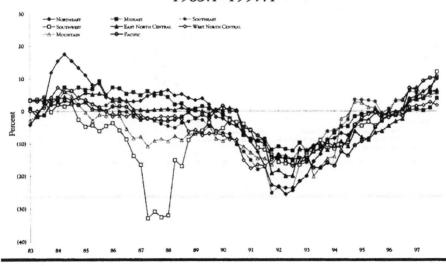

Exhibit 5: Income Return by Division, 1983:1–1997:4

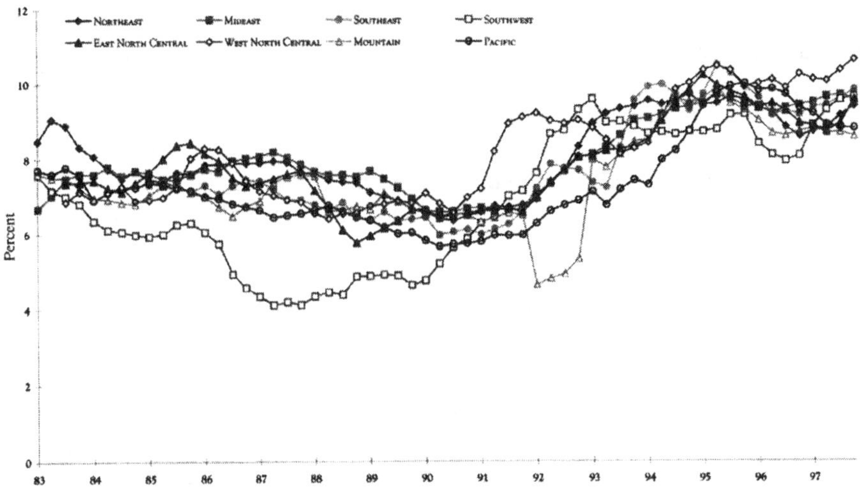

Deterioration in the demand/supply relationship is expected to reduce value. Growth in the regional economy influences forward-looking expectations of value and adds to demand in ways that are not measured by the direct demand variable. The same is true for a change in income growth. A change in income influences future price appreciation by capturing the persistent nature of growth expectations. The national financial markets affect property value through the pricing mechanism of the real estate market. For a given set of local real estate conditions, property values vary with opportunity costs in other investment markets, as well as the future risks associated with the real estate sector. Higher opportunity costs or higher future risks increase required return for investment and so decrease property value. While the relationship between demand and supply captures the specific risk of the real estate market, the impact of general economic and financial risks can only be captured by including national financial markets indicators in the equation. Finally, changes in the inflation rate will lead to real estate value movements, as real estate is at least a partial hedge against inflation.

THE INCOME EQUATION

Changes in office income are largely determined by the sector's unique long (five to seven years) lease structure. Changes in market conditions are reflected in rents paid by new tenants, but not by existing tenants.[5] New leases generally represent only a small fraction of the total rental income for all but brand new buildings. All else being

---

[5] With the exception, of course, of inflation passthroughs.

equal, an unexpected rise in inflation increases *marginal* rental rates and overall operating costs, whereas *overall* rental movements correspond more with long-term trend, or expected, inflation. Besides inflation, another important determinant of income is the relationship between demand and supply. Such a relationship can be reflected in two ways: the absolute demand for space and the intensity of use of space. Growth in demand, meaning more office workers, will generate demand for more office space, but can also create more crowding in the current amount of space. While a change in absolute space usage is reflected in new leases and new rents, the intensity of use of space affects the price when, or if, the crowding is relieved, probably at lease renewal.

SOURCES OF OTHER DATA

Other major data and sources that are included in the models are the historical vacancy rates, new office supply, and office demand. The regional historical vacancy rate is used as an indicator for the interaction between demand and supply. It is the weighted average of metropolitan vacancy rates obtained from various brokerage firms. New office supply is estimated with data from F.W. Dodge, which tracks the square footage of contract awards for new office development. Given that time is needed for each contract award to be actually put into place, an equally weighted distributed lag of contract awards is used as the indicator of new supply. Finally, RFA provides employment data, which are the base for the calculation of office demand. Office demand is a combined result of the regional employment structure, demand for office space by various economic sectors, and the comparative regional concentration of these sectors.

ESTIMATING THE MODELS

The regional models consist of a number of equations, three of which are structural, as described above. The rest of the equations are identities, simple (or not so simple) equations that do not depend on statistically estimated coefficients.

The structural equations are those that determine the percentage change in value, the percentage change in income, and the amount of supply. The identities turn the history and forecasts of economic variables into office demand, differentiate between expected and unexpected inflation, determine the spread of the yield curve, calculate regional economic growth, estimate the intensity of office use, and project the change in vacancy rate from the change in supply and demand. Of course, income and total returns are also calculated from identities.

These equations were run for each of the eight NCREIF divisions. In a formal sense the equations for one region are seemingly unrelated to the equations for another region. In other words, the supply in the West does not depend on the amount of supply in the Northeast, a reasonable assumption. Real estate construction requires a small portion of the labor, materials, and financial capital of the country, so construction in the West does not deprive the Northeast of the resources it needs to build. However, econometricians note that these types of equations often contain residuals (the forecasting errors) that are related. It is easy to see why. If there is a REIT crunch (something that is not and cannot realistically be included in the model), the flow of capital to construction will be more constrained everywhere and the equations will overpredict construction in all the regions. The residuals for supply will all be positive. Wouldn't it be nice if one could use the knowledge about an overprediction in one region to improve the predictions in the other regions? Econometricians call such a method, a "seemingly unrelated regression," or SUR, model. The estimations used the SUR technique.

RESULTS OF THE MODEL ESTIMATION

As mentioned above, the first step in a forecasting model (after all the data preparation and planning) is the estimation of the coefficients in the various equations. Using the seemingly unrelated regression technique, the equations were estimated for percentage change in value and percentage change in NOI by region. In some regions, individual variables did not help the equation, or actually hurt it by producing a movement in the wrong direction (e.g., in one case higher inflation made values fall). The offending variables were removed from those regions and the model estimations were rerun. The results are presented in Exhibits 6 and 7 for the value and income equations, respectively. For each variable in each region, the estimated coefficient and the t-statistic are shown. The t-statistic is a measure of whether the coefficient is random or whether there is a relationship between that variable and what we are looking for. Some of the sizes of the coefficients do not suggest an intuitive meaning unless you know the units in the original data. However, for the percentage change variables, the connection is clearer. For example, a one percentage point decrease in vacancy rate in the Pacific region results in a 1.3% increase in values. The overall quality of the model is measured by its goodness of fit (R^2), which is also presented. They range from 0.837 (Mountain) to 0.971 (Northeast) for the value equations and from 0.617 (Pacific) to 0.924 (Southwest) for the NOI equation.

For each region, the demand/supply relationships, interest rate spread, and percentage change in income are key determinants of changes in value. Economic growth is also a principal factor in all but the Mideast region. Inflation affects value in the Northeast, Pacific, and Southeast regions. Office values were found to be less sensitive to vacancy rates in those regions that experienced severe oversupply and large vacancy rates swings than in regions with relatively stable demand/supply relationships. For example, a one-unit change in the office vacancy rate leads to a 0.77% decrease in value in the Mountain region and 1.02% to 1.15% decrease in the two southern regions, whereas a similar change leads to a 4.09% decline in value in the Northeast. This happens because the Northeast has a relatively low and less volatile vacancy rate over time, so a one-unit change in vacancy is more significant. The only exception to this rule is the Mideast, where, although the historical vacancy rate is low and stable, the value is relatively insensitive to the change in vacancy rate.

Exhibit 6: Seemingly Unrelated Regression Results for Percentage Change in Value

	NE	ME	SE	SW	EN	WN	M	P
Vacancy Rate	-4.098*	-0.283*	-1.023*	-1.156*	-1.363*	-0.941*	-0.770*	-1.341*
	(-12.21)	(-1.69)	(-11.14)	(-7.78)	(-6.10)	(-10.56)	(-6.91)	(-7.26)
Interest Rate Spread	-1.742*	-2.641*	-2.098*	-3.538*	-2.061*	-1.362*	-1.880*	-1.705*
	(-5.77)	(-7.25)	(-5.30)	(6.44)	(-4.61)	(-4.67)	(-4.09)	(-3.93)
% Change in NOI	0.016	0.525*	0.024	0.083*	0.099*	0.025	0.052*	0.275*
	(0.28)	(9.32)	(0.54)	(2.31)	(2.48)	(0.79)	(0.72)	(3.66)
Economic Growth	0.247*	—	1.672*	1.444*	0.903*	1.481*	0.922*	1.954*
	(1.39)		(13.67)	(3.92)	(3.89)	(8.10)	(2.93)	(9.00)
Current Inflation	1.290*	—	0.345*	—	0.289	—	—	0.591*
	(6.25)		(1.27)		(0.85)			(2.33)
Lagged SUR Residual	0.785*	0.724*	0.690*	0.667*	0.689*	0.852*	0.725*	0.721*
	(9.62)	(11.90)	(9.04)	(6.23)	(8.21)	(12.99)	(8.56)	(7.34)
Constant	57.70*	7.026*	9.493	23.12*	18.19*	6.036*	8.604*	15.55*
	(11.36)	(3.70)	(4.53)	(5.68)	(5.13)	(3.77)	(2.59)	(5.12)
R2	0.9709	0.8730	0.9239	0.8652	0.8695	0.9107	0.8370	0.8999

Notes
t-statistics are in parentheses
* indicates that the estimated coefficient is statistically significant at the 0.10 level

Exhibit 7: Seemingly Unrelated Regression Results for Percentage Change in NOI

	NE	ME	SE	SW	EN	WN	M	P
Vacancy Rate	-3.451*	-0.225	-0.404*	-1.78*	-0.735*	-0.969*	-0.722*	-1.014*
	(-20.28)	(-1.00)	(-3.34)	(-12.23)	(-1.28)	(-2.42)	(-6.91)	(-3.59)
Unexpected Inflation	—	-1.860*	-0.329	—	—	—	-0.267	—
		(-6.08)	(-0.60)				(-0.49)	
Expected Inflation	2.833*	1.827*	1.826*	2.870*	5.470*	3.424*	1.531*	0.209
	(8.21)	(4.23)	(2.31)	(3.52)	(6.40)	(2.85)	(4.14)	(0.33)
Intensity of Demand	—	-0.193*	-0.072*	—	-0.295*	-0.246*	—	—
		(-5.50)	(-1.39)		(-2.83)	(-2.18)		
Real Interest Rate	—	—	—	—	—	1.617*	—	1.450*
						(2.01)		(3.45)
Lagged SUR Residual	0.921*	0.646*	0.731*	0.929*	0.819*	0.793*	0.689*	0.676*
	(10.93)	(6.41)	(7.79)	(19.50)	(10.54)	(9.90)	(7.80)	(6.45)
Constant	38.85*	59.74*	29.44	29.09*	72.84*	61.23*	4.025	7.248*
	(13.68)	(5.29)	(2.17)	(6.15)	(3.35)	(2.27)	(1.02)	(2.11)
R2	0.8926	0.8530	0.7489	0.9244	0.7334	0.7837	0.7381	0.6174

Notes
t-statistics are in parentheses
* indicates that the estimated coefficient is statistically significant at the 0.10 level

Office vacancy is a principal determinant of the growth in income in all regions except the Mideast. As expected, income goes up when the vacancy rate comes down. Meanwhile, the impact of the intensity of the demand/supply relationship on income growth is seen in four regions — the East North Central, West North Central, Mideast, and Southeast, where income is negatively related to the inventory/demand ratio. Expected inflation moves income in the right direction in all regions. However, the impact of unexpected inflation on income is statistically significant only in the Mideast. The results confirm the argument that expected inflation is generally built into lease contracts. Finally, the real interest rate significantly influences income in two regions, Pacific and West North Central. In terms of the magnitude of the impacts, unit changes in vacancy rates produce between 0.22% (Mideast) and 1.78% (Southwest) declines in income. A unit change in expected inflation increases income by 0.21% (Pacific) to 5.47% (East North Central), whereas a one-percentage-point change in unexpected inflation decreases income by 0.33% (Southeast) to 1.86% (Mideast).

RESULTS OF THE FORECASTS

The models were simulated over the entire historical and future period, 1983–2002. The results are presented in Exhibit 8.

The time range from 1983 to 1997 in these figures represents a "within-period" test of the model because it tests how well the model can predict the data used to estimate the model. This test is not as silly as it sounds. In fact, it is a necessary first step in determining the quality of a model. Equations with bad variables and random (insignificant) or incorrect coefficients will produce poor within-period forecasts. The analysis suggests that the models for value and income capture history very well.

A more difficult test is examining out-of-period forecasts. Since these models were estimated using data only through 1997, one can now look at how well they predicted the 1998 NCREIF returns. With one exception, the forecasts of capital appreciation and income return were lower than the NCREIF estimated values. In all cases, forecasts of total returns were lower than the reported total returns. The "best" forecasts of total return were in the Northeast, Mideast, Southeast, East North Central, and West North Central regions. For these five areas, the average absolute errors were between 1.7 to 2.8 percentage points. However, average absolute errors for total returns were 5.7 to 7.4 percentage points for the Southwest, Mountain, and Pacific regions. For these regions, the historical coefficients of variation (standard deviation divided by the mean) were among the highest of the eight regions. It appears that relatively large average absolute forecasting errors appear in regions with large return swings.

Exhibit 8: Model Forecasts by Division, 1983–2002

Northeast

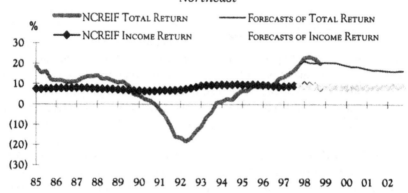

Mideast

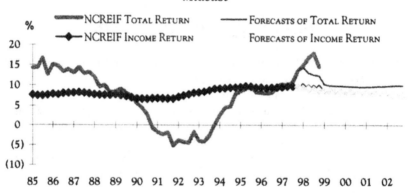

Southeast

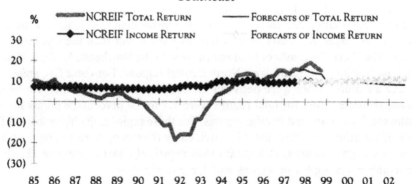

Exhibit 8 (Continued)
Southwest

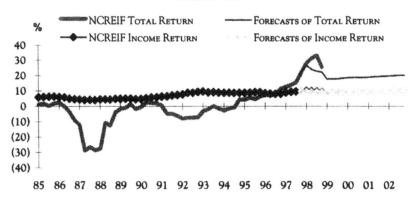

East North Central

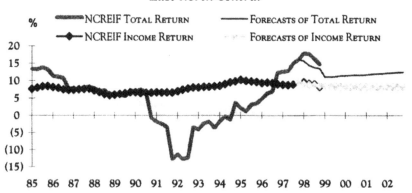

West North Central

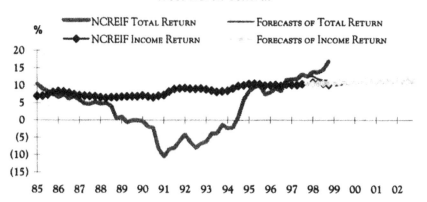

Exhibit 8 (Continued)
Mountain

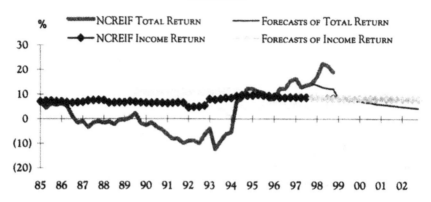

Pacific

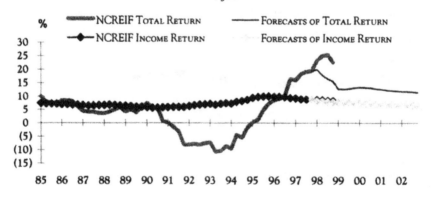

This out-of-period test was indeed a challenge because reported returns in 1998 for all regions were at, or higher than, historical maximum returns between 1983 and 1997. The SUR models used only data from 1985 to 1997. Further, total returns were at double-digit levels in all regions only after 1996:4. So, the magnitude of total returns observed in 1998 typically corresponded to only the last five quarterly observations used to construct the SUR models. Extremely wide variations in total returns were evident historically, from large negative values to large positive ones. Despite this pattern, the forecasts of total returns were, remarkably, in double digits and near the maximum levels of the 1983–97 period. It appears, therefore, that the SUR models performed well even though forecasts of total returns were lower than the reported returns.

CONCLUSIONS

Regional analysis clearly adds value. It allows for the identification and assessment of those factors that drive property value, income, and, ultimately, investment return. The determinants of these critical variables were found to be reasonably consistent across regions, meaning that similar explanatory variables were important and that the signs of the coefficients were generally consistent. However, significant differences exist across regions in the extent to which the dependent variables are driven by each factor. The estimated coefficients are not statistically the same across regions.

This structural specification works better in some regions than in others. This finding is partly because of the imperfection of the underlying data in the NCREIF index, which is based on properties that are not evenly distributed across or within regions at a moment in time or through time. Despite the fact that some of the differences lack intuitive explanation, the empirical results of this work still support the need for simultaneous geographic and economic diversification in the construction of real estate investment portfolios.

The success of structural analysis can translate into success from a forecasting perspective. The within-sample predicted values of the change in value and income for the eight regions replicate history very well. The forecasts of total returns and the associated components of capital appreciation and income return are, in most cases, reasonable. Compared to actual 1998 returns, the 1998 forecasts are evidently conservative and less dynamic. This result is not surprising given that in 1998 most regions booked record high returns. What is important is that the models produced double-digit forecasts of returns, matching or exceeding historical highs. Looking further out, the forecasts from the models suggest a trend of total returns either leveling off or sliding down. This trend is, in fact, occurring now. In general then, the models produce very plausible and useful forecasts.

Chapter 13

REITs' Real Estate Market Exposures

Bret R. Wilkerson, CFA

How much of the Dallas office market is in publicly traded hands? Can one get exposure to the Milwaukee warehouse market through the public markets? Where are the REITs concentrating new investment opportunities? Investors in equity real estate, either via the public or the private markets, must be knowledgeable about both the concentration of REIT investments and the flow of REIT capital. This is necessary so that intelligent choices can be made about how to participate in a particular market cycle and how to develop sharp strategies for creating and disposing of private equity in the context of an active REIT market. With the recent increased securitization of real estate, greater (but not yet great!) information is available to investors.

Of the four quadrants of real estate investing (public equity, private equity, public debt, and private debt), public equity is the smallest. Total market capitalization of the quadrant is roughly half the size of public debt, the next smallest. Private investment continues to dominate all equity investment in real estate. However, the rate of growth of public real estate equity capital in the mid-1990s was tremendous, capturing the attention of real estate investors. REIT expansion has been ad hoc and has grown at an unsustainable rate. The sector has grown for growth's sake, with little thought given to real estate cycles or the diversity of the portfolio.

As an emerging investment market in a mature industry, REITs provide an opportunity for intelligent investors to make informed decisions, and to make a significant amount of money. This was done fairly easily from 1995 to 1997, with tremendous industrywide annual returns. However, in 1998 REIT performance was extremely disappointing to those who had come to expect 20% total returns. It is likely that the underlying real estate performance now matters to investors in public real estate.

This chapter demonstrates where the REITs have focused their marginal investment dollars, and reviews the markets in which REITs had an early impact, in order to more completely understand the implications of the growth of REIT ownership in individual markets. While it is important to note trends in real estate cycles at the national level, it is becoming increasingly apparent to Wall Street that individual markets perform very differently from one another. For these reasons, trends in REIT investment at both the national and local levels will be discussed.

Reprinted with revisions with permission from *Mortgage Banking* Magazine, July 1998, pp. 32–42, published by the Mortgage Bankers Association of America.

METHODOLOGY AND CALCULATION OF EXPOSURES

The research concentrates on the real estate markets in which REIT properties are located and on the fundamentals and performance of those markets. Individual REITs' expected performance is forecast based on the theory that markets (*and the combination of markets*) matter. By first estimating each REIT's exposure to individual markets and property types, and then applying forecasts for each market, one can discern if a REIT is fighting an uphill battle to increase funds from operations (FFO), or if the public market should be rewarding growth that results from being in the right place, and a combination of right places, at the right time.

Property & Portfolio Research, Inc.'s DMRs™, driven by the interaction among supply, demand, and the influence of capital markets, are used. Because net operating income and capital value are modeled separately, the value of real estate in each of 60 cities and four property types can be estimated over time and into the forecast period.

The other data required to examine the REIT's degree of penetration in a market are those pertaining to individual REIT portfolios, including the date of acquisition, date of disposition, location, square footage, percentage ownership, and type of each property. These data are based on those gathered by SNL Securities and published in its REIT Datasource product. Combining the time series of property exposures to individual cities and property types with that of capital values and the market capitalization numbers noted above, a time series of REIT exposures to each city and each property type is created. While the absolute numbers of how much of each major market is owned by REITs are interesting, the relative allocation of capital is even more informative. Rank ordering the REIT markets gives us a significant amount of information about the flow of capital since 1993.

THE NATIONAL LEVEL — TRENDS TO WATCH FOR

Since 1993, a massive wave of real estate investments has been converted from private to public ownership. Exhibit 1 shows REIT ownership as a percentage of total market capitalization of the 60 major metropolitan areas for each of the four property types since 1993. The apartment sector has seen the greatest percentage of property converted to public ownership, growing from a 3.1% share at the end of 1993 to 11.3% by mid-year 1998. The retail sector, which in 1993 had the greatest percentage of property in REIT hands, has grown comparatively slowly because of reduced acquisitions and generally declining values, from 4.6% to 9.2% (this situation may be reversed in 1998 with several major portfolio acquisitions such as Simon DeBartolo's purchase of CPI). The warehouse sector has increased dramatically, from a mere 1.9% share to 9.3%. Finally, the wave of office REIT IPOs over the past two years, as well as the "nationalization" or "superregionalization" of those office REITs via acquisitions, has increased the amount of office space held publicly from 1.6% to 9.7% of the total in the 60 major markets.

Exhibit 1: REIT Ownership by Property Type as a Percentage of Total Market Capitalization

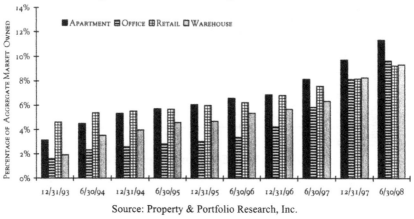

Source: Property & Portfolio Research, Inc.

The timing of these acquisitions by property type on an aggregate level demonstrates some interesting, and disturbing, trends. The apartment and office sectors provide two opposite and extreme examples of REIT acquisitions and market timing, as shown in Exhibit 2. Each chart plots the quarterly annualized change in the increase in REIT ownership of the aggregate market versus the total return. The apartment REITs, on an aggregate level, appear to be making pretty good timing decisions. When returns are low (and, therefore, pricing is less aggressive), they have increased the pace of investment. The correlation between the pace of acquisition and the return is –0.14 (lower is better), showing that there may be a link between low acquisition prices and investment. The warehouse REITs also appear to grow the most when markets are soft; the correlation for them is –0.23. Overall, it appears that some of these REITs are skilled at buying low (the ancillary, selling high, has yet to be seen).

On the other hand, the wave of office properties entering the REIT format has increased concomitantly with the increase in returns (correlation 0.66!), further evidence that supports the plethora of anecdotes about office companies paying higher prices. The office sector is clearly the most volatile of the four sectors we track in terms of total returns and values. If an investor is capable of timing the market, high-risk assets can best be taken advantage of using a trading strategy. However, the legal structure and financial constraints of the REIT format make this more difficult. The worst possible action is to load up an office portfolio with property at the peak of the cycle, exactly the cliff that office REITs are headed toward! While the near-term fundamentals in the office market suggest a few more good years of performance before development completely overwhelms demand, clearly office REITs now look to be a recipe for disaster not too far down the road. In retail, the correlation is 0.37, reflecting a slowdown in 1995 and 1996, when Wall Street was less apt to provide capital to a sector that had (rightfully) been beaten down. As stated earlier, retail acquisitions are on the rise as more and more investors begin to see the retail recovery.

Exhibit 2: REIT Growth versus DMR, by Property Type

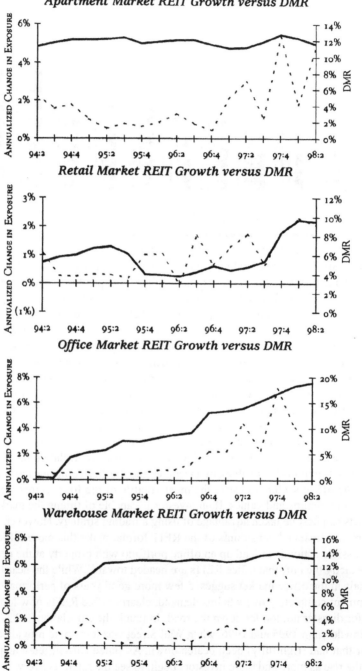

It is also interesting to note the drop-off in acquisition pace in 1998 (especially in office), with REITs perhaps realizing that their cost of capital is not as low as was once thought. Dramatically lower stock prices don't help either!

THE LOCAL LEVEL —
WHERE THE RUBBER MEETS THE ROAD

Differentiation becomes more apparent and the analysis is even more profound at the individual market level, especially to those who believe that investment capital is a significant driver in real estate cycles. The 10 markets with the largest percentage of REIT ownership by property type as of mid-year 1998 are shown in Exhibit 3. Among the cities for apartment investment, it is not surprising that each of the top 10 are either in the rapidly growing Southeast or in Texas. There has been a heavy concentration of apartment REITs in this region since the beginning of the cycle. Since the recession of the early 1990s, each of these metropolitan areas has experienced outstanding employment growth and strong net in-migration, two of the key ingredients that apartment investors rely upon. While the office sector has provided a stark contrast, with total REIT ownership significantly lower and recent growth rates of acquisition much higher, the list of markets where REITs are the most prevalent is again dominated by the Southeast. Somewhat surprisingly, Philadelphia and Bergen-Passaic make the list, reflecting the strength of a handful of "superregional" companies in that area and their appetite for suburban office space. The retail sector is second only to apartments in terms of the number of cities with greater than 10% REIT ownership, with 24 cities surpassing that benchmark. More geographically spread out, retail demonstrates a much less discernible regional trend, perhaps because of the historical emphasis of the retail REITs on venue rather than geography. In addition, a relationship with a national retailer is more beneficial to an owner with retail properties in multiple metropolitan areas. Finally, in the warehouse sector, in which there are relatively fewer REITs, the markets that make the list generally fall into two categories: major national distribution hubs where the REITs have a huge development capability, and smaller subregional hubs where the REITs can dominate the market.

For each of the sectors, the 10 markets with the lowest percentage of REIT ownership are shown in Exhibit 4. Across the board, the cities tend to fall into three groups: markets with large market capitalizations, those markets traditionally dominated by non-REIT investors, and underdemanded markets. In the larger markets, such as Los Angeles apartment and Seattle retail, it would take an enormous amount of absolute dollar investment to generate a marginal increase in the percentage of ownership. Others, such as the Boston apartment and the Kansas City office markets, have been traditionally dominated by other types of real estate investors. Most of the markets shown in Exhibit 4, however, fall into the last category — the underdemanded. The Hartfords, Honolulus, and Milwaukees of the world continue to suffer on the demand side of the equation, even as the rest of the nation experiences a tremendous demand for real estate. Occupancy rates have not moved much in these markets (and in many cases have moved in the wrong direction), and rent levels have not provided the story that is necessary to attract REIT capital. When faced with daily pricing in the public markets, REITs are forced to grow FFO as fast as possible, and, therefore, they refuse to dilute any of today's growth with acquisitions in markets that will detract from current income.

Interestingly, at year-end 1993, there were 21 markets where the REIT universe did not have any exposure. Today there are only six: Albuquerque warehouse, Honolulu apartment, Honolulu office, Honolulu warehouse, Newark apartment, and Pittsburgh office. Only in the retail property type can an investor get some exposure to all 60 major metro areas. While the apartment sector is often considered to be the most mature in terms of the public markets because of the number of companies that went public in the 1993–1994 period and also because of recent mergers, there are still two major markets that have no REIT investment! Most of the six markets with no REIT investment are not large markets — but that certainly does not preclude the possibility of finding good investment opportunities there. Nor does it mean that an investment in one of these markets may not be beneficial to a REIT. Low correlations of returns with those in the current portfolio can be very helpful in managing cash flow, a factor that will become more important and more apparent to REITs as they enter the later stages of the cycle.

This analysis concentrates only on those portions of REIT portfolios within the 60 major metropolitan areas. Data on the market conditions within each of these cities and property types are available. Therefore, investors can make educated decisions regarding the real estate fundamentals and expected performance of those investments. However, hundreds of properties in smaller MSAs, and many that do not even lie in a defined metropolitan area, also exist in the REIT universe. In addition, many REITs traditionally focus on "non-core" property types such as hotels, self-storage, golf courses, prisons, auto dealerships, and timber. These investments clearly add to the "accidental" collection of assets that happens to be publicly traded and likely overrepresent those asset classes. Taking one of the most extreme examples, REIT investors who are underweighted in hotels may only be underweighted when compared to a REIT index, but could be severely overweighted when compared to the true universe of investable real estate. Tracking the REIT index is not at all the same as tracking the true real estate investment universe.

Exhibit 3: Largest REIT Ownership by Market by Property Type at Mid-Year 1998

Apartments MSA Name	REIT Ownership Percent	Office MSA Name	REIT Ownership Percent	Retail MSA Name	REIT Ownership Percent	Warehouse MSA Name	REIT Ownership Percent
Memphis, TN	52%	Raleigh, NC	21%	Columbus, OH	18%	Nassau-Suffolk, NY	25%
Dallas, TX	44%	San Jose, CA	20%	Orlando, FL	18%	Indianapolis, IN	24%
San Antonio, TX	44%	Philadelphia, PA	17%	Newark, NJ	17%	Cincinnati, OH	22%
Houston, TX	42%	Atlanta, GA	17%	Atlanta, GA	17%	Chicago, IL	20%
Atlanta, GA	42%	Austin, TX	16%	Middlesex-S-H, NJ	15%	Nashville, TN	19%
Jacksonville, FL	41%	Jacksonville, FL	16%	Austin, TX	15%	Richmond, VA	19%
Richmond, VA	38%	New Orleans, LA	15%	Indianapolis, IN	15%	Columbus, OH	17%
Charlotte, NC	37%	Orlando, FL	15%	Washington, DC	14%	Memphis, TN	17%
Phoenix, AZ	36%	Bergen-Passaic, NJ	14%	Baltimore, MD	14%	San Jose, CA	16%
Austin, TX	34%	San Diego, CA	14%	St. Louis, MO	14%	Austin, TX	15%

Source: Property & Portfolio Research, Inc.

Exhibit 4: Smallest REIT Ownership by Market by Property Type at Mid-Year 1998

Apartments MSA Name	REIT Ownership Percent	Office MSA Name	REIT Ownership Percent	Retail MSA Name	REIT Ownership Percent	Warehouse MSA Name	REIT Ownership Percent
Newark, NJ	0.0%	Honolulu, HI	0.0%	San Jose, CA	2.9%	Honolulu, HI	0.0%
Honolulu, HI	0.0%	Pittsburgh, PA	0.0%	Boston, MA	4.0%	Albuquerque, NM	0.0%
New York, NY	0.9%	Hartford, CT	0.7%	Fort Worth, TX	4.3%	Norfolk, VA	0.5%
Bergen-Passaic, NJ	0.9%	Oklahoma City, OK	0.8%	Riverside, CA	4.5%	Pittsburgh, PA	0.5%
New Orleans, LA	1.0%	Kansas City, MO	1.1%	New Haven-Stamford, CT	4.7%	New Haven-Stamford, CT	0.6%
Boston, MA	1.3%	New Haven-Stamford, CT	2.0%	Milwaukee, WI	4.9%	West Palm Beach, FL	1.2%
Nassau-Suffolk, NY	1.6%	Albuquerque, NM	2.8%	Kansas City, MO	5.0%	Hartford, CT	1.7%
Middlesex-S-H, NJ	1.7%	Fort Worth, TX	3.2%	Tucson, AZ	5.0%	New York, NY	1.8%
Los Angeles, CA	1.7%	Tucson, AZ	3.4%	Norfolk, VA	5.4%	Ventura, CA	1.9%
Pittsburgh, PA	1.9%	Miami, FL	3.4%	Seattle, WA	5.6%	Tucson, AZ	2.5%

Source: Property & Portfolio Research, Inc.

WHY THOSE MARKETS?

The above data beg the question, why those markets? What are REITs looking for? The answer is clearly that these companies are publicly traded and must meet today's earnings expectations. Earnings are driven by rapid growth in occupancies and rent levels. These, in turn, are driven by demand relative to supply. A wave of apartment REITs went public in 1993 and 1994, at a time when nationally there was a tremendous amount of new demand. As a result, continued acquisitions at reasonable capitalization rates were accretive to FFO and, therefore, spurred a tremendous amount of REIT investment, especially in the faster growing cities. Exhibit 5 illustrates those markets where the increase in percentage ownership by REITs since 1993 has been the greatest. In general, the list is again comprised of those markets with great demand.

However, real estate is still a cyclical business, and strong demand begets a response in construction. New supply generally overresponds to the signal and hence, the cycle ensues. In addition to the overall growth, the historical standard deviation of each market's returns has been calculated and ranked by property type. Note that most of the markets in Exhibit 5 rank very poorly in terms of risk (lower ranks are better). Especially in office, and to a lesser degree in apartment and retail sectors, there is a concentration on more volatile markets. As seen in 1997, when it became apparent to everyone that Atlanta apartment was overbuilding, the public market began looking only at the supply side of the equation and responded by beating down the stock prices of those companies that were heavily concentrated in the market. Markets that experience strong waves of demand, such as Atlanta and Dallas, tend to overreact by generating the most new construction and are, therefore, more likely to have greater volatility in performance.

Wall Street has given REITs a mandate to grow, and apparently not much direction on what else will be rewarded. This has two major implications for REITs and their choice of markets. First, with a significant amount of capital to allocate, REIT investment tends to be in those markets with the greatest liquidity. Liquidity is minimal at the cyclical trough when pricing is the most favorable to new investments; it is also poor at the top when performance is the most robust and investors tend to hang on to their assets. The greatest amount of trading tends to occur on the way up the cycle — as a result, most of the cities with the largest percentage of REIT investment are those that are well into the recovery phase. Second, once the cyclical peak is approached, and pricing becomes too expensive to continue to make accretive acquisitions, REITs are forced to take on extra risk. This can come in the form of "opportunistic" investments or in the form of increased development. Risk is a double-edged sword, and while it can be a powerful tool when used at the right point in a cycle, taking on excess risk at or near the peak is more likely to be harmful.

Exhibit 5: Growth of REIT Ownership of Markets 1993-1997

MSA Name	Percent Owned 1993	1993 Rank (by PT)	Percent Owned 1997	1997 Rank (by PT)	Growth	Volatility Rank
Apartments						
Jacksonville, FL	9%	15	41%	6	32%	40
Dallas, TX	13%	8	44%	2	31%	58
Salt Lake City, UT	0%	53	30%	13	30%	46
Phoenix, AZ	6%	18	36%	9	30%	39
Memphis, TN	23%	1	52%	1	29%	9
Houston, TX	14%	6	42%	4	28%	55
Charlotte, NC	11%	12	37%	8	26%	8
San Antonio, TX	19%	4	44%	3	24%	54
Atlanta, GA	20%	2	42%	5	22%	52
Nashville, TN	6%	19	27%	15	21%	49
Office						
Raleigh, NC	1%	39	21%	1	20%	14
Philadelphia, PA	1%	37	17%	3	16%	25
Bergen-Passaic, NJ	1%	47	14%	9	14%	34
San Jose, CA	6%	2	20%	2	14%	35
Atlanta, GA	4%	9	17%	4	13%	52
Dallas, TX	2%	23	14%	11	12%	48
Orlando, FL	3%	15	15%	8	12%	41
Austin, TX	4%	5	16%	5	12%	45
New Orleans, LA	3%	12	15%	7	12%	22
San Francisco, CA	2%	22	14%	12	12%	15
Retail						
Middlesex-S-H, NJ	4%	27	15%	5	11%	48
Columbus, OH	8%	6	18%	1	10%	10
Orlando, FL	7%	10	18%	2	10%	55
St. Louis, MO	4%	34	14%	10	10%	15
Las Vegas, NV	2%	46	12%	17	10%	29
Bergen-Passaic, NJ	4%	28	13%	12	9%	30
Jacksonville, FL	3%	37	12%	18	9%	44
Indianapolis, IN	6%	13	15%	7	8%	11
Richmond, VA	5%	23	13%	13	8%	54
Tampa, FL	5%	21	14%	11	8%	19
Warehouse						
Nassau-Suffolk, NY	1%	34	25%	1	23%	51
Richmond, VA	0%	50	19%	6	19%	26
Nashville, TN	2%	21	19%	5	16%	44
Indianapolis, IN	8%	4	24%	2	16%	5
Columbus, OH	1%	28	17%	7	16%	1
Chicago, IL	4%	7	20%	4	15%	6
Cincinnati, OH	8%	5	22%	3	14%	17
Atlanta, GA	1%	39	14%	13	14%	35
Memphis, TN	3%	12	17%	8	14%	31
Orange County, CA	1%	41	14%	14	13%	52

Source: Property & Portfolio Research, Inc.

CONCLUSIONS

Both public and private equity investors can benefit from this knowledge when setting investment strategy. Whatever the format in which real estate is held, or how often it is priced, the long-term driver of performance will be the underlying property and the market in which it is located. REITs provide investors access to (slightly) more liquid assets, daily pricing, and the benefits of portfolio effects. However, as demonstrated, the REIT universe is clearly not even a close proxy for an index of the U.S. real estate market.

Because of their need to meet expectations today, REITs have less flexibility when it comes to managing tomorrow's portfolio. This does not suggest that they should ignore the cycles of the markets they are invested in, but rather that they need to pay extra attention to those markets and their respective cycles. In particular, they need to pay attention to the interaction of those cycles, so that when one market suffers from overbuilding, there are other exposures in the portfolio that are in the "sweet spot."

This means two very important things to REIT investors. At this point it is not possible to hold "core" real estate in the public form. As shown above, there are a number of markets in which the REIT universe is heavily overweighted, and a number where it is heavily underweighted. Also, there is excess risk in the public markets in terms of the markets in which REITs happen to be invested and of the sectors that are represented, above and beyond the extra volatility associated with daily pricing and the overall impact of the stock market.

Investors in private equity, who continually run up against REITs in attempting to acquire property, should think about a number of factors, depending on their investment strategy. First, in terms of acquisition/disposition strategies, excess capital is flowing into a number of cities, probably pushing cap rates lower than would be suggested by fundamentals. Concentrate acquisition on those markets where supply relative to demand is in check and where the REITs are underweighted, and focus disposition in those markets where demand is strong and where the REITs are increasing their exposures. Second, for a development strategy, those markets where REITs are ramping up their exposures appear to be excellent target markets. Finally, when considering swapping properties for REIT shares, an investor must consider where the company's portfolio is concentrated, the risk of the portfolio, and what the additional properties will contribute in the context of the overall portfolio.

REIT investments and capital continue to play an increasing role in the real estate market. As an emerging market in an old industry, educated investors will continue to be able to take advantage of arbitrage between the public and private markets through a better understanding of the REIT universe.

Chapter 14

Timberland Investments

John D. Wilson, Ph.D.

T he scene could be the offices of any large pension fund. A diverse group of professionals are busily tending to their fiduciary duties: analyzing, acquiring, selling, and managing assets to produce the desired financial results for the fund. Accountants check cash flows and calculate returns. Financial analysts calculate betas and correlation coefficients, and contemplate optimal asset-allocation strategies. Economists gather data and make forecasts. Asset managers prepare for a site visit, donning heavy coats to ward off briars and ticks, and hard hats for protection against "widowmakers"; their thick trousers are tucked into high-top boots in case of rattlers and water moccasins...hold it right there! Briars? Ticks? Falling branches? SNAKES? What kind of assets are these?

Over the past decade, timberland has come into its own as a viable (and even desirable) target for institutional investors seeking to enhance investment performance. Solid returns and positive portfolio diversification benefits have engendered substantial interest within the investment community, with foresters wearing gray suits and struggling with "efficient frontiers," and finance wizards puzzling over terms like "sustained yield" or "Lidgerwood skidder system."

WHAT IS TIMBERLAND?

Timberland can be simply defined as forest land which either currently grows or has the potential to grow timber of *merchantable* quality and quantity. In other words, land can be classified as timberland whether it is fully stocked with mature timber, partially covered with young saplings, or even if it is bare ground ready for planting. The merchantability criterion rules out forest land in preserves as well as those lands that can only produce poor quality or scant quantity of timber. The U.S. has nearly 740 million acres of forest land, of which 480 million acres is classified as timberland.

Timberland, like forest land in general, can yield a number of products or uses, major examples being wood and wood fiber production, recreation, watershed protection, and wildlife habitat. While owners often extract payment from recreational users of their lands (e.g., for hunting, fishing, and camping), sales of timber account for most of the owners' revenues; therefore, timber growth and value are the focus of this chapter.

WHO OWNS IT...AND WHERE?

Ownership can be broadly classified as public or private. Of the more than 480 million acres of timberland in the United States, nearly 100 million are federally owned and 35 million owned by state and local governments. Nearly three-quarters of the federally owned timberland is located in the Pacific Northwest and the Rockies. Private lands are held by individuals and trusts, corporations (most often wood products companies), and, recently, institutional investors (who currently own less than 1% of the private timberland in the United States).

Ownership may also be differentiated on the basis of the nature of ownership. It may be outright, fee simple ownership of the land and all associated "rights," or partial ownership of selected attributes such as timber-cutting rights, mineral extraction rights, hunting or other recreational usage rights, or the underlying land itself. For example, it is not unusual for a wood products company to negotiate a sale of timberland but retain timber-cutting rights to ensure a steady supply of wood for one of its mills.

Timberland is located on all continents except Antarctica and across all climatic zones. Perhaps best known to the general public are the extensive rainforests covering much of the world's tropics. These forests are the source of various high-value woods used for furniture, interior finish, and other specialties. For indigenous peoples, they are an important source of food, fuel, medicine, and many other products.

Therefore, there is substantial tension between those who would use the forests and those who would protect them. Tropical rainforests are by nature extremely fragile and are essentially depleted permanently by timber harvesting. Many tropical nations are beginning to protect their forests and constrain harvesting. Because of these constraints, ownership patterns, the underdeveloped and uncertain markets for tropical woods. and potential environmental backlash, timberland in tropical areas is generally out of bounds for investment purposes.

The temperate zones produce most of the timber harvested and sold in major world markets. Their forests supply the majority of the solid wood used in construction as well as the wood fiber for paper product production. Important traditional producing areas include Canada, the U.S. South, and Pacific Northwest, Russia, Scandinavia, and China. New Zealand and Chile are emergent producing areas as recently planted stands come online and begin to grow significant amounts of timber.

Most of the existing timberland in the temperate zones has been harvested and managed for many years, and has a well-developed infrastructure both for harvesting and end-product production (e.g., efficient transportation systems and modern, large-scale mills). A notable exception are the vast forests in Siberia and far eastern Russia, where there is scant infrastructure for exploitation of natural timber. Political and economic constraints are very likely to prevent the serious utilization of this resource base for many years.

WHAT DOES TIMBERLAND PRODUCE?

Commercial timber species can be broken down into two major categories: *hard-woods* and *softwoods*. Hardwoods, also known as *deciduous* or leaf-bearing trees, have relatively dense, heavy wood with short individual fibers (for example, maple, oak, and eucalyptus). They often grow in mixed stands, i.e., forests with a number of interspersed species. Hardwoods are found across climatic zones, although tropical rainforests are almost exclusively composed of hardwoods; hardwoods account for a declining proportion of the forest species mix as one moves from the equator toward the poles.

Softwoods, also known as *conifers* and needle-bearing trees, have lighter, softer wood with somewhat longer fibers (for example, pine, fir, and spruce). Because of their growth and reproductive characteristics, they are often found in relatively homogeneous stands in which the trees are of the same species and quite close in age and size. While softwoods are also found across climatic zones, they increase in proportion relative to hardwoods the farther away one moves from the equator. The fastest-growing, most densely stocked softwood forests are located in the temperate zones.

While geographical location determines a certain amount of use (e.g., indigenous peoples use whatever species are close at hand for fuel and shelter), the species' physical characteristics are the primary determinants of end use. Indeed, there are notable exceptions to these generalizations, but for the most part specific, commercial end-product production and quality requirements are best satisfied by specific categories or even single species of trees. While wood from almost all species has historically been widely used for fuel, most of the modern demand on commercial timberland is to satisfy the need for solid wood and veneers for construction and furniture, and wood fiber for pulp-based paper and related products.

With their harder and often more attractive wood, hardwoods provide the best source for furniture and construction finish materials. As such, they are often high-value species, although quality requirements make it difficult to find growing stock suitable for conversion into end products. They are, moreover, relatively expensive to manage and take a long time to grow to harvest age. Synthetic materials and metal now compete with hardwoods in end-use markets, although, because of custom and their aesthetic qualities, hardwoods are still often preferred. In recent years, high-quality hardwood veneers covering less expensive core materials have substantially replaced the use of solid wood for furniture and interior paneling.

Although not generally the preferred source due in part to their shorter fiber lengths, hardwoods are used in the production of paper and related products, especially high-quality fine papers. But if a steady and reasonably priced softwood supply exists, hardwoods are usually only a lower-cost alternative wood fiber.

Softwood timberlands are the dominant source for both construction lumber and wood fiber for pulp manufacture in the developed world. The wood is easily worked and relatively strong for its weight, and has structural characteristics that make it especially desirable for pulping processes. Metal, synthetics, and stone are substitutes for softwood lumber; hardwood fiber, non-tree fibers (e.g., *bagasse* from sugar cane), recycled wastepaper, and synthetic materials are substitutes for softwood fiber in pulp manufacture. In general, however, both cost and quality give softwoods a competitive edge over alternative materials.

WHAT AFFECTS TIMBER GROWTH?

Timberland is a dynamic entity. Not only can the trees on it be harvested, but, over time, they grow in size (and most often in quality) and, therefore, value. Individual trees, and stands of timber, exhibit a *sigmoid* growth curve, which can be segmented into three phases: growth rate accelerates during the young or *emerging* growth phase, decelerates during the *established* growth phase, and eventually plateaus during the *mature growth* phase. Value growth follows a similar pattern, augmented by the fact that as trees grow in size, they also grow in quality and make the transition from lower-value uses, such as fiber for pulp, to higher-value end-product uses, including lumber and veneer. It should be noted that only trees which have reached certain threshold stem diameters can be used for lumber or veneer production, while wood fiber for pulp can be extracted from any tree regardless of size.

Very young stands of timber may be considered for a period of some years to be *pre-merchantable*, having no or very limited possibilities for harvests, therefore, limiting yield income. At the other end of the growth spectrum, very mature stands of timber may effectively stop growing in value as slow growth and natural die-off combine to produce a static value stand.

Different species exhibit substantially different growth rates. Geographical and topographical location, affecting the quantity of sunlight and water as well as soil characteristics, have a significant impact on timber growth. Forests undergo natural birth, growth, and death processes. A *natural* stand, one that has not been planted (a *plantation*), may have started on bare land through wind-borne or animal-carried seed, or on a former forest site through vegetative reproduction (i.e., sprouting from the roots or stumps of harvested or burned trees). Seedlings or sprouts grow into saplings and then into mature trees. Stands eventually reach equilibrium, where death and decay are matched by growth of existing trees and *ingrowth* of new ones. This dynamic equilibrium may last indefinitely or until destroyed by wind, fire, pest infestation, or harvest activities.

Another important determinant of the rate of growth is forest management. Various forest management techniques, known as *silvicultural* practices, are used by trained foresters to either protect stands or enhance their growth characteristics and, therefore, value. Protection measures may include the creation of access roads for fire control, cutting fire breaks or establishing wind breaks to mitigate losses from fire and wind, or pest extermination and removal of diseased trees to reduce pest infestation damage.

Management practices which can enhance growth rates or wood quality are numerous and varied. Existing stands can be *thinned*, which enables the remaining trees to grow at a faster rate. Thinning can be noncommercial, or the harvested wood may be sold if a market for it exists. Trees can be *pruned* (i.e., the limbs removed for a portion of the stem) which results in the growth over time of clear, knot-free wood for high-value lumber or veneer production. Stands may also be *culled* of diseased or inferior trees. Chemical fertilizers may be applied to enhance growth rates.

On bare ground, either former farmland or harvested timberland, new stands can be established in plantations. Where natural stands may consist of a number of species of varying ages, plantations are usually *even-aged* and generally a *monoculture* (i.e., containing only one species). The trees are planted in evenly spaced rows at a density pre-determined to yield optimal growth. Seedlings are selected from genetic stock characterized by fast growth of desirable quality. Appropriate ground preparation and weed treatments can improve stand establishment and growth. The homogeneous nature of the stands and their orderly physical characteristics also reduce harvesting costs.

WHO INVESTS IN TIMBERLAND?

Timberland is owned around the world by various public and private entities, including individuals, partnerships, corporations, institutional investors, and governments. Individuals have often owned timberland as part of, or contiguous to, farmland. More recently, wealthy individuals or groups of individuals operating in partnerships have invested in timberland.

Governments have always held large areas of forest land. English monarchs, for example, viewed colonial American pine forests as a vital source of wood for ship masts, emblazoning desirable trees with "broad arrows." Colonists caught removing these trees for their own use were punished with death. Local governments may own forest land to protect water supplies. The U.S. government currently owns millions of acres of forests, holding some as preserves and others as timberland, with timber-cutting rights put out to bid.

Forest product companies in the U.S. have long held large tracts of domestic timberland, using them to supply their mills with sawtimber and pulpwood. In retrospect their investment and harvesting activities can be considered as exploitative; beginning in the 1800s and proceeding to the present day, companies cut huge tracts of timberland in the Northeast, the North Central states, the Southeast, and the Pacific Northwest. Trees were harvested and the lands abandoned to regenerate naturally. The fact that forests did grow back on cut-over lands attracted forest product companies back to once-abandoned areas. The physical and economic realities of a constrained fiber supply, once viewed as seemingly limitless, have forced these companies to invest in forest management and plantation forestry to ensure a steady supply of wood in the future. They have also had to look outside of the U.S. for sources of fiber in competitive global markets.

Institutional investors are relative newcomers to timberland. By the early 1980s, pension funding had grown dramatically and plan sponsors, encouraged by the dictates of ERISA and state legislation, were seeking ways to diversify their investment portfolios away from fixed-income securities. Alternatives included stocks and commercial real estate. At the same time, forest products companies were carrying vast areas of timberland on their books at what was perceived to be below-market value, making these firms susceptible to takeovers; the forest products companies also viewed timberland sales as a possible source of capital to expand their operations. As a result, institutional investment in timberland has risen to more than $4 billion, the management of which is primarily in the hands of timberland investment management organizations (TIMOs).

Institutional investors have traditionally become timberland owners either through fee simple purchase of tracts of land or by investing in separate account products offered by large insurers. Early in 1998, two large forest products companies combined their land holdings into one separate entity, forming the first timberland-based real estate investment trust (REIT). The smaller levels of investment necessary and the relative liquidity of these publicly traded instruments may make timberland a more palatable investment option for a wider spectrum of investors.

WHAT ARE THE SOURCES OF RISK AND RETURN FOR TIMBERLAND?

Returns from timberland are realized through the sale of timber and/or the land itself. During the period of ownership, harvests of timber can yield cash flows; these harvests could range from *intermediate* cuttings to final removal and sale of all the standing timber. It is conceivable that no harvests ever take place during the tenure of ownership, and that the return would, therefore, be predicated on the difference between original purchase and final sale prices of the land and timber together.

The rate of return is affected by a number of factors that contribute to the growth in value of the timber and land components. Timber is a dynamic entity since it grows over time. Biological growth is relatively stable and predictable, but varies across species and geographical regions. In the United States, for example, western timber grows at an average 2.4% per year, northern timber at 3.4%, and southern timber at 6%. Some locations outside of the U.S., particularly in the southern hemisphere, are said to exhibit higher growth rates. These average rates of growth vary within regions because of rainfall, soil conditions, topography aspect, and species composition. In general, softwoods display faster growth rates than hardwoods. Many timber investment managers view biological growth as the most important factor in generating returns, claiming that it will account for 50% to 70% of the return on investment.

As trees grow in size, they also grow from lower-value uses to higher-value uses. Trees reaching sawtimber diameter jump in value. Later diameter increases enable harvesting for the production of high-value veneers.

Growth, both in size and quality, can be enhanced through forest management practices, as discussed earlier. Of course, the decision to manage timberland must weigh the value of the enhancements and the time required for them to take effect against the costs, sometimes substantial, that come with more intensive forest management.

Returns for forest investments are significantly affected by changes in the prices of the forest products. Demand for timber is derived from the demand for end products such as lumber and paper. As their prices rise or fall, so do those for the primary input, wood fiber. Paper and lumber prices are impacted by population growth, interest rates, prices of substitutes, and the general level of economic activity. The value of the underlying land can be affected by changes in demand for land for alternative uses (e.g., residential or agriculture).

In general timber supply is relatively stable and predictable, but it can be affected by government actions. National governments are large owners of timberland with multiple goals, which influence the level at which national timberlands can be harvested. One example is in the U.S. Pacific Northwest where, during the early 1980s, large amounts of timber put out to bid depressed prices; more recently, cutting restrictions put in place to protect endangered wildlife species have caused sawtimber prices to rise significantly. Governments in South Africa and New Zealand are privatizing some national forest land, which may have an effect on wood supply. In the 1970s, Brazil gave financial assistance to private landowners to plant their acres with trees, which now represent a source of wood supply which would not have otherwise existed.

Another important source of returns for investments in timberland are financial management practices, especially with respect to acquisition (and eventual disposition) of timberland and the intermediate sales of timber itself. Timberland transactions are predicated on thorough appraisals, which must take into account not only the value of the land and timber, but also the market environment in which the investment exists. This requires that investment managers have (or can hire) a depth of knowledge in forestry, financial analysis, and economics to ensure that the agreed-upon price represents fair value. Harvests, the proceeds of which provide cash flow and can constitute a substantial portion of the investment's total return, require the same knowledge base plus a more fundamental knowledge of local timber buyers and loggers so as to maximize returns.

Risks can be categorized as physical or economic. Physical risks include damage or destruction from pests, disease, fire, wind, or volcanic eruption. Although they receive widespread public attention, these risks are generally not a major consideration for investment-quality timberland owners. They account for, on average, timber losses of less than one-half of 1% per year, and can be substantially mitigated on individual holdings through forest management practices.

Economic risk factors include substitution by alternative materials and government intervention, as discussed above. The most significant economic risk factor is the volatility of price for harvested timber. Pacific Northwest Douglas Fir sawlog prices dropped from $300 per thousand board feet in 1980 to under $100 in 1984 and then headed up to $600 in 1993 before stabilizing between $200 and $300 during the late 1990s. It should be noted that, over time, timber price increases have exceeded inflation rates. This price volatility is characteristic of that region, which is strongly influenced by federal timberland policies. Timber prices are much less volatile in the Southeast and even less so in the Northeast, albeit prices are lower in both these regions.

Another timberland risk factor for investors to consider is the asset's relative illiquidity. Sales and subsequent harvests of timber take time to plan, negotiate, and complete. So can disposition of the timberland itself, especially given the very large size of individual investments and also, in the case of pre-merchantable tracts of timber, because of some investors' need for timely cash flows. Timberland is not, therefore, an appropriate investment vehicle for those who require liquid assets. On the other hand, timberland has a unique association with time, which investors can use to their advantage. For example, should timber prices sag, timberland managers may decide to delay harvests and sales of timber until such time as prices are more favorable. During this period, timber, unlike agricultural products, can be "stored" on the stump and will continue to grow in size and value, thereby mitigating negative price impacts on returns.

HOW HAVE TIMBERLAND INVESTMENTS PERFORMED?

In the early 1980s, a forest economist working at a major financial institution constructed timber price-based indices to estimate historical and to project future returns from hypothetical U.S. timberland investments as there were no reliable sources of return data for the asset class. Econometric models, based on existing, baseline U.S. macroeconomic forecasts, predicted that timber investments equally divided between the Pacific Northwest and the Southeast could be expected to yield a 17% nominal return. Some dozen years later, it is interesting to examine the results of actual investments made during the period and compare them to this early estimate.

Institutional Property Consultants, Inc. reported in 1993 that aggregate annual returns for all timberland funds and separate accounts had averaged 11.5% between 1984 and 1992, after inflation. The CPI-U averaged nearly 3.9% over this period, resulting in a nominal return of 15.4%.[1]

The use of timber prices as the basis for indices of timberland returns was necessary in the past as there was no central auction market, such as the New York Stock Exchange, to provide an accurate assessment of timberland performance. As a possible substitute for hypothetical return estimates, NCREIF has, since the end

---

[1] "A Timberland Investment Update," October 1993.

of 1994, assembled and published the NCREIF Timberland Index. NCREIF combines income, expense, sales and purchase, and appraisal data provided by John Hancock, Prudential, and Forest Investment Associates on investments managed by those firms and estimates, on an ongoing basis, returns by U.S. region. Results indicated that the investments across all regions have achieved total returns ranging annually from 11% to 37% before inflation. Also of interest is the difference between the regional results. Consistent with earlier hypothetical index work, Pacific Northwest, Southeast, and Northeast returns rank in declining order.

These index measures have been criticized on two grounds. One is that investments managed by John Hancock dominate the Southeast index, and represent the entirety of both the Pacific Northwest and Northeast indices, thus presenting an inaccurate picture of the universe of U.S. timberland investments. Also it has been noted that, in an attempt to report values "marked to market" on a quarterly basis, the investments are valued using appraisals that some analysts believe understate the volatility of the returns. Still, the data from actual timberland property transactions help provide potential and existing investors with a more accurate way to assess timberland investments.

Readers will note the relatively high level of historical returns reported for timberland. One consultant said that returns were artificially high because of soaring wood prices caused by a late 1980s boom in housing construction, combined with harvesting restrictions in the Pacific Northwest. At least one manager agrees, and feels that the region's timberland is currently overvalued, presenting a good opportunity to divest. In part, these concerns reflect the volatile nature of Pacific Northwest timber prices and investment returns.

Also important is the fact that many of the early investments were made at a time when many forest products companies were offering timberlands for sale to remove these often undervalued holdings from their books and render the companies less susceptible to hostile takeovers. With this scenario past, investors may no longer be able to take advantage of what was likely a buyer's market for timberland. What portion of historical returns can be attributed to that particular scenario has not been estimated.

While there is a need to view past returns with some circumspection, historical results give at least some measure of the performance characteristics of the asset class. The estimates warrant further consideration of timberland as a portfolio return enhancer, encouraging a further look at its prospects in the future.

WHAT'S THE OUTLOOK FOR TIMBERLAND INVESTMENT PERFORMANCE?

Managers seem to have taken the past and its aberrations into account as they project timberland's performance into the future. Their expected returns for U.S. timberland consistently stay within the 6% to 10% range after inflation, with 8%

being the number most commonly offered. Returns for domestic "niche" opportunities and for overseas investments are projected to be in the 10% to 20% range, with 12% as a standard target rate.

Compared to the reported returns of the first 12 years of institutional investment in timberland, these projections seem to indicate some caution on the part of the managers. They may not want to promise more than they can deliver, but their caution also indicates that there are currently more players involved in the timberland investment business than before, and that more accurate information about the investments is available. More participants and better information are prerequisites for a more competitive market, and, therefore, the excess gains received because of market imperfections are less likely to be duplicated.

However, the managers still have good reason to believe that timberland returns will be strong in the future. Basic demand/supply relationships, both domestic and international, will dictate rising real timber prices, conservatively estimated to grow over the long term by 1% to 2% annually. World population and real per capita income are projected to rise by 1.4% and 2% annually, respectively, boosting demand for wood, particularly as countries industrialize and develop more modern consumption patterns. If, for example, all countries in the world matched U.S. per capita wood consumption, harvests would have to be increased fourfold.

At the same time, harvests in some major traditional producing areas, including the Pacific Northwest and parts of Canada, are declining. In some places, such as the South Seas, inventories have declined. Inventories of privately owned timber in both the southeastern and northwestern U.S. are also projected to decline. As demand in the rapidly expanding Pacific Rim economies grows substantially in the near and long-term future, these supply reductions will be particularly important. Offsetting some of the supply constraints will be increased harvests of fast-growing plantation forests in New Zealand and Chile, more efficient utilization of harvested wood, and substitution of nonwood materials. These factors will account for a portion of the anticipated growth in demand, but analysts uniformly believe that demand/supply equilibrium will be attained primarily through higher real timber prices.

HOW DOES TIMBERLAND FIT INTO AN INVESTMENT PORTFOLIO?

Early work with timber indices showed timber returns to be only slightly or even negatively correlated with the returns from stocks and bonds. With better indices, these results have held up over the years and have beneficial diversification implications for portfolios. Timberland investment marketing efforts during this period have routinely touted the asset as a portfolio enhancer, enabling investors who mix timber with a stock and bond portfolio to achieve a higher level of returns at any specified level of risk.

The often-repeated marketing claim that the addition of timber to an investment portfolio will substantially change that portfolio's risk/return characteristics must be viewed with care. Few investors, a notable exception being the State of New Hampshire, have let the timber component of their portfolios exceed or even reach 1% of total assets. A small allocation to a powerful diversifier will certainly help, but cannot be expected to alter the basic risk/return characteristics of the overall portfolio.

HOW ARE THE INVESTMENTS MANAGED?

A discussion of timberland investment strategies must include a discussion of TIMOs. Although each TIMO has a different strategy and a particular management structure, they all have some common strategic and operational characteristics.

TIMOs provide essential services in investing in timberland as they possess the requisite technical and financial knowledge. Their management decisions require a solid knowledge of forestry. As products are often sold into local markets using local harvesting companies, it is important that the organizations have, or have access to, people familiar with local market conditions and forest product–related companies. Finally, TIMOs must possess the economic and financial skills in order to understand and take advantage of broad economic and industry trends both in managing properties as well as acquiring and disposing of them. Often, a forest economist takes the lead in this area.

No matter whether TIMOs perform all or some of the foregoing functions in-house, contract out a portion of them, or enter into joint ventures with companies specializing in one or more specific areas of expertise and/or local knowledge, they all agree on the importance of employing the entire range of needed skills.

WHAT ARE THE STRATEGIES FOR
TIMBERLAND INVESTMENT?

While their individual strategies may differ, TIMOs rely on two strategic considerations to yield investment performance: biological growth and market opportunity. Biological growth is often heralded as the primary force behind successful timberland investment performance. Timber is said to be unique in that, regardless of whether prices rise or remain flat, the asset will grow in value as the trees continue to grow in size and into higher-value product classes. Growth, therefore, mitigates the risk of price fluctuations and, say the managers, represents a solid (and dominant) component of return on investment. This reasoning often leads managers to pursue and promote investments characterized by rapid tree growth resulting from species composition, management intensity, and/or geographical location.

From an economist's perspective, this strategic argument seems suspect; theory would suggest that future growth in value because of predictable biological growth should be accounted for in the initial cost of investment. Fine quality wine provides a corollary example. Over time spent in storage, fine wine grows in quality and, therefore, value. The initial price for this wine includes its current value (should it be opened, or "harvested," prematurely), plus its incremental quality-growth value discounted appropriately to account for risk and the opportunity cost of holding the "asset" over time.

The managers' argument that biological growth per se is a major component of returns probably should be rephrased; excess returns can be attributed to timberland's biological growth because of an excessively high discount rate given the level of risk associated with the investment. The effective overstatement of risk is particularly pronounced for young, emerging stands and for international timberland as well, probably because of an imperfect knowledge of the asset class and its characteristics. As more investors and more managers generate a higher level of transactions, it can be expected that the discount rate applied to the investment class will decline, and the effects of biological growth will eventually be more fully incorporated into timberland prices.

On the other hand, some managers argue that, with intensive forest management techniques, growth rates can be enhanced to produce significant increases in returns. Thinning of natural stands can enhance the quality and growth rates of the remaining trees. Plantations can benefit from high-quality genetic stock, fertilization, weed treatment, and other silvicultural techniques to produce a faster-growing forest. Returns from these management practices are based on the discounted value of the anticipated increase in growth and quality compared to the cost of the practices.

Market opportunity represents the other major strategic focus of TIMOs. (One could even argue that the timberland investment market's lack of recognition of the value of timberland's biological growth potential relative to risk represents yet another form of market opportunity.) Managers argue that particular age groups, species, or geographical locations present special opportunities that will result in higher returns.

A number of managers are concentrating on emerging and established growth stands as currently undervalued opportunities for investment. Implicit in this strategy is the belief that investors able to hold these relatively illiquid timberlands for a period of time, with little or no cash flow until the products harvested from the land will have increased substantially in value, will receive substantial returns as a reward for their patience. Most of these opportunities are to be found in the southeastern United States, which has relatively stable prices historically and the highest domestic biological growth rates. Some managers offer investments in mature growth stands with shorter investment horizons and the potential for positive cash flow. Rates of return, expected to be lower than for their younger counterparts, are predicated on the ability of the manager to invest when prices are discounted in depressed markets.

Some managers combine timberland investments from different regions and/or across different age categories in order to achieve diversification benefits within the asset class itself. Historically, returns between the regions have not been strongly correlated, so managers feel that they can offer an investment package that yields a higher rate of return for given levels of risk. One manager combines age group and regional purchases, but also looks at very specific subregions within the major producing areas, seeking out undervalued properties which present high-return opportunities.

Managers often focus on "high-quality, investment-grade" timberlands, primarily those currently under management for timber production and often consisting of intensively managed plantations. One manager, however, has taken a substantially different path and proposed investing not only in natural, unmanaged stands, but also in those that are stocked partially or predominantly by hardwoods. These stands in the southeastern United States are said to be undervalued, particularly given the rapid price rises of hardwoods, an often-ignored species group. Those stands with timber somewhat too small to be harvested for sawlogs would be the narrow investment focus so as to achieve the expected gains in value when the trees grow into the higher-valued sawtimber class. Again, this strategy assumes an imperfect market for timberland and, therefore, an opportunity for investors.

Other proposed market opportunity investment strategies include a focus on fast-growing species and stands in nontraditional areas; for example, rapid-growth hardwood eucalyptus planted on former sugar cane plantations in Hawaii. This timberland venture is primarily aimed at satisfying the burgeoning Pacific Rim demand for wood fiber, but can still be considered a domestic investment. Another example is investing in rapid-growth Radiata Pine plantations in Chile and New Zealand. These stands have demonstrated extremely fast growth, and currently are viewed as very undervalued. It is interesting to note that at least three major timberland investment managers are talking seriously about investments in these areas. While political risks are a consideration, there is very little exchange-rate risk as wood product commodities are traded worldwide on a U. S. dollar basis. Management costs are, of course, paid in local currency, but this risk can be partially offset by selling harvests in local markets. Other rapid-growth stands in, for example, Brazil and South Africa have high expected return potential associated with higher political risks.

HOW DO THE STRATEGIES FIT ON THE RISK/RETURN SPECTRUM?

For the purpose of simple categorization, these strategies can be assigned to four strategic groupings and placed on a risk/return spectrum as shown in Exhibit 1. Real return range estimates are based on a combination of historical evidence and comments by analysts and managers. While not for the most part highly reliable as point estimates for particular investment types, the ranges can serve as relative performance measures.

"Traditional Timberland" includes investments in established or mature growth stands located in one of the three commonly recognized regions of the United States held in unmixed timberland portfolios (e.g., established growth pine in the Southeast). Growth rates are moderate, but risks are relatively low because of greater liquidity and positive cash flows during the holding period. Return and risk variations within the group result from (1) the investment's location, Northeast/North Central being lower in volatility and return than Southeast and Pacific Northwest, and (2) the investment's age group, mature growth at the lower end and established growth at the upper end. Real return estimates run from 5% to 8%.

"Domestic Timberland Portfolio" includes investment strategies that may combine a number of regional and/or different-aged properties. Emerging growth stands may constitute a substantial portion of the portfolio and push returns toward the upper end of the range. Similarly, strategies that rely on careful analysis of performance of submarkets within regions and combinations of carefully selected properties within these submarkets may elevate returns. A number of managers propose to elevate returns while maintaining low risk levels by combining a large "core" component consisting of more traditional timberland investments with a smaller opportunistic component consisting of, for example, emerging growth stands or other high-return, high-risk investments. Real returns may run in the 7% to 11% range, with a higher level of risk because of the relative illiquidity and reduced cash flows associated with younger stands. It should be noted that a portion of the risk may effectively be reduced by the fact that the performance of the various properties within portfolios may not be highly correlated.

Exhibit 1: Strategies Grouped on Risk/Return Spectrum

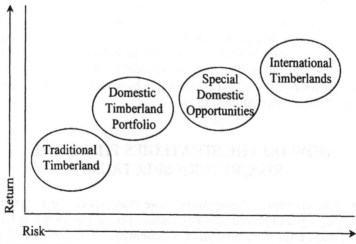

"Special Domestic Opportunities" are represented by such investments as Hawaiian eucalyptus or southern hardwoods. Real return estimates for these timberlands are in the 10% to 12% range, with an accordingly higher level of risk. As these are essentially new ventures, there is no (or little) historical evidence to rely on for assessment of return and risk estimates.

"International Timberlands" are represented by rapid-growing plantation investment outside of the U.S., particularly in New Zealand and Chile. Real return estimates range from 11% to 20%. There is relatively little U.S. investment experience with these timberlands, so the reliability of return and risk estimates is reduced. There is fairly uniform agreement among managers and analysts (both those pursuing the strategy as well as those who are not) that these international investments represent an opportunity for high returns, but have an unknown level of risk.

CONCLUSIONS

Historical evidence from the mid-1980s on, plus the indications given by hypothetical indices covering the years pre-dating institutional investment in timberland, shows timberland to have been a solid, high-return investment, especially for those who "took the leap" and invested in the early 1980s. While historical results should not be taken to indicate future performance of an asset class, they can be useful when comparing returns from different asset classes. In the absence of major technological or broad economic changes, one can assume that the relationships between the performance characteristics of various assets will not change dramatically.

In our swiftly changing world, however, it is difficult to extend historical trends directly into the future without considering the positive and negative impacts of change, particularly in a global context. On the positive side, world population and economic development continue at a rapid pace. Wood consumption is directly related to both factors. Pacific Rim countries, for example, which were very low-level wood consumers prior to World War II, are now beginning to consume substantial amounts of wood-based products, although they have a long way to go before their rates challenge the extremely high per capita consumption levels of the United States. As these and other world regions' economies continue to develop, as well as grow at rapid rates, world wood consumption will increase dramatically. At the same time, supply increases will be moderated by the fact that traditional wood-producing regions are experiencing declining harvests, which are, to some extent, offsetting productivity gains from more efficient fiber usage patterns and the increased growth rates seen in intensively managed plantations. Costs of substitute materials continue to be high relative to wood fiber, especially in terms of production energy requirements. These factors, as discussed earlier, lay the groundwork for continued increases in timber prices in the future. As timber has increasingly become a global commodity, and since the U.S.

is a major participant in world markets, timberland prices will be impacted by these trends, both internationally and domestically.

On the negative side, returns for timberland must be viewed cautiously, as the institutional investment framework for timber has changed. Many of the properties were purchased when the sellers (forest products companies) were anxious to divest themselves of timberland and the buyers (managers on behalf of pension funds) were relatively few. It is conceivable that the early and mid-1980s represented a "window of opportunity" domestically, during which investors received excess returns. Currently, forest products companies seem to be under less pressure from takeovers, and there are certainly more investment managers specializing in timberland. Acknowledgment of this change in environment is implicit in the timberland managers' more cautious, although still quite positive, projections for returns in the future.

In summary, primarily because of the underlying demand/supply fundamentals and the imperfect market for timberland investments (which does not fully recognize the asset's risk/return characteristics), timberland continues to be an investment class that presents a good opportunity for relatively high returns. The level of expected return and associated level of risk depend on the nature of the investment strategy selected and the expertise of the timberland investment manager.

Chapter 15

Agricultural Real Estate

John D. Wilson, Ph.D.

In order to truly appreciate the current and future economic environment for investing in U.S. agricultural land, we need to rewind to the mid-1970s and take a brief look at that period's events. World population had exceeded four billion, growing by 2.1% annually, and threatened to double within three decades. Paul Ehrlich and his colleagues were predicting famine by 1975. The first oil embargo underscored the concept of finite natural resources. Federal price supports contributed to the creation of large inventories of grain. America was viewed, and indeed viewed itself, as the "breadbasket of the world." Exports grew by more than 20% annually in the late 1970s. Net farm income doubled between 1971 and 1979 in response to export demand-driven (and expectation-driven) food price increases and increased production efficiency.

Farmers reacted rationally to what appeared to them, as well as to their creditors, as a future promising great gain to those who acted decisively. They bought land to increase farm size and output and invested heavily in new capital equipment, encouraged by the ready availability of financing provided eagerly at exorbitant rates by banks and large insurers. Loan-to-value ratios were kept in check, not by prudent underwriting, but rather by soaring land values. Between 1971 and 1981, farmland prices rose by 15% annually.

Then the balloon burst. The second oil embargo elevated petroleum prices and, therefore, production costs, hurting efficiency. This shock, combined with rampant baby-boom consumerism and inflammatory fiscal and monetary policy, led to an unstable economic environment in which the economy faltered while interest rates soared to record levels. World politics were unstable, e.g., Iran's hostage taking and the Soviet Union's foray into Afghanistan, the latter prompting a U.S. grain embargo on the Soviet Union.

The impact of these economic and political events on the farm was catastrophic. Fuel, fertilizer, and financing costs rose sharply. Exports peaked in 1981 after a 10-year run-up, and began a steady six-year decline. By 1983, net farm income had fallen to levels seen 10 years earlier. Farmland prices began a precipitous five-year decline, falling by 27% through 1987. Loan-to-value ratios suffered, farmers became unable to service their debts, farm auctions became commonplace, and banks and insurers became major equity owners of farmland. Managers who had enthusiastically pushed farmland as a profitable investment opportunity had to backtrack and spend the decade or so in abashed silence.

Fast forwarding to the present, the same formerly beleaguered asset managers are back in the marketplace offering agricultural land as a sound and rewarding investment yielding returns between 10% and 25%, reminding us that the U.S. is (again) the breadbasket of the world. Fiduciaries wonder, and rightfully so, if the promise is real or if history is preparing to repeat itself.

This chapter explores the demand and supply underpinnings of the markets for agricultural products, and, therefore, the advisability of investments in agricultural land. American and world economies are discussed, as is global agricultural supply. Different investment strategies are analyzed in relationship to the underlying market forces.

AGRICULTURAL DEMAND

Before looking at the market forces affecting agricultural investments, it is useful to briefly set forth the differences between the investment opportunities and how they are impacted by different economic variables, as well as to outline with a broad brush their relative investment performance characteristics. For the sake of clarity, this discussion is confined to two broad categories of agricultural product — row crops and permanent crops.

Row crops are what nearly everyone envisions when they are talking about agriculture in general: basic grains such as corn and wheat or the utility legume soybeans. Other important row crops include potatoes, tobacco, rice, and sorghum. While these crops are impacted by fluctuations in the U.S. economy, they also play a large export role, and are subject to global demand variations. Investments in row cropland focus primarily on the land's productive capacity, because of, for example, soil quality and water availability. Crops are seasonal and can be stored for periods of time; hence, supply response to demand changes can be made on a seasonal basis. Severe weather generally impacts only one crop season. Row crops are "staple" goods for both home consumption and livestock feed, and demand for them can be characterized as relatively inelastic. Investment returns are considered to be moderate and relatively low-risk.

Permanent crops include those produced by orchards and vineyards: citrus, apples, nuts, and wine and table grapes. These products are more specialized in that the bulk of investor value resides above the ground in trees and vines that are "permanent" producers of seasonal crops. Many of these crops do not store as readily as row crops, and developmental orchards and vineyards require many years of care before their first harvest; supply response to changing levels of demand is slow. Per acre development costs are substantial. The demand for permanent crop agricultural products is generally more elastic than that of row crops. Because of all these characteristics, permanent crops are significantly higher than row crops on the risk/return spectrum.

Exhibit 1: World Population and Economic Trends

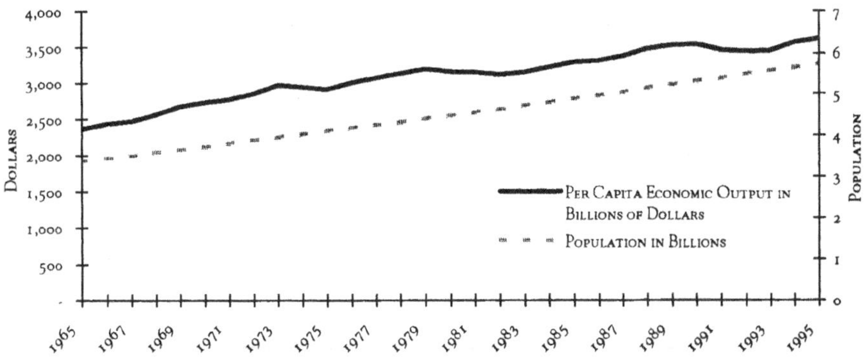

Sources: U.S. Bureau of the Census, World Bank, IMF

Agricultural demand, regardless of product classification, is subject to population growth, changes in income levels, and changes in taste (although much of this is related to changes in income). (See Exhibit 1.) Row crops are particularly impacted by global population and income/taste changes, given American agriculture's significant exposure to the world's grain and soybean markets.

Although population growth has slowed from more than 2% in the 1960s to 1.6% currently, rapid growth continues, especially in Asia and Latin America. China's population exceeds 1.2 billion (with some estimates closer to 1.4 billion) while the often-ignored Indian subcontinent contains 1.2 billion people; each entity is more than four times the size of the U.S. population which grows at a rate under 1% annually. World population has doubled in the 40 years since 1960.

Global per capita income growth, while relatively steady, has averaged under 1% annually. While the African, Latin American, and formerly Soviet-influenced economies are beginning to recover from recent years of instability and show signs of increased economic growth, the emerging Pacific Rim economies until their recent downturn grew rapidly, between 7% and 10% per year. Associated with changing income levels are changing tastes, a good example being the growth in meat consumed per capita, which has doubled since 1950, reflecting growth in incomes (see Exhibit 2). China now accounts for nearly half of the world's total production of pork, and its total consumption of red meat exceeds that of the U.S. Growing meat consumption has important implications for grain markets. Given the limited capacity of rangeland to accommodate larger herds of livestock, much of the increased meat production expected in the coming years will come from feedlots: each pound of poultry, pork, and beef added in feedlots requires two, four, and seven pounds of grain, respectively.

Per capita grain production, also depicted in Exhibit 2, demonstrated growth in the 1960s and 1970s, but in the 1990s fell to levels of 30 years earlier. Exhibit 3 shows the inevitable result of population growth and falling per capita production: the reduction of world grain stocks. Mid-1990s inventory declined to the lowest level, in terms of days of reserve, seen in 40 years. This will undoubtedly place upward pressure on grain prices over the next few years if stocks are to be rebuilt to their former levels.

The U.S. has experienced strong growth in agricultural exports since the early 1970s. For example, it currently accounts for nearly half of the world's production of corn and soybeans and more than two-thirds of world exports of those commodities, although grains did experience a decline during the mid-1980s from peak export levels of 1980–81 (these levels have since been reattained). While nowhere near the volume of grains, exports of fruits, nuts, vegetables, and meat products have grown substantially as world income levels rise, tastes change, and GATT and NAFTA open trade doors (see Exhibit 4).

Exhibit 2: World Agricultural Production
(kilograms per capita)

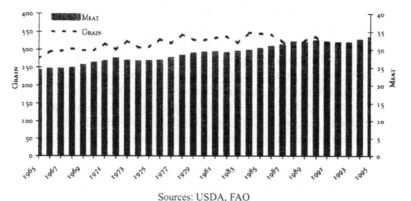

Sources: USDA, FAO

Exhibit 3: World Grain Inventory

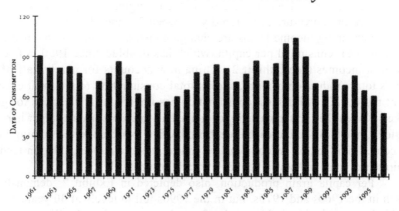

Source: USDA

Exhibit 4: U.S. Agricultural Exports

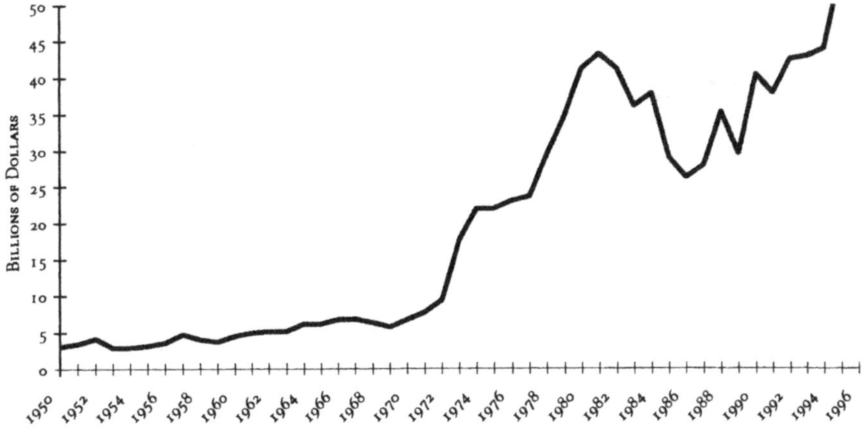

Source: USDA

U.S. population growth has slowed to under 1% annually, but personal income has continued to grow at rates of more than 3% in real terms in recent years. This, combined with steadily, if moderately, growing per capita incomes in the rest of the world, has positive implications for the more income-sensitive permanent crops such as fresh fruit, nuts, or wine grapes. Domestic per capita consumption of tree nuts, for example, has grown by 40% since 1970. While domestic per capita consumption of such products as wine and citrus fruits has remained stable or shown slight declines, total production and production value have, in spite of some volatility, generally risen.

For example, the value of production for both almonds and grapes more than doubled between 1986 and 1997. Production quantities and prices rose over this period, but displayed significant volatility year to year. Tree nuts, in general, have seen significant export demand growth over the past 10 years, with exports nearly doubling and absorbing the bulk of expanded production. For the sake of perspective it should be noted that all fruit and nut production had grown to approximately 5.5% of total farm cash receipts by the mid-1990s, from about 4% in the 1960s and 1970s; vineyards and nut orchards account for less than 1.5% of the value of farm production annually.

The general outlook for agricultural products is good. Domestic and global population and income growth will inevitably result in increased demand for food. Income growth will, in particular, play a significant role in elevating the demand for meat as well as fruits and nuts as higher-value products are added to the world menu. Increased meat production will exacerbate already growing worldwide grain demand. The key to the performance of agricultural investments in the future lies in how the world's agricultural production systems are able to meet this demand.

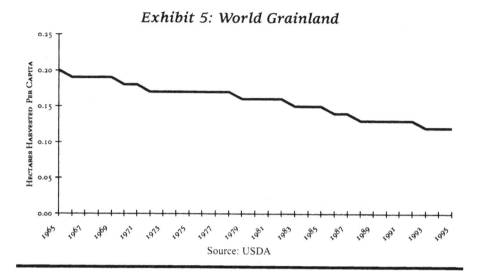

Exhibit 5: World Grainland

Source: USDA

AGRICULTURAL SUPPLY

What is true and not subject to argument is that the world's land area is finite. It follows that agricultural land itself is also finite, although the percentage of land dedicated to agricultural production can change as can the productivity of that land. What is apparently true but subject to argument is that the world's agricultural lands' ability to feed a growing population is reaching its limit and, therefore, markets may see dramatic price rationing of food in the coming years.

As Exhibit 2 shows, per capita grain production rose or remained stable over the two decades prior to 1985 (it has fallen off since then). This occurred in spite of a dramatic reduction in the per capita area of grainland harvested. World population is indeed bumping up against constraints of land available for agricultural use. There are essentially no new agricultural lands available for production. "Creation" of new agricultural lands can only be achieved at the expense of forestland, but it will not be of the same quality as existing agricultural land. True, there are marginal tracts which could produce food at an inefficient level, but these will only be brought into production when prices rise significantly. Agricultural land is, however, constantly subject to the development pressures of a burgeoning population. For example, it is estimated that 1% of the prime agricultural land in China succumbs to development pressure each year. Worldwide, land made useful for agricultural purpose by irrigation is subject to pressure from the growing demand for diversion of water to cities. The area of irrigated land grew by 80% between 1961 and 1992, but has recently leveled off or even declined. Perhaps 10% of this land is afflicted by increasing salinity levels, decreasing crop yields. These trends, combined with rapid population growth, have led to a decline in per capita grainland harvested, as shown in Exhibit 5.

Exhibit 6: U.S. Agricultural Productivity Indices
(1982 = 100)

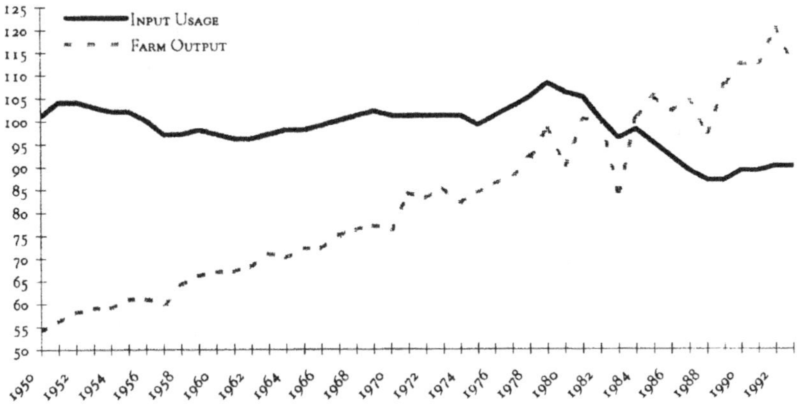

Source: USDA

In spite of what appears to be a relative reduction in resources used for agriculture, the world has not experienced the widespread famine predicted in the 1970s (the starvation in recent years in drought- and war-ravaged central Africa gave a limited preview of what many had predicted on a wider scale). This greater global stability occurred because of advances in growing methods and improvements in plant varieties.

Biological research helped develop plant varieties that had greater output per acre and were relatively more resistant to diseases, pests, and drought. Similarly, better planting techniques and equipment improved yields and consistency of results season to season. Exhibit 6 shows that U.S. agriculture became increasingly efficient, and output per unit of input has risen steadily over the years. One of the biggest factors in increasing productivity worldwide has been the substantial growth in the use of irrigation. Irrigated land currently represents but 17% of the world's agricultural land, but accounts for the production of 40% of the world's food supply.

Exhibit 7 shows the tremendous growth in the global use of fertilizer to enhance productivity. By 1988, fertilizer use was 10 times higher than in 1950. Fertilizer use is responsible for a significant part of the productivity gains in global food production. In the U.S., however, fertilizer use has leveled off, as increased applications beyond current levels would be unprofitable. Over the past eight years, world fertilizer use has dropped, particularly in the former Soviet Union. It is expected that this trend has begun to reverse itself and that fertilizer will see increased use in Latin America, Eastern Europe, and the Indian subcontinent.

Increased fertilizer usage, growth in irrigation, and enhanced technology have all contributed to expanded food production worldwide, and have staved off the gloomy predictions of the mid-1970s. However, as implied in Exhibit 3, while meat production per capita is still rising, grain production per capita has declined, suggesting that population growth may be pushing against cropland capacity constraints. Soybean production per capita has also leveled off during the past decade, after seeing strong growth in the 1960s and 1970s.

The permanent crop supply and its potential to expand is harder to estimate over the long run because of the availability of land for orchard or vineyard development. Between 1986 and 1995, while the row cropland–harvested area declined by 2%, the fruit- and nut-bearing area grew by 7%, from 3.4 to 3.7 million acres (compared to more than 300 million acres of row cropland). Expansion capacity is limited not so much by scarcity of available appropriate land as by the high development costs associated with planting a vineyard or orchard. Permanent cropland may be characterized as having about 80% of its value in the trees and vines above ground; per acre development costs for a modern apple orchard can run upward of $20,000 beyond the cost of the land itself. After initiating development, the owner then must wait for 5 to 10 years before seeing positive cash flow from the planting.

MARKET IMPLICATIONS

It is clear that population and income growth will have substantial impacts on agricultural markets. As evidenced by the "retirement" of large farm tracts in this country as uneconomical and by the relatively low level of fertilizer utilization in much of the rest of the world, outright food shortages in the coming years on a worldwide basis are unlikely. The needs and wants of a growing population can be met, but doing so will entail higher production costs, which will necessarily translate into higher prices for agricultural commodities. Also, given the ability to grow more food economically than its local markets can absorb, U.S. agriculture will benefit strongly from an even more robust export market than the current one (in spite of the strong dollar), a situation enhanced by growing overseas economies and more open trade policies.

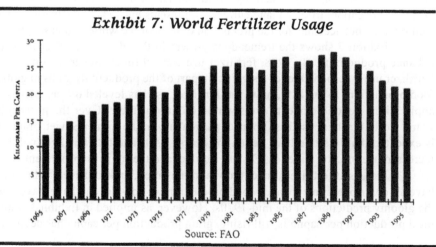

Exhibit 7: World Fertilizer Usage

Source: FAO

Exhibit 8: Farm Income and Land Values

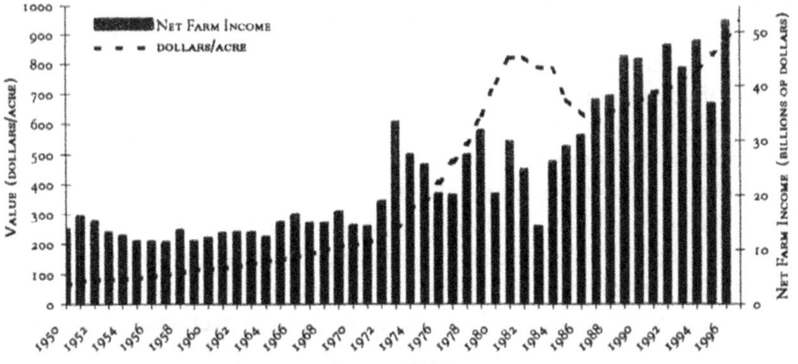

Source: USDA

Exhibit 8 shows that farmland values reflect net farm income. Agricultural exports (see Exhibit 4) have supported net farm income to the extent that, had there been no export market, net farm income in much of the 1970s and 1980s would have been negative or minimal. On the heels of (and, more important, in expectation of) large increases in agricultural exports, farmland values rose on average by 15% annually between 1972 and 1982. Land prices dropped as exports fell in the early to mid-1980s, and have begun to rise again along with exports, albeit at a more moderate 4.7% rate annually from 1987 to 1997. World demand and supply characteristics for basic commodities strongly imply a continuation and strengthening of this recent trend in farm incomes and land values over the coming years. Little on the horizon, short of widespread war or world economic depression, appears likely to change this scenario.

Similarly, growing world income levels will lead to an increased demand for higher-value agricultural products — permanent crops such as almonds, walnuts, grapes, and apples. While per capita consumption of fresh fruit in the U.S. has risen slowly over the past decade, per capita consumption of dried fruit and tree nuts has declined or remained stable. During the same period export levels (on a quantity basis) for both fruits and tree nuts have doubled as world demand levels have grown.

AGRICULTURAL LAND INVESTMENT STRATEGIES

Of the more than $900 billion of agricultural land in the U.S., less than 1% is currently owned by institutional investors. The events of the 1980s seemingly chastened investors into looking at agriculture with a healthy amount of skepticism, such that, although there is evidence of some heightened interest in agricultural land, there is no excess pressure on land prices stemming from investor activity. Managers still find agriculture a relatively hard sell, especially given the continuing strong performance of the securities market.

Managers continue to sell agriculture on the basis of its portfolio balance characteristics and its potential for producing high rates of return. In most cases, the former attribute can be noted and then brushed aside as somewhat irrelevant to investors as agriculture represents, or would represent, such a small component of the total investment portfolio as to render enhancements to the efficient frontier relatively insignificant. The latter attribute of potentially high returns is what currently attracts some investors.

What is most interesting in the strategic approaches offered by the managers is the differentiation they employ between row and permanent crop investments. Row cropland is presented as a relatively low-return but stable, low-risk investment. Returns are predicted to be nearly equally divided between income and appreciation, each in the 4% to 6% range, corresponding well to current rents averaging 5% and recent land value appreciation averaging nearly 6% in recent years.

Permanent croplands, such as vineyards and fruit and nut orchards, are touted as investment vehicles likely to produce annual returns as high as 25%, primarily through annual income. Permanent crops' growing stock depreciates over time as the plantings mature and get closer to replacement age, such that managers are hesitant to ascribe any significant portion of return predictions to appreciation, although in recent years permanent crop properties have, in fact, shown value increases.

Where returns to row cropland are acknowledged to be almost entirely predicated on the global market conditions for the commodities grown, managers are quick to point out that high returns from permanent cropland are based on the proficiency of operations management, the production efficiency of new growing stock and planting techniques, and the ability to obtain favorable long-term marketing contracts. The irony in the managers' approach is palpable; they open with concerns about the world's ability to provide China with basic commodities and, therefore, the anticipated dramatic demand-driven price impacts, and close with nonmarket reasons for investing in high-value permanent crops. What is missing in their presentations is the linkage between growing world population and income, and the demand for U.S. exports of high-value permanent crops. These have clearly grown over the past decade and will continue to do so, barring economic or political upheaval.

The caveat lies in the difference in the nature of the demand for row and permanent crops. Basic commodities can be characterized as being demand-inelastic relative to such crops as almonds or wine grapes. It is conceivable, and likely, that rapidly rising world market prices for grain would negatively impact the demand for higher-value, relatively demand-elastic permanent crops as overseas (and domestic) consumers spend a higher portion of their food budget on staples, leaving less disposable income available for higher-value foods. However, assuming that world markets will adjust more gradually to growing demand and that incomes continue to demonstrate solid growth, the general outlook for continued strength in exports of permanent crops looks promising although each specific crop type may experience differing levels of success in world markets.

Part III

Public and Private Debt

Chapter 16

Creating a Performance History for CMBS

George J. Pappadopoulos, CFA

Commercial mortgage-backed securities (CMBS) are publicly traded bonds that are secured by portfolios (pools) of individual mortgages on commercial real estate. The cash flows available from the combined mortgages are distributed on a hierarchical basis known as the *tranche structure*. As a result, different classes of bonds are formed based upon the priority of the cash flows, and each bond's credit risk generally increases as its priority to the cash flows decreases.

Investor appetite for CMBS has been extremely high. With the exception of a slight downturn in 1995, issuance has grown steadily throughout the 1990s, and few investors would argue that this market is not here to stay.

More important, the overall tightening of spreads indicates an insufficient supply of this product. Increasing investor demand has drastically reduced the premium above comparable corporates across all rating levels, and this is occurring even as lenders bring increasing supply to the market.

This compression suggests that investor expectations regarding the market must either be strong or else many have forgotten the pain of the last real estate cycle. Being curious, we at PPR thought it would be interesting to postulate what might have happened to investments in these securities had they, in fact, been available over the past 15 years.

We do not mean to suggest that now is an inopportune time to invest in these securities. Instead, we want some insight into these tightening risk compensation levels by attempting to understand how different types of tranched mortgage pools would behave at various points in the real estate cycle. Exactly how might these securities have responded during the last downturn? If we can get a grasp on this, we can draw some inferences about whether the current tightening is rational or wishful.

It is obvious that no actual performance data exist for performing such a task. Fortunately, PPR's Derived Market Returns (DMRs™) allow for the needed "re-creation" of history by econometrically modeling historical real estate collateral performance. Overlaying the individual investment structure on the collateral then produces the pertinent results.

Exhibit 1: Property & Portfolio Research CMBS Model

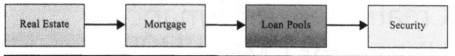

THE MODEL

The primary tool utilized for this analysis is the Property & Portfolio Research CMBS Model. This proprietary model links the cash flows of the security directly to the cash flows of the underlying real estate, as shown by Exhibit 1. Distinct market behaviors drive real estate cash flows and asset valuations that affect the mortgage cash flows via the "normal" operation of a mortgage or through the borrower's default decision. Next, these cash flows directly impact the cash flows of the overall loan pool, which, in turn, affect the performance of the tranched securities.

The link begins by first modeling the real estate collateral on a market by market, property type by property type basis. We do not need to use broad-based approaches to the issues of the incidence and costs of default; we simply observe how each market behaved and, therefore, how each loan performed.

At the real estate level, the PPR model is grounded in a thorough econometric estimation of historical and future performance of real estate assets at the property type/urban area level (DMRs). These comprehensive forecasts of capital value and net operating income capture the interactive dynamics among demand side, supply side, and capital markets variables. They provide the model with a well-researched, empirical view on what has transpired and what is likely to transpire, market by market, property type by property type. The benefit of this approach lies in carefully outlining the substantive differences in the underlying economic fundamentals that occur between individual real estate market and property type pair — differences that affect the security.

The result is a rigorous and thorough environment for forecasting individual loan and mortgage pool performance. At the mortgage level, default is now viewed within the context of a time series of localized market-pricing information, and is based on contemporaneous pricing ratios. These factors are crucial to the borrower's financial decision regarding the loan, and our increased understanding of this information is, therefore, crucial to the accurate assessment of value at the security level.

Additionally, the embedded DMRs allow the model to forecast critical rating ratios and thereby enable the appropriate application of time and risk sensitive interest rate spreads. The reward is a complete time-series backcast and forecast of mark-to-market pricing of mortgages, pools, and securities.

THE BASE LOAN POOL

The underlying pool of mortgages available to construct the securities consists of individual loans made in each of our covered markets (60 MSAs by four property types — 240 markets). The relative size of each loan is weighted by PPR's estimate of each respective market's capital value, as broken out by property type, at the time of *each* loan origination. In other words, each year of originations reflects the structure of the U.S. real estate equity market at that point in history. A new set of originations is added at the beginning of each year, thus forming a return index composed of more than 10,000 individually modeled loans originated over a 15-year period (1982–1996).

The loans of this index are further weighted by the gross amount of yearly commercial mortgage originations as measured by American Council of Life Insurance's (ACLI) data. Therefore, origination cohorts of heavier volume have a greater effect on the pool. Again, all loans in each cohort were assumed to be originated at the beginning of the year.

The base loan utilized is a 10-year, call-protected bullet loan. That is, each loan is originated with a 10-year term to maturity, has equal quarterly principal and interest payments reflecting an amortization period of 30 years, has the entire remaining principal balance due at maturity, and has a prepayment lockout. No further term extensions or workouts were assumed to occur. In other words, any nondefaulted loan is assumed to pay off in full at maturity. On the other hand, defaulted loans are foreclosed at the value of the collateral less costs.

Other contract terms were adjusted to reflect a range of perceived risk. Loan-to-value ratios (LTVs) of 50%, 70%, and 90% were used to represent our low-, mid-, and high- risk strategies. The associated debt service coverage ratios (DSCRs) were 1.5×, 1.35×, and 1.2×, respectively.

The contract rates applied to each set of loans were also derived from ACLI data. The average rate of ACLI originations, by quarter, by property type, were used for 70% LTV loans. To account for differences in risk, contract rates were set 100 basis points below the respective average ACLI rate for 50% LTV loans, while contract rates for loans of 90% LTV were set at 100 basis points above the respective average ACLI rate.

POOL AND TRANCHE SELECTION

In order to obtain a range of comparative investment options, we compiled four separate pools and each individual loan pool was carved into three hierarchical tranches. The tranche structure in all cases was a very typical sequential pay configuration of the type found in numerous offerings, and the assumption was made that the servicer would not make any advances to cover a defaulted loan. In all cases, tranche size was set to obtain a AA-rated senior bond, a BB-rated mezzanine bond, and a residual, first-loss junior bond.

All four pools are composed of loans underwritten in all 60 MSAs and four property types covered by PPR as weighted by the index setup described earlier. Each pool, therefore, conforms to the capitalized value of the U.S. real estate market by property type, but does not necessarily constitute an efficiently diversi-fied portfolio on a mean-variance basis. Each individual pool does differ by prop-erty type mix and individual loan risk mix (50%, 70%, or 90% LTV).

The first mortgage pool consisted of all loans in the base index as speci-fied above. This large pool then represents a mix of all four property types and all three levels of individual loan risk (LTV = 50%, 70%, and 90%). Although the second pool also contained an equal property-type mix, in this case only high-risk (90% LTV, 1.2× DCSR) loans were part of this four-property-type pool. A third, more conservative, pool was formed by underwriting only mid-risk, apartment loans while the final pool included only high-risk office mortgages.

RESULTS

The return series displayed in all of the following exhibits represent the year-over-year total returns of a full investment in the index. That is, the returns assume you bought additional securities each year as they became available, and that these were added to your CMBS portfolio. Therefore, the returns represent those on a portfolio composed of 15 years' worth of continued investment in securities of that particular pool type. The price of each individual security was determined by discounting the future, default-adjusted cash flows at the appropri-ate time-sensitive, risk-adjusted rate.

Exhibit 2 contrasts returns from investment in the senior (A-1) tranche across all four pools. Appropriately, the effect of interest rates is, of course, extremely strong, and the overall tandem, bond-like behavior is quite obvious. However, even in this protected tranche, there are distinct differences among the pools over time. Substantial return differences begin to occur quite early, and the more conservative mid-risk apartment pool clearly outperforms the pack during the very troublesome early 1990s. Note that the high-risk office pool takes a little longer to rejoin the other pools as the office cycle lagged the improvement in the overall real estate market. Interestingly, this higher-risk pool appears to have a bit more strength than the others through the forecast period.

While much of the reduction in returns for this protected senior tranche comes from changes in payment timing as a result of defaults, in contrast, the mezzanine (B-2) tranche bears more of the loss of principal because of foreclo-sure. This structure effect can be seen in Exhibit 3.

Note that forward-looking public markets price the heavy defaults of the high-risk pools quite early, and that the extremely poor performance of the office market has a particularly harsh impact. Once again, the more conservative mid-risk apartment pool outperforms the alternate investments into the early 1990s, but this trend reverses as the real estate markets improve. During this period of reduced risk, it appears that the extra rate consideration on the riskier loans is more adequate compensation for the investor.

Exhibit 2: A-1 Tranche by Pool

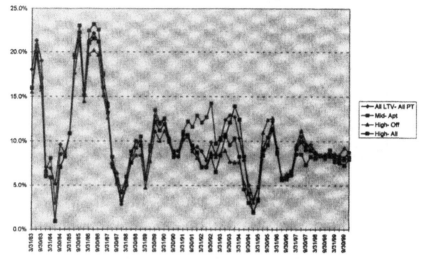

Exhibit 3: B-2 Tranche by Pool

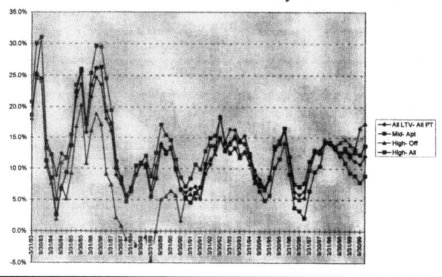

Finally, risk and property type differences fully express themselves within the junior (C) tranche. This tranche receives the full principal loss associated with foreclosure, and, as a result, the returns can be severely impacted by changes in pool composition. This result is clearly outlined in Exhibit 4, where we see very large differences in tranche returns as a result of the mix of the underlying collateral.

Exhibit 4: Tranche C by Pool

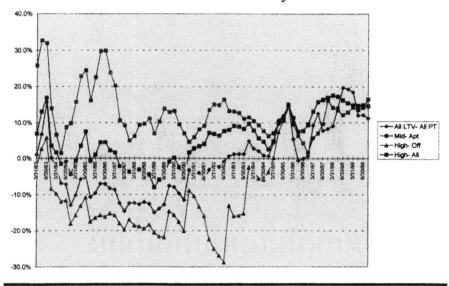

Pools containing any high-risk loans are strongly impacted over the complete cycle. Furthermore, it appears that it is primarily office collateral that accounts for most of the losses, as all pools underperform the pure mid-risk apartment pool. Interestingly, although the all-risk mix pool should be less risky overall, the lower compensation levels reduce returns compared to an all-property-type high-risk loan pool.

CONCLUSIONS

As investor demand dramatically reduces required risk spreads across all CMBS rating levels, one must question the fair risk-adjusted value of these instruments. Unfortunately, although the dramatic growth of CMBS issuance has brought this asset class out of its infancy, there is still little known about the long-term behavior of these derivative securities.

In an effort to better understand true tranche-level behavior, PPR's analysis attempts to outline tranche default-adjusted value for several different pool mixes of a general broad-based index of loan collateral. The intent is to uncover some long-term behavioral differences that may exist for tranched bonds underwritten by loan pools containing various levels of mortgage risk, and various property types.

Not surprisingly, the results do suggest substantial differences across all tranche types as a result of differences in the underlying pool mix. Pools containing higher-risk loans affect even the senior AA-rated bond, and the negative impact of such pools on the first loss tranche is extremely strong. In addition, differences in the underlying property types also affect all tranche levels, and we find that the more volatile office collateral is especially risky for the first loss and mezzanine bonds — although decidedly less so over the forecast period as the collateral is expected to outperform other property types.

So, even on such a broad-based, geographically diversified set of pools, applying a standard discount rate based solely upon bond rating may lead to inaccurate pricing and, hence, to improper compensation. Naive diversification is not necessarily the answer; therefore, proper modeling of each individual pool is crucial.

Furthermore, as spreads tighten, there is certainly less room for error. Fortunately, although the analysis constructed a broad indexed-type portfolio, the PPR model works at the MSA/property type level. It is, therefore, not only possible to understand the overall cycle, but it is also possible to predict particular market cycles, and to price individual securities appropriately.

Chapter 17

CMBS versus Whole Loans

George J. Pappadopoulos, CFA

What is the source of volatility of debt-related returns? What are its characteristics? More important, what structures are more protected? We believe that both whole loans and commercial mortgage-backed securities (CMBS) can play a valid role in portfolio composition. In fact, the risk/return characteristics of each differ and if these differences are understood, there is an opportunity to create a more efficient portfolio.

On the risk side, the "fixed" in fixed income is certainly more nebulous than it sounds. All debt structures are subject to volatility of total return, especially in a mark-to-market environment. One strength of the CMBS structure is that it segments the overall risk of a whole loan into separate components, each with their own distinct patterns of expected return and exposure to various market forces. In theory, CMBS allows an investor to choose more precisely the magnitude of risk he wishes to assume.

In order to assess the risk of the CMBS and mortgage worlds, an actual CMBS issuance was modeled and the return volatility of its component tranches was compared to that of the overall loan pool. We find that there are distinct differences in mark-to-market total return across the tranche spectrum as compared to whole loans. More important, the underlying causes of these differences can be individually identified.

Modeled pricing is based upon the forecasted risk of each piece (tranche or portfolio) and represents the price at which it should trade at any point in time. These forecasts are underpinned by a thorough econometric estimation of historic and future performance of real estate assets at the property-type/urban area level (using PPR's Derived Market Returns or DMRs™). The benefit of this approach lies in thoughtfully outlining the substantive differences in the underlying economic fundamentals that occur between the individual real estate markets that affect the price and the volatility of the security.

The Property & Portfolio Research model links the cash flows of the security directly to the most likely path of the cash flows of the underlying real estate. Distinct market behaviors drive real estate cash flows and thus valuation. These factors, in turn, affect mortgage cash flows because the cash flows and value of the real estate shape the borrower's default decision. A default stops the flow of both interest and principal repayment and accelerates (and usually diminishes) the repayment of the principal balance. These mortgage cash flows directly impact the overall loan pool which, in turn, affects the tranched securities.

Exhibit 1: Year-over-Year Returns

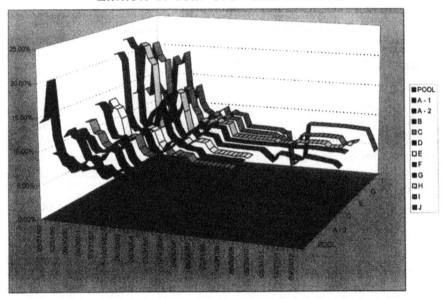

Because of the influence of DMRs at the mortgage level, default is based on contemporaneous pricing ratios and can be viewed within the context of current, localized market-pricing information. An increased understanding of these factors is, therefore, crucial in accurately assessing the investment.

Each loan's unique, performance-adjusted cash flows are then pooled and distributed according to the specific issue's tranche allocation structure. Additionally, the embedded DMRs allow the model to forecast critical rating ratios and, thereby, enable the appropriate application of time- and risk-sensitive interest rate spreads. Measures of risk are centered around the loan-to-value (LTV) and debt service coverage (DSCR) ratios which are, in turn, affected by the subordination levels set up by the tranche hierarchy. Accordingly, the pricing model properly applies discount spreads that coincide with the risk cohort of the tranche by basing the risk cohort upon these changing LTV and DSCR ratios. The reward is a complete time-series forecast of mark-to-market pricing of each tranche in the security, as well as of the entire pool.

The actual issuance used to analyze the differences in volatility contained 145 loans and was divided into a typical hierarchical structure consisting of 11 tranches receiving principal and interest payments. The year-over-year returns for each tranche are outlined alongside those of the entire pool in Exhibit 1. Although all tranches have a similar bond-like behavior attributable to interest rate shifts, they nonetheless display varying return dynamics. The overall pool return volatility appears to lie somewhere between the extremes displayed by the tranches.

This is an interesting observation, but how can one assess this conclusion more accurately? In order to better compare the tranche level volatility with those of the entire loan portfolio, the standard deviation of total return for the portfolio as a whole was calculated across the same lifespan as that of each tranche. For instance, since tranche A-1 gets paid off in the second quarter of 2004, the measure used to compare the whole loan portfolio against this tranche was the standard deviation of total returns of the portfolio through the second quarter of 2004. The results for all tranches are outlined in Exhibit 2.

The volatility of the whole loan pool is greater than those of the tranches in the more senior half of the issue (A-1 through E), and less volatile than the tranches in the junior half of the issue (F through J). Overall, this is consistent with intuitive risk arguments regarding CMBS, but the reasons for these results must be examined.

Three main factors should influence the volatility of returns: cash flow volatility, interest rate shifts as a result of general yield curve and spread movement, and discount rate changes as a result of a shift in risk cohort. A major factor affecting cash flow volatility is default (prepayment was not a factor in our analysis except as part of the foreclosure recovery process). The tranche priority structure shifts the direct losses to the bottom portion of the hierarchy, whereas the pool retains all the impact of the losses (albeit to a smaller degree because of its aggregated size). On the interest rate side, differences in the duration of each tranche and of the pool will affect the relative impact of any shift in rates.

Rather than comparing these factors for every tranche, four tranches were chosen that appear to be representative of several important points along the tranche spectrum. The following discussion focuses upon tranches A-1, E, F, and J, because A-1 is the most senior bond, J is the most junior bond, and E and F are the mezzanine pieces that define this CMBS's turnover point for a tranche that is more volatile than the portfolio of whole loans.

Starting at the top of the structure, the return dynamics of the A-1 tranche are significantly different from those of the entire loan portfolio. Both the returns and the volatility of the senior A-1 piece are lower than those of the pool, yet these distinctions do not arise because of major differences in cash flow volatility.

Exhibit 3 compares the actual cash flows distributed to the A-1 tranche with those received by the entire pool. Although the overall magnitude is, of course, different (A-1 is only a portion of the pool), the flows move in sync. Except for the final period in which A-1 gets paid off and excess principal is distributed to the next tranche, the cash flow pattern is nearly identical. This result makes sense as the senior tranche receives not only its proportional interest payment, but also all of the pool's principal payments.

Exhibit 2: Standard Deviation of Total Return
(Pool calculated over same time horizon as each tranche)

	A-1	A-2	B	C	D	E	F	G	H	I	J
Tranche	0.95%	1.50%	1.36%	1.44%	1.95%	1.97%	3.48%	4.14%	3.78%	3.62%	3.59%
Whole Loan Portfolio	3.25%	2.86%	2.86%	2.84%	2.84%	2.84%	2.43%	2.43%	2.43%	2.43%	2.38%

Exhibit 3: Actual Cash Flows Pool versus Tranche A-1

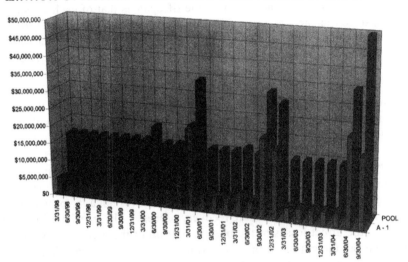

There are indeed some cash flow differences resulting from foreclosure losses which are not well displayed by the exhibit. The senior tranche is the last to get hit by these losses, whereas the pool as a whole has no protection against such exposure. Therefore, the loan portfolio does have some increased volatility relative to the A-1 tranche because of these losses, but the losses for this particular pool happen to be relatively minor and do not have a dramatic effect on the overall returns of the pool. If the default experience were greater, the difference in volatility could grow significantly so it is not safe to conclude that in general there is little cash flow difference between the pool and the "safest" tranche.

If cash flow volatility is not a major factor driving the return differences in this example, one might look at sensitivity to changes in the interest rate. Exhibit 4 outlines the duration for each tranche alongside that of the loan portfolio. Tranche A-1 does, in fact, have a shorter duration than that of the overall pool. Although this difference will certainly make the A-1 tranche less sensitive to changes in the discount factor, the size of the discrepancy does not appear to be large enough to account for the significant differences in return patterns between this tranche and those of the pool.

What then drives the different patterns of total return and volatility? The answer lies with interest rates, but it has more to do with altered discount rates as a result of changes in the risk of the tranche and the pool over time. Basically, tranche A-1 is invariant with respect to the credit risk cohort that it occupies over time. Exhibit 5 displays the time series of risk cohorts for the four tranches, and as we can see, A-1 starts out as a AAA bond and remains one through its maturity.

Because of high subordination levels, this tranche is well insulated from default losses and remains "safe" through maturity. A more stable tranche in terms of risk will produce more stable discount rates and, therefore, more stable returns.

Exhibit 4: Duration: Whole Loan Pool versus Tranche

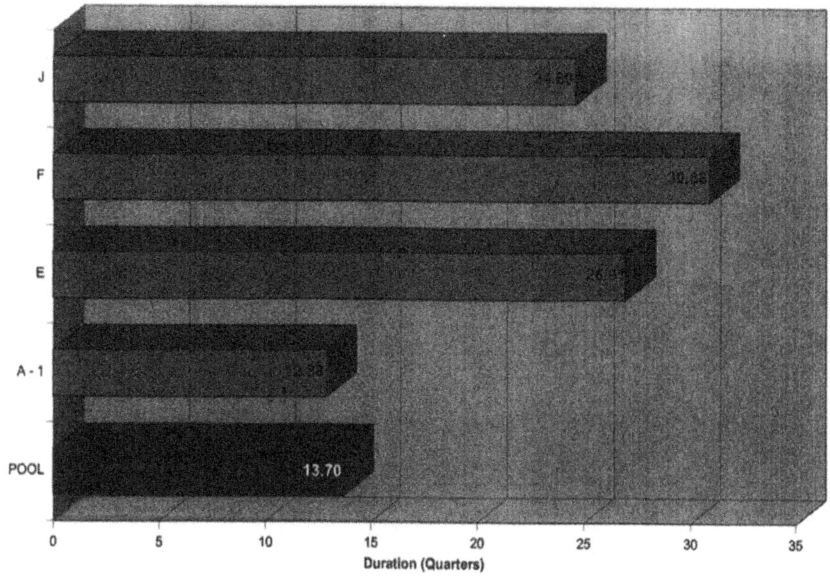

By applying this credit-sensitive discounting methodology to the loan portfolio, each loan is separately rated (and priced). Therefore, there is a higher probability of multiple-rating shifts occurring at any particular point in time, and although each individual shift is not necessarily large as a percentage of the pool, the greater aggregate variation in loan values does have an impact on the portfolio. In other words, tranche A-1 and the overall pool are subject to similar shifts in the yield curve and to time-dependent changes in same-rating spreads, but the spread changes of a move in risk cohort are more volatile in total for the individual loans of the pool. The riskiness of the individual loans is not protected by the subordinated structure found in the security, and so the risk levels are more idiosyncratic.

To compound the matter, the individual loans are more likely to have a longer duration than that of the A-1 tranche. Thus, spread changes will have a more dramatic effect on value. Furthermore, the change in spread tends to be more dramatic for shifts at the lower end of the risk spectrum. That is, the spread change of an upgrade from B to BB is greater than the spread change of upgrading from AA to AAA. The individual loans are certainly more likely to have a lower rating than the AAA tranche A-1, and a greater spread change will have a greater effect on volatility of value and total return.

This important aspect of spread movement comes into play in examining the next three tranches, E, F, and J, but before looking at the effects of interest rates, one must first compare cash flows. Because of the considerable differences in tranche size compared with the size of the pool, reviewing the percentage change in each period's cash flow from that of the prior period made for a better direct comparison.

Exhibit 5: Tranche-Rating Cohorts

Date	A-1	E	F	J
12/31/97	AAA	BBB	BB	BB
3/31/98	AAA	BBB	BB	BB
6/30/98	AAA	BBB	BB	BB
9/30/98	AAA	BBB	BB	BB
12/31/98	AAA	BBB	BBB	BB
3/31/99	AAA	BBB	BBB	BB
6/30/99	AAA	A	BBB	BB
9/30/99	AAA	A	BBB	BB
12/31/99	AAA	A	BBB	BB
3/31/00	AAA	A	BBB	BB
6/30/00	AAA	A	BBB	BB
9/30/00	AAA	A	BBB	BBB
12/31/00	AAA	AA	BBB	BBB
3/31/01	AAA	AA	A	BBB
6/30/01	AAA	AA	A	BBB
9/30/01	AAA	AA	A	BBB
12/31/01	AAA	AA	A	BBB
3/31/02	AAA	AA	AA	A
6/30/02	AAA	AA	AA	A
9/30/02	AAA	AA	AA	A
12/31/02	AAA	AA	AA	A
3/31/03	AAA	AA	AA	AA
6/30/03	AAA	AA	AA	AA
9/30/03	AAA	AA	AA	AA
12/31/03	AAA	AA	AA	AA
3/31/04	AAA	AA	AA	AA
6/30/04	AAA	AA	AA	AA
9/30/04	AAA	AAA	AA	AA
12/31/04		AAA	AA	AA
3/31/05		AAA	AA	AA
6/30/05		AAA	AA	AA
9/30/05		AAA	AA	AA
12/31/05		AAA	AA	AA
3/31/06		AAA	AA	AA
6/30/06		AAA	AA	AA
9/30/06		AAA	AA	AA
12/31/06		AAA	AA	AA
3/31/07		AAA	AA	AA
6/30/07		AAA	AA	AA
9/30/07		AAA	AA	A
12/31/07		AAA	AA	A
3/31/08			AA	BB
6/30/08			AA	BB
9/30/08			AA	BB
12/31/08			AA	BB
3/31/09			AA	BB
6/30/09			AA	BB
9/30/09			AA	BB
12/31/09			AA	BB
3/31/10			AA	BB
6/30/10			AA	BB
9/30/10			AA	BB
12/31/10			AA	BB
3/31/11			AA	BB
6/30/11			AA	BB
9/30/11			AA	BB
12/31/11			AA	BB
3/31/12			AA	BB
6/30/12			AA	BB
9/30/12			AA	BB
12/31/12				Unrated
3/31/13				Unrated

Exhibit 6: Cash Flow Comparison: Change in Cash Flows as a Percentage of Last Period Cash Flow — Pool versus Tranche E versus Tranche F

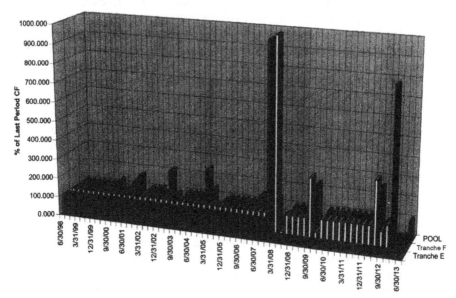

Note: The vertical axis is intentionally limited to a maximum of 1,000 in order to better display the values centered around 100. As a result, the two large values posted in the period 12/31/07 are substantially truncated. For tranche E the value was 6,183; for tranche F, 1,596.

Exhibit 6 outlines these cash flow patterns for both tranche E and tranche F versus those of the entire pool. Other than at the point of payoff (the result of sizable balloon payments in 12/31/07), tranche E's cash flows are much more stable than those of the pool. As a mezzanine tranche, E is protected from both default and prepayment. In fact, tranche E is not impacted by the foreclosure losses inherent in this pool. Therefore, in this particular CMBS issue, stability is the major factor contributing to the lower volatility of returns of tranche E versus that of the overall pool.

Examining the effect of changes in interest rates, one finds that two factors add to the volatility of returns for tranche E. These are its longer duration (see Exhibit 4), and its multiple-rating shifts (see Exhibit 5). Although these factors do add to the volatility of returns (note that tranche E has a greater standard deviation than tranche A-1), it appears that the combined magnitude of these factors when compared with those of the pool is not significant enough to overwhelm the effects of its very stable cash flows. That is, as opposed to the case of tranche A-1, the greater valuation impact caused by longer duration and more significant rating changes does make tranche E's volatility closer to that of the pool's, but the combined impact of these two factors does not push the volatility of tranche E beyond that of the pool.

Note, however, that this is not the case for tranche F, which, as shown in Exhibit 6, has relatively more stable cash flows than those of the overall pool, yet a greater volatility of returns. In this case, the greater duration relative to the pool combined with a larger impact from the spread shifts caused by ratings changes do, in fact, make the returns from this tranche more volatile than the returns of the pool of loans.

The key to understanding this tranche lies in recalling that the magnitude of spread change as a result of a rating shift increases as one goes down the rating spectrum. The crucial point for this tranche F lies at the upgrade it receives from BB to BBB in 12/31/98 (see Exhibit 5), where the spread contraction for the shift amounts to 135 basis points. Compare this to the 35 bp move for the tranche E shift in 6/30/99 and it can be seen why this tranche's returns have much greater movement. It is also important to note that this shift occurs fairly early on, when the duration of this tranche is still substantially longer than that of the pool (duration generally decreases through time), thereby imparting even stronger effects.

Note that removing this credit-rating shift from the return series of tranche F produces an overall volatility of returns closer to that of tranche E. It is, therefore, crucial to understand the exact dynamics of the tranche structure and the underlying pool in making determinations of volatility.

Finally, tranche J is the most junior piece of the CMBS under review, and as such is the first to receive the impact of direct foreclosure losses. The effect of these losses becomes quite evident by reviewing Exhibit 7. The gaping hole from 12/31/99 through 9/30/01 is the direct result of several foreclosures. The relatively larger cash flows ensuing to the pool during this timeframe are the recovery payoffs from the property liquidation sale. Only tranche J, on the other hand, bears the loss and does not benefit from any recovery proceeds; instead all recovered principal flows to the senior tranche.

These cash flow losses obviously have a direct impact upon the return for tranche J, and are reflected in its increased volatility. In addition, increased volatility results from changing discount rates. Referring back to Exhibit 5, there are six cohort shifts over the life of this tranche. Furthermore, many of these occur at the lower end of the rating area, where relatively larger spread changes result from a shift in cohort.

Several of these rating moves have a significant effect on tranche value. Exhibit 8 outlines the effect of various discount rate shifts on the change in market value for tranche J. Note the significant impact as a result of cohort factor shifts. Furthermore, cohort factor-caused shifts in value for the tranche will not be in sync with individual loan cohort changes at the portfolio level. This is different from the manner in which changes in the yield curve impact the pool and the tranches.

As the most junior piece in the hierarchy, tranche J is the last to receive principal payments. The longer duration of this tranche (see Exhibit 4) makes it more susceptible to interest rate movement, so even the yield curve factor, although in sync with timing and direction of those of the individual loans, is more likely to have a different magnitude of impact, thus creating greater volatility of returns versus that of the whole loan portfolio.

Exhibit 7: Cash Flow Comparison: Change in Cash Flows as a Percentage of Last Period Cash Flow — Pool versus Tranche E versus Tranche J

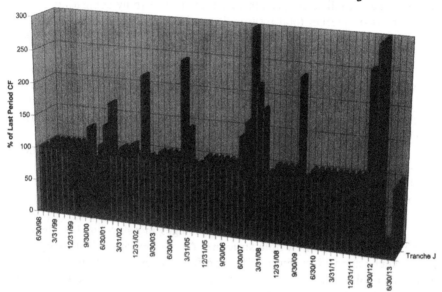

Note: The vertical axis is intentionally limited to a maximum of 300 in order to better display the values centered around 100. As a result, the two large values posted in the 12/31/07 period are substantially truncated. For tranche E the value was 6,183; for tranche F, 1,596.

Exhibit 8: Attribution of Value Change

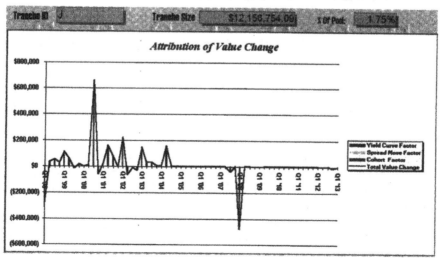

CONCLUSIONS

It is apparent that we cannot generalize about CMBS because the individual tranches behave so differently, as this chapter has shown by comparing the volatility of mark-to-market total returns. Likewise, there are distinct differences among individual tranche volatilities, the volatility of the loan pool as a whole, and the sources of volatility.

Overall, the more senior tranches are less volatile than the whole loan pool while the bottom portion of the tranche structure tends to be more volatile. The factors contributing to these differences center around: cash flow volatility, interest rate shifts as a result of general yield curve and spread movement, and discount rate changes as a result of a shift in risk cohort.

Cash flow volatility is dependent upon both the tranche structure and the make-up of the particular pool (each unique pool is likely to have differing default characteristics). Yield curve movement will affect all assets in the same manner directionally, but the magnitude of this effect is heavily dependent upon the specific duration of the security.

In general, it was the third factor (changes in risk cohort) that played a significant role across the whole structure. At the top, the risk stability of the senior tranche allowed its return to be significantly less volatile than that of the whole loan pool. It is important to understand, however, that in a pool with a substantial number of defaults the differences in cash flows between the senior piece and the entire loan pool will affect returns and their volatility more significantly. The result, however, will still be a less volatile asset because of the greater protection from default losses afforded to the senior tranche.

The mezzanine pieces define the crossover point at which the tranches become more volatile than the loan portfolio. The cash flows of these tranches are protected from both the top and the bottom and, therefore, tend to be very stable except for the final payoff period. Cohort changes, on the other hand, are dependent upon the structure hierarchy and the subordination level can affect risk changes differently for each tranche. As a result, mark-to-market total returns will also differ for each individual mezzanine piece. The longer durations of these pieces make them more sensitive to the shifts in discount rate, and at some point this impact is greater than the aggregated impact from the changes affecting the individual loans. In this particular CMBS, the F tranche was the piece that defined this crossover point.

Finally, the default impact on the junior tranche was certainly a factor that contributed to the relatively greater volatility of this bond. Although both the pool and this tranche absorb all losses from default, the very small size of tranche J (1.75% of the pool) makes its return much more susceptible to these losses than the pool's. As the first loss tranche, this bond is also more susceptible to changes in the value of the underlying collateral. Therefore, it encounters a substantial number of cohort changes. Furthermore, these changes tend to surround the lower portion of the risk spectrum, where spread moves as a result of a shift are more substantial than those occurring near the upper part of the spectrum. Combining this with the tranche's longer duration results in a more volatile level of mark-to-market total return.

Overall, these varying return and volatility differences between individual tranches and the whole loans bode well for portfolio construction. These differences create a reduced correlation of returns which, in turn, allows for construction of a more efficient portfolio when several of these tranches and/or whole loan pools are used. Note, however, that it is important to understand the specific pool and the structure of the specific CMBS issue. Returns are heavily dependent upon the particular collateral of the pool[1] and structure also plays an important role. Therefore, it is imperative to model each and every individual asset appropriately in order to obtain the best portfolio performance.

---

[1] Susan Hudson-Wilson and George J. Pappadopoulos, "CMBS and the Real Estate Cycle," *Journal of Portfolio Management* (Winter 1999). See, also, Susan Hudson-Wilson and George J. Pappadopoulos, "A Tale of Two Loan Pools," *Real Estate/Portfolio Strategist* vol. 1, no. 2 (Winter 1997).

Chapter 18

CMBS Loan Pool Comparisons

George J. Pappadopoulos, CFA

They were the worst of pools, they were the best of pools. . . the problem, of course, lies in determining which is which. In assessing the true risk exposure of commercial mortgage-backed securities (CMBS), numerous uncertainties must be properly addressed, and gauging default is certainly a major factor underlying an assessment.

Yet of the analytical tools that attempt to unearth the possible consequences of the borrower's embedded default put option, most do not appropriately adjust for the key factors that drive default. Two more commonly used techniques incorporated by many of the financial models are: (1) the fixed percentage rules of a conditional default rate (CDR), and (2) the random walk of property price incorporated by Monte-Carlo analysis. Unfortunately, each method may lead to grossly misleading results.

CDR makes the nonviable assumption that a fixed percentage of *each* outstanding loan defaults in *each* year. The approach makes no attempt to determine the probability of each individual loan defaulting, gives no consideration to specific collateral characteristics that incite default, and offers no judgment on the likely timing of default losses. Treating all loans in the same manner is a major shortcoming as loans that appear to be very similar may have drastically differing risk profiles. In fact, it is very likely that individual loans will have very different susceptibilities to default. Thus, the use of CDR is virtually a guarantee for erroneous pricing. Its virtue is ease of implementation; its weakness is that it is unrealistic.

The more sophisticated Monte-Carlo technique offers a far better solution than CDR, but its random assignment of differences across individual properties has drawbacks. Although Monte-Carlo tests for default on a loan by loan basis and may adjust for contract terms, this random walk hypothesis does not take into account the underlying economic factors that move individual markets and property types cyclically, yet often independently.

Market-level economic factors are major drivers of default, and should, therefore, be incorporated into any CMBS analysis. Differences at the MSA and property type levels will significantly affect property level performance, and, thereby, impart drastically different values for tranched bonds. Although this may seem obvious, most models do not properly address this critical influence on bond performance.

By utilizing a model that appropriately incorporates the effects of the multiplicity of real-world market behaviors on CMBS, it will be clearly illustrated why they should concern any CMBS investor. Basically, the following analysis will quantify bond price differences as a direct result of charges across: (a) metro areas, (b) loan contract terms, (c) origination cohorts, and (d) property types, all prevalent factors in most CMBS issues.

THE MODEL

The Property & Portfolio Research model links the cash flows of the security directly to the cash flows of the underlying real estate, as shown below. Distinct market behaviors drive real estate cash flows and valuation that affect resultant mortgage cash flows via the borrower's default decision. Next, these cash flows directly impact the overall loan pool, which, in turn, affects the tranched securities.

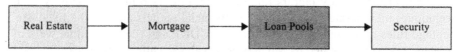

Most important however, the link begins by first modeling the real estate on a market by market, property type by property type basis. The benefit of this approach lies in its accurately outlining the substantive differences in the underlying economic fundamentals of individual real estate markets that affect the security.

At the real estate level, the PPR model is grounded in a thorough econometric estimation of historical and future performance of real estate assets at the property type/urban area level (Derived Market Returns or DRMs™). These rigorously constructed, comprehensive forecasts of capital value and net operating income accurately capture the interactive dynamics among demand side, supply side, and capital market variables, and are the true value-adding key to the model. DMRs provide the model with a well-researched, empirical view on what is likely to transpire, market by market, property type by property type, thereby eliminating the need for the broad generalizations used by the other methods.

The result is a precise and thorough environment for forecasting individual loan, mortgage portfolio, and security performance. At the mortgage level, default is now viewed in the context of current, localized market-pricing information, and is based on contemporaneous pricing ratios. These factors are crucial to the borrower's financial decision regarding the loan, and an enhanced understanding of the borrower's environment is crucial to the accurate assessment of the securities.

The unique, performance-adjusted loan cash flows are then pooled and distributed according to the specific issue's tranche allocation structure. Additionally, the embedded DMRs allow the model to forecast critical rating ratios and, thereby, enable the appropriate application of time- and risk-sensitive interest rate spreads. The reward is a complete time series forecast of risk-adjusted mark-to-market pricing of each tranche in the security.

THE PARAMETERS

To properly illustrate the pricing effects of differences in market location, property type, origination date, and loan contract terms, nine stylized loan pools were analyzed. To ease direct comparison, each pool contains individual loans that are all $25 million in size. Although principal payments in each case are scheduled over a 30-year amortization period, all notes are balloons, with outstanding principal due in full 10 years after origination, and with no further term extensions. Finally, all loan interest payments are calculated at an annual rate of 9.50% of the outstanding mortgage balance, and both scheduled principal and interest are due quarterly.

Exhibit 1 outlines the scenarios surrounding these base loans, and each applied change is highlighted. Static sensitivity analysis was performed by independently varying the four key default-pricing parameters. In general, higher risk timeframes for origination were used to aid the illustration of these critical pricing issues.

Actual pricing impacts that result from differences in market location, property type, origination date, and loan contract terms are outlined in Exhibits 2, 4, 5, and 6. Each will be reviewed in turn in the next section. A typical sequential pay, subordinated tranche structure with three tranches was used for the analysis, and the tranche sizes were assumed to be 70%, 20%, and 10% of the loan pool. Additionally, tranches were assigned contract rates of 9.00%, 9.50%, and 10.00%, respectively. The "Default-Adjusted Price" represents the ratio between the contract rate discounted present value of the actual default-impacted cash flows versus the original face value of the bond. In other words, the ratio captures the default impact on price as a result of shifts in the parameters.

THE RESULTS

Differences Across Markets

Scenarios 1, 2, and 3 represent equal size pools comprised entirely of loans on office properties originated at the same point in time with identical contract terms and underwriting ratios. As a result, these three pools would look virtually identical when analyzed by most financial models. In other words, even though the underlying real estate assets are located in different markets, traditional analysis would produce indistinguishable pricing differences and offer no guidance on which may be the better pool.

Although each pool incorporates typical/acceptable characteristics for geographic diversification, PPR's econometrically based model suggests that each one is, in fact, characterized by distinctly different default risk profiles. A slight shift in pool geographic mix produces variances in both loss severity and loss timing. In short, the unique economic cycles of each market produce a different set of defaults and foreclosure losses for otherwise equal loan pools.

Exhibit 1: Scenario Outline

Scenario	Pool	Property Type	Origination Date	Loan-to-Value	Debt Service Coverage	Projected Foreclosure Date
1	Atlanta 2 Boston 2 Salt Lake City 2 San Francisco 2	Office	3/31/88	70%	1.40	12/31/92
2	Atlanta 2 Boston 2 Los Angeles 2 Salt Lake City 2	Office	3/31/88	70%	1.40	12/31/92 9/30/95
3	Hartford 2 Kansas City 2 Phoenix 2 San Francisco 2	Office	3/31/88	70%	1.40	9/30/95 9/30/92
4	Hartford 2 Kansas City 2 Salt Lake City 2 San Francisco 2	Office	3/31/88	70%	1.40	9/30/95
5	Hartford 1 Kansas City 1 Salt Lake City 1 San Francisco 1	Office	3/31/88	75%	1.30	9/30/94 9/30/93 6/30/93
6	Atlanta 1 Kansas City 1 Salt Lake City 1 San Francisco 1	Office	3/31/88	75%	1.30	9/30/92 9/30/93 6/30/93
7	Atlanta 4 Kansas City 4 Salt Lake City 4 San Francisco 4	Office	3/31/90	75%	1.30	3/31/93
8	Boston 1 Hartford 1 San Francisco 1	Office	3/31/88	75%	1.30	9/30/94
9	Boston 3 Hartford 3 San Francisco 3	Apartment	3/31/88	75%	1.30	

For example, the only change between the pool of Scenario 1 and that of Scenario 2 is the substitution of a loan from Los Angeles for one underwritten in San Francisco.

Yet Scenario 1 experiences only one foreclosure in late 1992, while Scenario 2 gets hit by the 1992 foreclosure as well as by an additional foreclosure almost three years later in the third quarter 1995. Furthermore, the pool of Scenario 3 encompasses four different, geographically dispersed markets and has yet a third type of experience.

Exhibit 2: Bond Pricing

Delta	Tranche	Scenario	Initial Size	Default-Adjusted Value	Default-Adjusted Price
MSA	A-1	1	$70,000	$70,000	$100.00
		2	70,000	69,962	99.95
		3	70,000	69,973	99.96
	B-2	1	$20,000	$19,136	$95.68
		2	20,000	13,862	69.31
		3	20,000	13,196	65.98
	C	1	$10,000	$3,321	$32.21
		2	10,000	2,964	29.64
		3	10,000	2,813	28.13

Exhibit 3: Default-Adjusted Price by Scenario

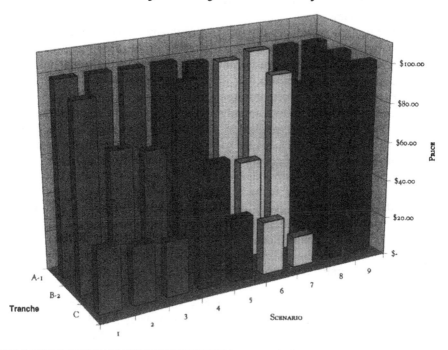

It is clear that the market cycle differences that affect the underlying collateral flow through to affect the bonds. Moreover, it is evident in Exhibits 2 and 3 that even the senior A-1 tranche is not necessarily immune from the effects of these differences. The single default of Scenario 1 is not enough to affect the A-1 tranche, but the second default produced by the pools of Scenarios 2 and 3 does produce a slight negative value impact, even in this "safe" tranche.

Although there is no loss of actual principal for the bond as a result of the second foreclosure loss, there is a shortfall of incoming loan contract payments during the delayed foreclosure process. Assuming the servicer makes no advances, the senior bond suffers because there is not enough current cash flow to cover the full interest payment during this foreclosure lag period.

This cash flow shortfall also causes a problem for the B-2 tranche under the first three scenarios. Until the proceeds from the foreclosure are available to pay down the senior tranche, there is not enough cash flow to cover the interest due to the mezzanine B-2 tranche. Once the A-1 tranche principal has been reduced, its interest payment requirements decrease, and there is enough cash flow to cover the current interest due to the B-2 tranche.

The second default that occurs in both Scenarios 2 and 3 does much more damage to the mezzanine tranche. The principal of this tranche absorbs some of the foreclosure loss under both of these scenarios because the first loss C tranche is eliminated prior to bond maturity. The effect on B-2 is evidenced by its drastically reduced pricing.

The junior C tranche is the first to absorb any foreclosure losses, as evidenced by its extremely low pricing under all the first three scenarios. More important, material pricing contrasts continue to result from the market cycle differences underlying each scenario.

Furthermore, it is worth noting the pricing differences between Scenario 2 and Scenario 3. There are two defaults in each case, yet pricing discrepancies still exist. The difference is explained by disparities in market cycles. The pricing variance is caused not only because of the differences in timing between the defaults of these two scenarios, but also because of the differences in the severity of the loss for each particular foreclosure.

Actual loss severity, being a function of property value, is, of course, strongly affected by market economic cycles. Neither a CDR nor a Monte-Carlo–produced random property price variable is equipped to quantify these critical differences properly. The PPR model, on the other hand, models severity as a function of contemporaneous property value forecasts on a market by market basis, not as a generalized function of the original loan amount, or a random property price.

Since tranche A-1 does not directly shoulder any of the foreclosure losses, the slight pricing difference between Scenarios 2 and 3 is generated merely by a matter of timing. On the other hand, tranche B-2 takes a larger hit from the particular foreclosures encountered in Scenario 3 than it did from those foreclosures in Scenario 2, and this is once again reflected in the bond pricing. Finally, although tranche C is retired before maturity in both Scenarios 2 and 3, the varying interplay between default timing and severity once again combines to alter pricing. Overall, these results clearly illustrate that the location of the collateral is crucial to effective pricing of the security.

Exhibit 4: Loan Contract Terms

Delta	Tranche	Scenario	Initial Size	Default-Adjusted Value	Default-Adjusted Price
	A-1	4	$70,000	$70,000	$100.00
Loan		5	70,000	68,492	97.95
Contract	B-2	4	$20,000	$19,299	$96.49
Terms		5	20,000	10,763	53.82
	C	4	$10,000	$4,606	$46.06
		5	10,000	3,264	32.64

Differences Across Contract Terms

By reviewing identical sets of collateral secured under different loan to value and debt service coverage parameters, Scenarios 4 and 5 illustrate pricing differences that may occur as a result of differing loan contract terms. Certainly, an increase in loan to value ratio from 70% to 75%, and the decrease of debt service coverage ratio from 1.4 to 1.3 should combine to form a much riskier set of loans.

All tranches do, in fact, bear out this assertion. Remember, a CDR model would not have even considered these differences. Furthermore, while a Monte-Carlo approach would illustrate the same conclusion in a general sense, PPR's model makes an additional contribution by breaking this risk out by geography and property type. This more reflective forecast of property price allows for a more accurate forecast of the borrower's default decision.

The results outlined in Exhibit 4 illustrate that the additional defaults that occur under the riskier set of contract terms affect pricing at all tranche levels. Recall that no advances are considered to be made by the servicer, and the resultant cash flow shortfall during the default period, therefore, reduces the value of the senior A-1 tranche.

Furthermore, although the mezzanine B-2 bond does absorb a slight loss of principal in Scenario 4, the far greater foreclosure losses of Scenario 5 take a serious toll on this tranche. Fittingly, the B-2 pricing suffers dramatically from the difference in collateral contract terms.

Finally, it is interesting to note that despite the fact that in both scenarios the C tranche is completely consumed by foreclosure losses, there is still a pricing difference because of the timing of those principal losses. The single default of Scenario 4 occurs much later than any of the defaults in Scenario 5 and the resultant tranche-level cash flow differences translate directly into altered pricing.

Differences Across Origination Cohort

Scenarios 6 and 7 both encompass pools of loans that would be virtually indistinguishable to many pricing models and have the exact same collateral originated on the exact same contract terms. The key difference, however, is the date of the original underwriting.

Exhibit 5: Origination Cohorts

Delta	Tranche	Scenario	Initial Size	Default-Adjusted Value	Default-Adjusted Price
	A-1	6	$70,000	$67,827	$96.90
		7	70,000	70,000	100.00
Origination	B-2	6	$20,000	$10,245	$51.22
Cohort		7	20,000	18,656	93.28
	C	6	$10,000	$2,746	$27.46
		7	10,000	1,587	15.87

The results in Exhibit 5 show that this case comparison is, in fact, similar to the last. Once again, foreclosure period cash flow deficiencies impact even the most senior tranche. In addition, the greater number of defaults in Scenario 6 lead to a much higher default loss, which, in turn, overpowers much of the principal of the mezzanine tranche, and tranche B-2 pricing suffers appropriately.

Most intriguing, however, is the fact that in this set of scenarios, the junior tranche displays a very counterintuitive result. Even though the pool of Scenario 6 has a much greater foreclosure loss than the pool of Scenario 7, tranche C is worth more in Scenario 6 than in Scenario 7.

The backdrop for the explanation lies in the fact that in either scenario, tranche C does not survive the initial foreclosure. Furthermore, note that the first foreclosure in Scenario 6 occurs 18 quarters into the life of the pool, whereas the opening foreclosure for Scenario 7 occurs only 12 quarters after origination of the pool. As a result, tranche C receives more cash flow under Scenario 6 simply by staying alive longer.

In other words, this out-of-the-money tranche is behaving very similarly to an interest only piece that receives payments only while it has a notional principal balance outstanding. Such timing factors are crucial, and, thus, it is clear that knowledge of the property market's cycle at the point of origination is critical to a proper evaluation of the prospective performance of the bond.

Differences Across Property Types

The final comparison of Scenario 8 versus Scenario 9 deals with underlying performance differences that can occur when the collateral is located in the same urban areas, but is not the same property type. While both office properties and apartments represent sizable sectors of CMBS issuance, traditionally they have not experienced the same patterns of market cycles. By directly contrasting these two property types, characterized by identical contract terms underwritten in identical markets, at an identical point in time, we can analyze the effect of cycle differences on bond pricing.

In these scenarios, the apartment pool of Scenario 9 performs better than the office pool of Scenario 8 (no defaults versus one default), and in neither case is there enough of an effect from foreclosure loss to affect the senior A-1 tranche.

Exhibit 6: Property Type

Delta	Tranche	Scenario	Initial Size	Default-Adjusted Value	Default-Adjusted Price
Property Type	A-1	8	$52,500	$52,500	$100.00
		9	52,500	52,500	100.00
	B-2	8	$15,000	$12,948	$86.32
		9	15,000	15,000	100.00
	C	8	$7,500	$3,035	$40.46
		9	7,500	7,500	100.00

On the other hand, the foreclosure loss of the office default that occurs in Scenario 8 affects both the mezzanine and junior tranches. The obvious result of this increased absorption of losses are the pricing differences outlined in Exhibit 6. In this case the particular market economic conditions during this timeframe strongly favored apartment performance over office performance, and the bond pricing appropriately reflects that distinction. It is, therefore, apparent that knowledge of the type of collateral is also crucial to proper evaluation of the bond.

CONCLUSIONS

Although mortgage default risk is commonly understood to be a major pricing factor for CMBS, existing analytical methods do not appropriately adjust for the factors that drive default. PPR's analysis has conclusively outlined substantive pricing differences as a direct result of modest changes in normally overlooked or overgeneralized parameters.

Markets behave differently and naive diversification will not necessarily reduce diversifiable and manageable sources of risk. Loan pools that appear to be equally well diversified may, in fact, behave quite differently, and unexpected results may occur if a full range of parameters is not considered. It is, therefore, far better to have a well-informed opinion of an individual property market's economic cycle, for the consequences will indeed flow through to the security.

Furthermore, the analysis illustrates the need to have an understanding of this specific macroeconomic behavior of markets as it combines with differences in timing, contract terms, and property types. These parameter differences should not be assumed away or managed with broad-scale simulation. Instead, they should be, and can be, appropriately modeled.

Part IV

Allocation Across the Real Estate Asset Class

Chapter 19

Modern Portfolio Theory Applied to Real Estate

Susan Hudson-Wilson, CFA

M odern portfolio theory (MPT) has increasingly gained general accep-
tance as the preferred method for intelligently diversifying pools of real
estate assets. Prior to the 1990s there were few individuals in the real
estate investment community who would have given serious consideration to the
use of MPT in designing a real estate portfolio; today there are few serious investors or investment managers who do not currently use, in a more or less rigorous
fashion, the principles of MPT to help them manage their real estate portfolios.

MPT: A LONG, SLOW ACCEPTANCE

Long used in the creation of portfolios in and across the public markets, MPT did
not begin to find a home in real estate until the 1980s. The two most important
reasons for this lengthy delay were the lack of data for analysis and blind adher-
ence to the belief that each real estate asset was unique. Until the creation of the
NCREIF Property Index in 1982[1] there was no publicly available real estate
return series. Even after the creation of the index years passed before it contained
enough information to allow even a rudimentary diversification study. And, it
was not until the crash of the late 1980s and early 1990s that real estate investors
*fully appreciated the role of cycles in the performance of individual assets and
portfolios of assets.* The role of the market cycle became apparent to anyone with
more than one investment in Houston, New York, Los Angeles, or Anytown,
U.S.A. The role of the portfolio should now be apparent to all but the most obsti-
nate as a simple example will demonstrate. Exhibit 1 presents the performance
histories for three very different cities and property types. Portfolios constructed
using varying allocations across these different bets would have produced very
different results as measured in return, in risk, and in risk-adjusted return (see
Exhibit 2).

---

[1] Although established in 1982, the NCREIF Property Index contains historical data beginning in 1978.

Exhibit 1: Total Annual Returns

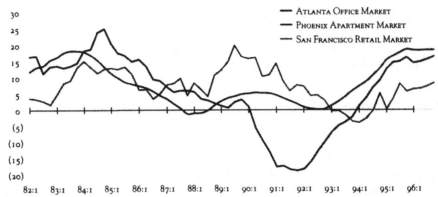

Exhibit 2: Portfolio Performance 1982:1–1996:4

	Return (%)	Risk (%)	Return per unit of Risk (%)
Market Neutral 33% Atlanta Office 33% Phoenix Office 33% San Francisco Office	7.04	6.10	1.15
50% Atlanta Office 50% Phoenix Apartment	6.96	8.55	0.81
50% Phoenix Apartment 50% San Francisco Retail	7.77	4.30	1.81
50% Atlanta Office 50% San Francisco Retail	6.40	6.68	0.96
90% Atlanta Office 10% Phoenix Apartment	5.86	11.07	0.53

The equal weighted, or naïve, portfolio produced a decent return at a bearable level of risk, but a small degree of care used in market selection and allocation would have caused both the return to rise and the risk to fall. Risk-adjusted performance would have improved greatly. In contrast, poor selection and poor allocation would have produced quite unacceptable performance results. Careful portfolio construction can make or break the performance of a pool of assets. This is a "done deal"; further debate is only distracting, not useful.

Since cycles are obviously relevant, investors are finally ready to think seriously about them and about risk management.

INPUTS: HISTORICAL AND FORECAST RETURNS

Despite the growing availability and integrity of performance databases, two serious shortcomings presented another major speed bump on the road to the use of

MPT: there were no forecasts of expected returns available and the return series that were available were too aggregated, revealing little about the meaningful differences at the urban area and property type levels. Really detailed forecasts of performance were in short supply. It was many years before even basic modeling techniques were brought to bear on the problem, and still more years before the level of sophistication in this area began to approach that of other economic disciplines. It turned out that the modeling was difficult and made more so by the fact that, initially, the NCREIF index did not cover even one economic cycle. Any attempts at modeling that would be sensitive to a variety of regimes were futile. Well, time has largely addressed this problem. Today there are nearly 20 years of data covering two complete economic cycles. The challenge now is to disaggregate the broad indices to reveal the performance of markets at the interesting and useful urban area and property type levels.

This disaggregated data are needed because MPT isn't MPT without three crucial inputs:

• Expected returns,
• The riskiness or volatility of each return, and
• The cross correlations among the returns.

Historical and forecast returns on a market by market, property type by property type basis are needed to calculate these inputs. It is essential that these data be consistent across time, geography, and property types. Idiosyncratic information does not cut it when asset allocation is the goal.

There are two possible solutions to the problem of obtaining the data necessary for the modeling. One is to model the required data and the second is to collect the data property by property, city by city. Let's deal with the latter approach first. In order to build a database of sufficient statistical integrity, one would need at least 30 properties in each city for each property type, quarterly over a long enough historic time period. Assuming that 60 cities and four property types were worthy of pursuit, data on 7,200 properties evenly distributed over cities and property types would have to be assembled and maintained! Perhaps someday the World Wide Web will make this possible, but for now it is not. Even NCREIF tracks fewer than 3,000 properties, and they are certainly not even remotely uniformly distributed across urban areas and property types.

So Plan B — model the behavior that did and will occur in each city and property type pair based on market fundamentals and capital market drivers. This is what PPR has done. This is the source of the data used in Exhibit 1. The PPR Derived Market Returns (DMRs™) are modeled estimates of the historical and forecast performance of real estate for 60 urban areas and four property types. They are quite revealing.

THE DISCOVERY OF MEANINGFUL DIFFERENCES

Creating the data is a necessary, but hardly a sufficient, condition for creating a portfolio model. The PPR return model produces results for 240 urban area/property type pairs and there is not a portfolio analysis package that can, or should, incorporate so many assets. Thus, the next step is to unearth the "dimensions of diversification." How many truly differentiable investment choices are there available in the U.S. property markets? The statistical technique of cluster analysis provides the means to discover the sectors (to borrow a term from the stock and bond markets) of the U.S. property market.

Clustering of individual return series, to identify groupings of similar and dissimilar markets, actually solves two problems — one practical, one conceptual. First, it makes the analysis of a large number of markets possible. As discussed above it is simply not reasonable to put 240 assets into an asset allocation model and expect to produce sensible results. The results could easily be meaningless as the optimizers are dogmatically wired to search out and use the "best" assets, even if an asset is only best by 0.0001 of a basis point. Forecasting has come a long way but isn't quite up to that standard of accuracy yet!

This leads to the conceptual purpose of clustering. PPR doesn't believe there are 240 unique real estate markets in the U.S. (this really flies in the face of old guard thinking, which holds that *each asset* is unique!), but rather that there are collections of urban areas and property types that share patterns of behavior. In other words, some groups of markets have very similar expected returns and historical return profiles. Clustering such markets together shows that certain economies move similarly (a tip of the hat to the economic location proponents). However, the performance of a market is only partially attributable to its economic structure; the supply side of each market and the effect of capital market influences on returns must also be considered when identifying groups of comparable markets. Exhibits 3 and 4 show two sample office market clusters and make clear the reality that while demand side drivers are sometimes very important (as in Exhibit 3), they are not the only influence on performance as demonstrated by the members of the cluster in Exhibit 4. Richmond is a state capital, but Kansas City and Memphis aren't. Memphis and Richmond are southern cities, but Kansas City isn't. Returns are clearly produced by the complex interrelationships among demand, supply, and capital market factors such as inflation and investment opportunity costs.

Therefore, clustering serves to rigorously answer the question of which markets are complements and which markets are substitutes in the context of a portfolio. An additional virtue of clustering is that in the execution stage, one has choice. The portfolio model is indifferent with respect to the investor's use of one market in the cluster over another to execute an allocation. Thus, the practical aspects of buying and selling, such as relationships and temporal pricing inefficiencies, can be exploited.

Exhibit 3: Sample Office Market Cluster 1

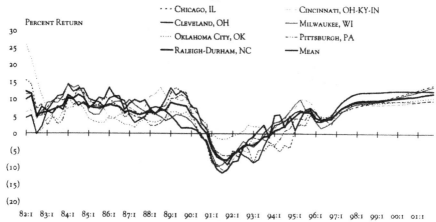

Exhibit 4: Sample Office Market Cluster 2

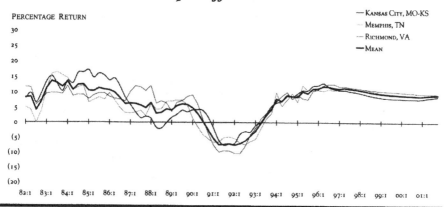

UNDERSTANDING THE BIG PICTURE — WHAT'S POSSIBLE?

After understanding how markets relate to one another it is time to gain an understanding of the nature of the investment universe. To do this a market efficient frontier is constructed. Efficient frontiers in any asset type context describe the highest attainable returns associated with each level of risk. Each point on a frontier represents a portfolio allocated in a specific way over all the investments in the model. The frontier is called "efficient" because it provides insight on the highest return for each level of risk and the least risk for each level of return. There are many nonefficient portfolios, but they are less desirable since the same return could have been earned while assuming less risk or, for the same level of risk a greater return could have been achieved. Return is the benefit, risk is the cost — why pay more than you have to?

Exhibit 5: Efficient Frontiers Through Time

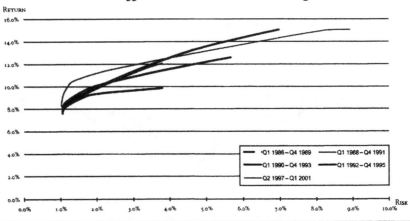

The frontier itself communicates a wealth of insight. Long frontiers suggest that the assumption of market risk is rewarded; short frontiers suggest that market risk is not worth assuming. A flat shape to the frontier suggests that the assumption of *additional* risk is incrementally less well rewarded, while a steeper frontier suggests that the assumption of increasing levels of market risk will be increasingly well compensated. *The frontier alone provides investors with sufficient information to establish real estate investment policy. It's a huge source of insight.* Exhibit 5 presents a succession of frontiers calculated using expected returns in different time periods. Each frontier uses a four-year forward time horizon to calculate the expected return.

Follow the market cycle by looking in turn at the 1986–89 frontier (number 1, the peak of the last cycle), the 1988–91 frontier (number 2, decline from peak return of 300 basis points, flattening and shortening shape), and the 1990–93 frontier (number 3, further deterioration of return of another 200 basis points and significant flattening along with additional shrinkage). The frontiers of the late 1980s through the early 1990s told the story loud and clear — the risk/reward relationship in the real estate markets was not pretty and was deteriorating. Next observe the frontier describing the investment opportunity set from 1992–95 (number 4, longer, steeper, higher). The market turning point is well and clearly marked. Today's frontier (number 5) describes the prospective period from 1997–01 and suggests that current real estate markets reward the investor appropriately. This said, it is worth noting that the new frontier is longer than the initial frontier. *This suggests that the same level of return that was achievable in the last cycle will again be achievable in the current cycle; however, to achieve that return, it will be necessary to invest in riskier markets in this cycle than in the last one.* In examining the portfolios that underlie the frontier at the respective end points, it is evident that while in the last cycle the high return could be achieved with portfolios dominated by retail assets, in this cycle it takes portfolios dominated by office assets to produce the same gain. This cycle is therefore a riskier cycle.

Exhibit 6: Current Efficient Frontier and Sample Portfolio

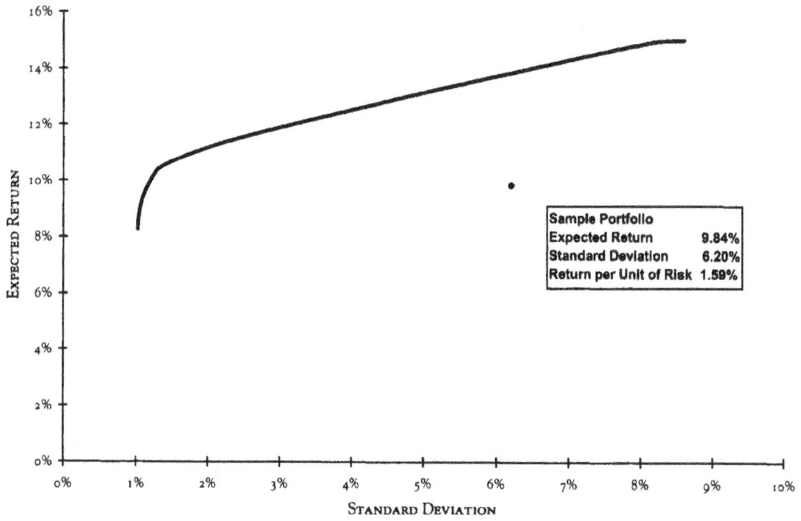

Sample Portfolio	
Expected Return	9.84%
Standard Deviation	6.20%
Return per Unit of Risk	1.59%

Future frontiers are likely to continue to exhibit rising and lengthening shapes, right up until the moment when the cycle turns, once again.

ASSESSING YOUR PORTFOLIO

Given a knowledge of the expected investment environment, it is possible to assess a particular portfolio within that context. Questions like: *How am I doing?* (and *How can I do better?*) can be answered. In order to put the portfolio into the modeling framework, data on what is in the portfolio (and where it is located) and on the value of each asset are needed. This is pretty basic stuff. The portfolio's allocation across the clusters of different investment behaviors is then easily seen and the implications of this allocation for portfolio return and risk are readily calculated. Exhibit 6 shows a sample portfolio in relation to the current efficient frontier. Now it is possible to assess the situation. Is the portfolio efficient? How much is any inefficiency costing the investor? (Calculate the opportunity cost by measuring the basis point spread between the frontier and the portfolio at a constant level of risk.) And, most important, *What can be done about it?*

CONSTRAINTS

The frontier shown in Exhibit 6 is unconstrained. That is, it assumes that the investor has perfect mobility and can re-weight investments to create a portfolio right on the efficient frontier at zero cost. This would be great, but in fact is rare. For most real estate portfolios three kinds of constraints may influence investment behavior: constraints on what you can sell (because of the illiquid structures of certain investments), constraints on how much capital you can invest (because of overall asset allocation targets or execution capacity), and constraints on the structure of the portfolio you are willing to hold (because of the use of benchmarks and/or tracking error rules and/or policy restrictions on certain types of assets). By incorporating these constraints into the portfolio, one may easily construct the constrained efficient frontier faced by the investor, which represents the investor's investment opportunity set.

This analysis serves two purposes. The first is to identify the incremental investments that will most improve the current portfolio. The second is to identify current holdings that are impediments to performance. Taken in tandem they are the beginning of a road map for identifying both targeted acquisitions and dispositions plans. Also at this point one can compare the constrained and the unconstrained frontiers to determine the cost to the portfolio of continuing to labor under these constraints. This exercise is important in determining if the constraints placed on the portfolio are justified from both a risk/return and a cost/benefit basis. If the constraints cannot be justified on either dimension, perhaps serious thought should be given to removing them.

CONCLUSIONS

Having set up the quantitative framework for the analysis, it can now be worked hard. The investor knows what the investment universe looks like, what the current portfolio looks like, how unalterable investments restrict mobility, how much progress could be made given any fixed level of incremental investment over the forecast period, which clusters offer the greatest benefit if exposure to them is reduced and which offer the greatest benefit if exposure is increased, choices within clusters, and enough to act with confidence!

The next time the phone rings with a great deal, the investor has a frame of reference with which to say yes or no. Investment opportunities can thus be rapidly advanced or taken off the list of investments requiring further due diligence. Portfolio modeling does not substitute for due diligence on investments that fit the portfolio's needs, but it certainly helps the investor figure out what deserves the time and expense of due diligence and what doesn't. A tremendous efficiency for both sellers and buyers.

Portfolio modeling can get you a long way down the road, but the rest of the job gets done the old fashioned way, investment by investment.

A final and important aspect of building this framework is the ability to repeat it on an ongoing basis. Stock and bond portfolio managers re-weight their portfolios with astounding frequency, in some cases daily. While it is clearly not feasible to re-weight real estate portfolios so often, it is important to keep abreast of shifts in the market, and to adjust the portfolio as needed. When the benefits of shifts in the allocation outweigh the costs of shifts — *shift*! This means that an empirical analytical framework becomes part of the fabric of the portfolio management process. It's worth it, as the value will be captured in greatly reduced transaction and due diligence costs, more productively used staff time, and, most important, more reliable and more understandable portfolio performance. Portfolio modeling makes sense and can be executed. What possible rationale can there be for not doing it?

Chapter 20

Cross-Quadrant Asset Allocation

Susan Hudson-Wilson, CFA

Robert E. Hopkins Jr.

In recent years, cross-quadrant (public debt, private debt, public equity, and private equity) asset allocation has received considerable attention. Previous research has explored[1] the issue of cross-quadrant investing vigorously, asking such questions as:

- whether adding investments in the public equity and public and private debt quadrants to investments in the basic private equity quadrant provides any value to the real estate investor (it does);

- whether a multi-quadrant investor would have outperformed a single-quadrant private equity investor through the past, nasty cycle (they would have); and

- whether defining real estate as a four-quadrant adventure rather than a one-quadrant adventure impacts the overall stock, bonds, bills, and real estate allocation question (it does).

Carrying the analytics to the next logical step, Property & Portfolio Research, Inc. (PPR) built a very detailed, very specific cross-quadrant asset allocation capability. This new level of inquiry actually allows investors to analyze their entire current real estate portfolio in the context of the full-blown cross-quadrant model. As with the private equity modeling presented in Chapter 19, investors can see how they fit in the larger, and probably more relevant, world of debt and equity, in public and private markets. Until now it has only been possible to think theoretically about the best way to allocate an open-minded portfolio; now it is possible to think specifically.

The chapter begins with a description of data assembly, moving beyond a general approach to the definition of the behavior of each quadrant and using the

---

[1] Susan Hudson-Wilson and Bernard L. Elbaum, "Diversification Benefits for Investors in Real Estate," *Journal of Portfolio Management* (Spring 1995), pp. 92–99; Susan Hudson-Wilson and Daniel P. Guenther, "The Four Quadrants: Diversification Benefits for Investors in Real Estate — A Second Look," *Real Estate Finance* (Summer 1995), pp. 82–99.

far more detailed behavioral data to simulate the performance of three smart investors (a high-risk/return investor, a moderate risk/return investor, and a low-risk/return investor) in *each* of the quadrants. Every investor seeks to create and maintain as efficient a portfolio as possible *within each quadrant*, using realistic assumptions about investment and disposition costs as well as advisory fees. The problem was approached at this level of detail since it is rare that actual investors experience the performance of an *index* representing a quadrant (the NAREIT index, for example). In fact, most investors approach the investment mission with an eye to outperforming an index or other benchmark! Of course, different investors have different goals and objectives so it is inappropriate to "represent" all investors' past and hoped for performance with a gross measure of index (or worse) performance. Thus, investors have different appetites for risk and different needs for return. They are trying to do the *best* job possible, not just the average job.

MODELING EFFICIENT STRATEGIES WITHIN EACH QUADRANT

PPR's secret weapon, and the basis for virtually all the real estate performance research, is the Derived Market Return (DMR™). PPR's proprietary modeling and forecasting methodology are the basis of predicted performance of aggregate and local area real estate markets. This model has been under development for more than 13 years and is used by large, sophisticated, institutional real estate investors domestically and internationally.

At the national level the methodology separately estimates equations for the net operating income (NOI) and capital value (CV or appreciation/depreciation) components of total return (the basic data come from NCREIF and are far from perfect, but that issue is addressed by the manner in which the data is applied). The equations seek to quantitatively identify the factors that drive the performance of real estate markets. Some of the factors used in the model include: demand for space, the structure of the economy (the distribution of employment over sectors), the supply of space (stock and changes at the margin), depreciation rates, inventory, the vacancy rate, the propensity to build new space, space usage factors by employment sector, general economic well-being (captured by the unemployment rate and income per capita), construction costs, the inflation rate (past, current, and prospective), stock per user, short-term interest rates, long-term interest rates, and the spread between the long and short ends of the yield curve. The equations are estimated over history and are updated twice a year.

To capture the performance of local real estate markets, PPR applies these equations at the local level and re-solves the equations over the historical and forecast time periods. This captures the behavior (volatility and performance) of 240 local markets (60 urban areas and four property types). The basic performance data are then used to model the historical and prospective performance of the universe of investments in each of the quadrants of the real estate investment universe. Some examples of DMRs for a set of very different cities and the four property types within each city are presented in Exhibit 1. Next, the discussion centers on the performance of the assets available for investment within each quadrant and then how the historical and forecast performance of the three smart investors was modeled in each quadrant.

Exhibit 1: DMRs, Selected Cities
Hartford

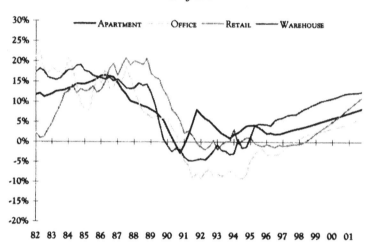

Los Angeles

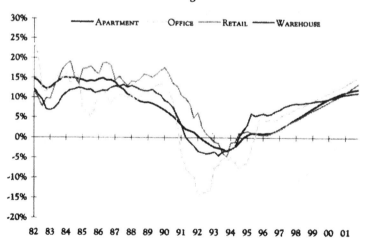

Exhibit 1 (Continued)
New York

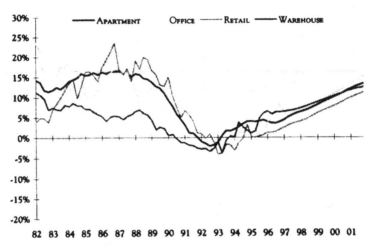

Dallas

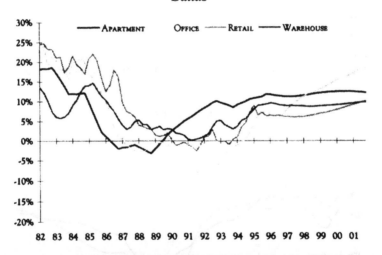

THE WITHIN-QUADRANT MODELING PROCESS

Using the Derived Market Returns described above, the performance of individual real estate investments made within each quadrant and of multiple *strategies* (*combining* various individual investments) within each quadrant was replicated. The modeling of the strategies accounted for transactions and investment advisory costs, and for the fact that these cost[2] are different for each of the quadrants. Some restrictions were then imposed on the volume of re-balancing that was permitted within the less liq/*ing "best practice" portfolio management techniques.* The methodology for maximizing performance within each quadrant is explained below.

The Public Equity Quadrant

In order to model the past and prospective performance of the assets in the public equity quadrant, the next step was to identify a universe of more than 140 individual real estate investment trusts (REITs) and constructed a data set capturing the property type and geographic composition, or allocation, of each REIT. This in itself is not a trivial exercise as the data describing REIT composition are not well organized or easily accessible. The database developed is unique to PPR.

Each REIT's weighting across geographies and property types was determined and applied to the DMRs, creating "Main Street" REIT DMRs. These time series revealed the performance of each REIT in the investment universe as if they had been traded in the private market. Clearly REITs are not traded in the private market so the model was enhanced to econometrically include data on the cycle and pricing of the public securities market. This yielded an estimate of how each REIT in the universe of the public equity quadrant behaved over history and is expected to behave over the forecast period. Exhibit 2 presents an example of a Main Street and a Wall Street REIT DMR.

Exhibit 2: Cluster 2 — Snowbelt Apartment DMRs

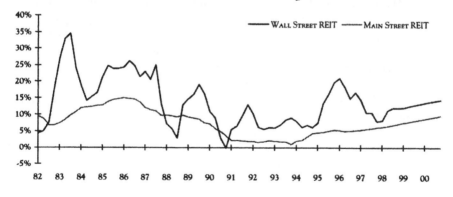

---

[2] The costs assumed in the modeling were as follows (transaction costs were applied to both acquisitions and dispositions):

	Transaction Costs	Management Costs
Private Equity	100 bp	100 bp
Private Debt	40 bp	80 bp
Public Debt (low and moderate risk)	20 bp	50 bp
Public Debt (high-risk)	75 bp	100 bp
Public Equity	25 bp	40 bp

The next step was to design portfolios of REITs that were sensible and useful to the three different types of investors described earlier. It was necessary to conduct efficient frontier analysis within the quadrant to find the portfolios of REITs that could be held by each of these hypothetical investors in order to satisfy their goals.

But, how many truly different REIT investment behaviors are there? What are the dimensions of diversification in the REIT world? The idea was to group the similar REITs and separately group the different REITs. This step was important for both practical and theoretical reasons. From a practical perspective it is impossible to place a very large number of any kind of individual assets into a mean variance model. The modeling software will not accept extreme numbers of assets and, even if it were technically possible, the results produced would be very close to meaningless. From a theoretical perspective the process makes sense; each REIT does not represent a unique pattern of behavior. Certainly REITs that share exposures to similar property types and geographies ought to share some behavioral characteristics. It would be really weird if there were 140-plus unique behavioral patterns in the REIT universe!

So the efficient frontier modeling began by seeing which assets behaved similarly and which were different. The similar REITs were grouped together as clusters of REITs, which were, in effect, substitutes for one another. The REITs that were in different clusters were, in effect, complements to one another. This caused the REIT universe of more than 140 REITs to form a handful (well, two handfuls) of clusters of REITs.

The investment characteristics of each REIT cluster were then entered into the mean variance model (the model requires expected returns, standard deviations of returns, and cross correlations) and a separate efficient frontier was calculated for each and every time period, quarterly from 1984 through 2000. It was necessary to observe and document the performance that would have been experienced by each of the hypothetical investors over the course of the historical and forecast time period. A total of 64 frontiers were calculated and three time series produced representing three different investor track records of quarterly public equity performance.

It is important to note that each of the investors' performances were optimized performances, representing three smart investors carefully adjusting the mix of their portfolios over time. These were not "buy and hold" portfolios, and the investors were subject to the payment of transaction fees and investment advisory fees so the time series that result are net of all fees. Exhibit 3 presents the three time series for the three strategies in the public equity quadrant. It is interesting to see that although the three strategies follow a similar path over time (stock market influences), they do produce some serious spreads in performance, particularly in the up cycles. All three strategies, although labeled high-, medium-, and low-risk/return, are really all pretty high (especially when compared with the private equity strategies). The convergence in some time periods is created when there is really very little that distinguishes one REIT cluster from another, so any choice is virtually as good as any other.

Exhibit 3: Performance for Low-, Moderate, and High-Risk Investors in the Public Equity Quadrant, 1984–2000

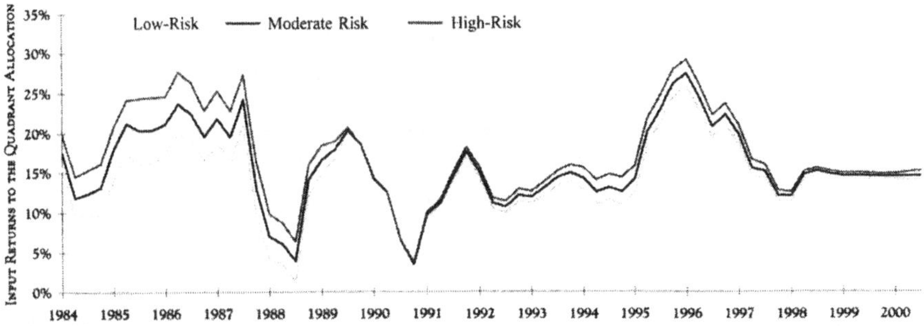

It is also important to note that the accuracy of the forecast for performance of the three whiz kids is seriously dependent upon the accuracy of the forecast for the S&P 500, which is one of the drivers of the model. The S&P 500 is forecast to return an average annual return of 5%. Is this too high or too low? Last year the return was north of 25% but one money manager predicted a negative 1% over the forecast. This is clearly the wild card in this forecast. (The 5% came from Regional Financial Associates, a well-known macro- and urban economic data vendor.)

The Private Equity Quadrant

The DMRs capture the investment experience of three smart investors in the private equity quadrant with return histories and forecasts for 240 separate markets. Again one faces the same issue that was evident in the analysis of the public equity quadrant — the need to discover the true dimensions of diversification. We executed a Cluster analysis grouped together the markets that could operate as substitutes for one another. In the private equity quadrant the 240 individual returns form 34 clusters. Exhibit 4 presents some representative clusters.

In order to define the historical and forecast performance of the three intelligent investors in the private equity quadrant, the usual inputs to the mean variance model were calculated — expected returns, standard deviations, and cross correlations — and the model was run quarterly from 1984 through 2000. As in the private debt modeling, portfolio rebalancing was constrained to ensure replication, as closely as possible, of the true manner in which private equity portfolios are managed. The magnitude of the transactions costs is great enough that it is truly better to let the portfolio become a bit suboptimal than it is to execute every trade the portfolio model would call for in the absence of costs. The performance track records amassed by the three private equity investors are presented in Exhibit 5.

The results were very interesting. In the best of times the spreads between the high- and the low-risk/return investors were very wide. It is possible to do risky things and get paid for it in good times. In bad times the three lines converged as there are few acceptable things to do. Every portfolio manager must go to ground in the same way in order to save the performance of the portfolio.

Look at the level of performance experienced in the bad times — it's nothing like NCREIF. This is because the investors were actively managing the portfolio and had forecasts of performance in order to do it! Granted, the hypothetical investors had perfect forecasts; so what would have happened had their forecasts been half as good? They would have underperformed these geniuses, but for sure, they would have outperformed the average investor.

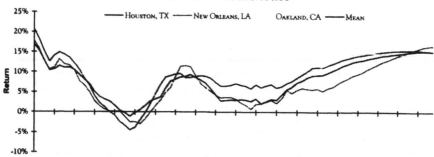

Exhibit 4: Selected Clusters
Cluster 34 — Warehouse

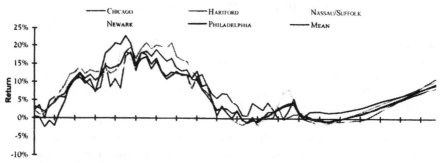

Cluster 22 — Retail

Exhibit 5: Performance for Low-, Moderate, and High-Risk Investors in the Private Equity Quadrant, 1984–2000

The lesson: use research and other means of gathering insights on market cycles, and act on your beliefs. You can earn yourself a whopping number of basis points just by listening and then acting.

The Private Debt Quadrant

In order to model the performance of the three careful and smart investors in the private debt quadrant, we again began with the performance data of the Derived Market Returns. In this case the DMRs represented the behavior of the collateral underlying the mortgage. Since DMRs are composed of income and value components, we can apply a wide range of types of mortgages (pretty much any mortgage you can design, we can model) to the basic collateral and then observe how each mortgage structure, applied to a range of property types and geographies, would have performed historically, and will perform over the forecast period.

A set of mortgages were modeled that were structured to represent the bulk of the U.S. mortgage market. The mortgages had the following attributes: 10-year bullets with 30-year amortization, locked to prepayment (equivalent to a yield maintenance provision), no workouts or extensions were permitted, and low, medium, and high loan-to-value and debt service coverage ratios (LTVs at 50%, 70%, and 90% and DSCRs of 1.5×, 1.35×, and 1.20×). The interest rates in each quarter were set as the average from the American Council of Life Insurance (ACLI) data series for the medium risk loan, with 100 basis points added and subtracted for the high- and low-risk loans. These mortgage structures were applied in a capitalization-weighted fashion to all 240 markets PPR covers and the flow of new origination capital was weighted in keeping with the flow of originations from the ACLI database. Loan pools were created by property type for a total of five different bases (four property types and the entire market) and three risk levels of loans creating 15 different mortgage substrategies from which the hypothetical high-, moderate-, and low-risk investors could choose. Each strategy represented the mark-to-market total return that the investor would have received had he or she chosen to invest in each mortgage structure. The 15 substrategies are plotted in Exhibit 6.

As in the analysis for the other quadrants, the various mortgage strategies were placed in a mean variance model and the efficient frontier model was run 64 times (one per quarter for the period from 1984 through 2000) to identify the performance track record of the three smart private-debt investors. The historical and forecast performance of participants in the private debt quadrant are presented in Exhibit 7.

A different (and intuitively satisfying) pattern of performance differences among the three investors emerges. The downside has a greater spread than the upside. Mortgages manifest greater downside divergence as different mortgages "blow up," depending on the property type and the geographies underlying the mortgages. On the upside, however, there is mainly coupon (and some improvement in credit quality, which raises the mark-to-market value of the mortgage) so even if the collateral underlying the mortgage is having a party, this excellent performance is not captured by the mortgage. Clearly the pattern of the returns suggests that interest rates matter a great deal as well.

Exhibit 6: Mortgage Return Series — 15 Strategies

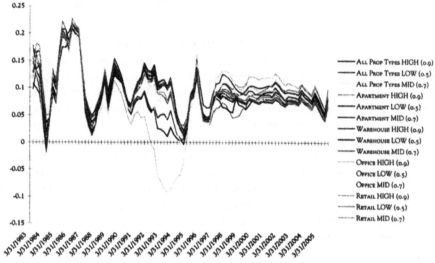

Exhibit 7: Performance for Low-, Moderate, and High-Risk Investors in the Private Debt Quadrant, 1984–2000

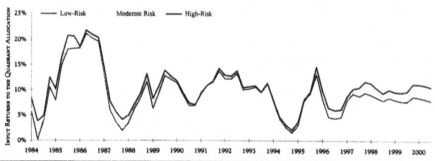

The Public Debt Quadrant

The modeling of this quadrant required adding a layer onto the modeling executed for the private debt quadrant — the layer that describes how the cash flows from both the interest payments and balloon payments are allocated to the various pieces of the bond structure that is wrapped around the pool of mortgages. In commercial mortgage backed securities (CMBS) there is a hierarchy of payout preferences setting forth which tranche of the security will be paid first, second, third, etc. as cash flows are received. The more secure tranches receive the first cash flows and are the most highly rated (AAA, AA, and A), the next most secure tranches are the BBB, BB, and B levels, and the less secure (i.e., further down in the pecking order for the receipt of cash flows from the underlying mortgages) are rated CCC, CC, C, and Unrated. At the most secure end of the security the asset behaves in a very debt-like fashion; as one moves down the tranches the equity-like component of behavior assumes a more important role.

PPR selected 12 strategies from among the almost infinite possibilities defined by loan-to-value and debt service coverage ratios, interest rates, property types, and geographical mixes. The selected strategies were intended to be representative of the range of investment behaviors available in the public debt quadrant and are presented in Exhibit 8.

Once again PPR needed to identify the portfolios and the performance for three investors with low-, moderate-, and high-risk/return profiles. Again 64 frontiers were calculated (repetition is the soul of good research!) using the mean variance inputs of expected return, standard deviation, and cross correlations. The resulting performance paths of the three investors are presented in Exhibit 9.

Exhibit 8: CMBS Return Series — 12 Strategies

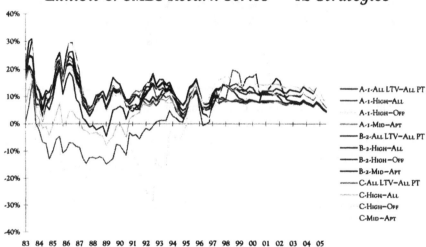

Exhibit 9: Performance for Low-, Moderate, and High-Risk Investors in the Public Debt Quadrant, 1984–2000

Exhibit 10: All Four Quadrants, All Three Strategies, 1984–2000

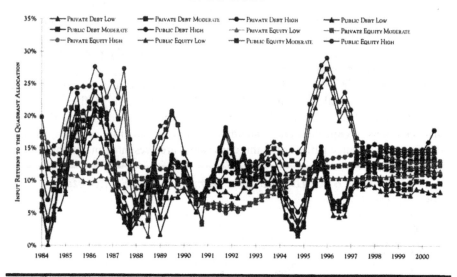

The result is both divergence in up markets and divergence in down markets as CMBS has both debt-like and equity-like investment characteristics. The generally favorable outlook for real estate markets results in a nice convergence over the forecast period.

CONCLUSION — ALL THE QUADRANTS TOGETHER

Exhibit 10 illustrates the performance histories and forecasts of each of the brave and wise investors. What a range of histories (note, however, none below zero)! What a spread over the forecast! There are definitely enough information and insights here for a portfolio manager to work with!

Index

Printed and bound by CPI Group (UK) Ltd, Croydon, CR0 4YY

16/04/2025

14658442-0011